MENDING BROKEN FENCES POLICING;

an Alternative Model for Policy Management

Redefining Police Resource Allocation and Performance Measurement on the Basis of Social Cohesion—An Alternative Model for Policy Management

Anil Anand,
BPHE, LLM, MBA, GEMBA

Copyright © 2016 Anil Anand

All rights reserved. No part of this book may be reproduced, stored, or transmitted by any means—whether auditory, graphic, mechanical, or electronic—without written permission of both publisher and author, except in the case of brief excerpts used in critical articles and reviews. Unauthorized reproduction of any part of this work is illegal and is punishable by law.

ISBN: 978-1-4834-4502-1 (sc)
ISBN: 978-1-4834-4503-8 (e)

Library of Congress Control Number: 2016900891

Because of the dynamic nature of the Internet, any web addresses or links contained in this book may have changed since publication and may no longer be valid. The views expressed in this work are solely those of the author and do not necessarily reflect the views of the publisher, and the publisher hereby disclaims any responsibility for them.

Any people depicted in stock imagery provided by Thinkstock are models, and such images are being used for illustrative purposes only.
Certain stock imagery © Thinkstock.

Lulu Publishing Services rev. date: 1/19/2016

CONTENTS

Preface vii
Introduction ix
Performance Management 1
Applying a Balanced Scorecard to Policing 14
Boundary, Beliefs, Interactive Controls, and Diagnostics 30
Community Policing 50
Intelligence-Led Policing 55
Balancing Community Policing with Intelligence-Led Policing 63
Integration of Participatory and Restorative Practices 68
Social Cohesion 84
Developing the Intelligence-Led/Community-Based Policing
Model (IP-CP) and Quality/Quantity/Crime (QQC) Model 105
Discretion 122
Selecting Performance Indicators 140
Diversity 156

Conclusion 167
Bibliography 169
Endnotes 183

PREFACE

Despite the enormous strides already made during the past decade, particularly with the adoption and expansion of community policing, there is much that police leaders can do to improve police-public relations. The urgency is particularly evident in cities across the United States and Europe, where an increasing number of police interactions over the past few years have ignited large, sometimes even national, protests against police policy and strategy, highlighting a gap between what police leaders feel they have archived in terms of public satisfaction, support, and legitimacy and the perception of bias among many marginalized communities. The decision on which one policing strategy is chosen over another, how many resources are allocated, and how strenuously the policy is applied resides primarily with the police and the units and subunits tasked with its enforcement. The scope and opportunity for police officers in impacting social attitudes and social policy are important elements that cannot be overstated. It has been suggested that "[t]he police are among the most important policymakers of our society. And they make far more discretionary determinations in individual cases than any other class of administrators; I know of no close second."[1]

It has always struck me as odd that despite the centrality of policing and security in modern society, few citizens truly understand how they are policed and the implications of to what and how their police leaders decide to respond. How do police leaders, for instance, decide when to apply one strategy—say community-based policing—over another, like intelligence-led policing? How do police leaders measure performance and success? Should these measures be based on quantitative preferences over qualitative, or should the preference be based on some other criteria? And how do police leaders define, allow, and control discretionary decision-making?

I hope that this book, *Mending Broken Fences Policing*, based on the notion of social cohesion, will contribute to a renewed dialogue on some of the contemporary issues in policing and perhaps even provide some practical alternatives to contemporary practices in police performance management, policy, and administration.

I would also like to take a moment to recognize that there is no work that is not in some way influenced by one's lived experiences, years of reading and learning, or the conscious and unconscious assimilation of the influences of one's mentors, coaches, and teachers. In the spirit of being as broadly based as possible in recognizing that all good research depends on the contributions of preceding research and that even original works are not immune to the influence of one's lived experiences, I therefore want to thank everyone who has contributed to the experiences that have allowed me to be able to write the following work. I would like to thank everyone who has mentored, inspired, and supported me and everyone who has taught me something through sharing his or her own lived experiences and works. I have applied the *Chicago Manual of Style* of reference, assessing it to be the best suited to this work. And while I have endeavored to reference or otherwise acknowledge the direct and indirect influence of the works of others, including academic and nonacademic, it would be marginal of me to pretend to have successfully identified and acknowledged every source of influence to my thinking and writing. I therefore want to, at the onset, extend my regret and apology for any oversight of those who should have been included.

In the end, I hope that everyone will benefit from the ideas, thoughts, and discussions this work might provoke and above all do some good.

INTRODUCTION

Although trust and legitimacy are often used interchangeably in policing, they are two distinct yet linked and codependent concepts. The level to which the public resorts to police for the coproduction of social cohesion and order is a reflection of the level of trust the citizens have in their police. And the degree to which police decisions are understood, complied with, and supported is a reflection of the legitimacy ascribed to the police and the rule of law to which the community is subject. Victims and complainants will call their police service for assistance to the extent that they feel safe in doing so and to the degree that they feel that their concerns will be addressed fairly. The scope of their willingness to call for help is a reflection of their trust in the institution of policing and the specific response that they expect from the responding officer. The extent to which observers of the process and events that unfold following engagement of the police feel that the engagement was fair, effective, and in keeping with the understanding and communication of laws within existing social standards is a reflection of legitimacy.

An example of the scope of engagement may include the range of offenses victims are willing to report to the police. In some communities, trust and legitimacy are developed to the extent that certain crimes, rape and domestic violence for instance, are reported with little hesitation. In contrast, other communities might be more likely to report other crimes but not rape and domestic violence. This then is a reflection of the trust and legitimacy ascribed to the police's ability to service a particular social issue.

Trust is a factor on which all personal and institutional interactions depend. Without trust, there can be no basis for a healthy and meaningful relationship between individuals, organizations, or communities. But trust is not a simple phenomenon to grasp. Because trust is not concrete, it is difficult to assess and measure. It is not always transparent or evident; it can be fleeting and fragile and represents a vague construct, the reality of which depends on how well involved parties are able to share and sympathize in each other's realities.

All relationships involve some form of conflict as well as opportunities for its resolution through a spectrum of strategies varying from avoidance, acceptance, negotiation, mediation, arbitration, and litigation to use of force. Relationships are, however, only strengthened when the parties find ways to enhance confidence and develop their abilities to tolerate, share, accept, sympathize, or embrace each other's frequently divergent realities, interests, positions, or expectations. The endurability of relationships and the trust on which they are formed depends on the parties' abilities to respond in meaningful and well-timed ways to their own evolving interests as well as the expectations of their counterpart.

In order to enhance the ability to respond to the unexpected but inevitable conflicts, democratic societies develop institutions and processes for facilitating civil society. Governments, for instance, have executive, judicial, and administrative branches that provide rules, interpret the application of rules, and guarantee the maintenance of systems designed to define and sustain social cohesion. The criminal justice system works to ensure that laws are applied fairly and equitably, that law and order guarantee the safety and well-being of all citizens, and that breaches of laws are remedied to restore trust and legitimacy in social systems. Trust is linked integrally to the actions and behaviors of the individuals and systems that represent the collective values and principles of the society constituted by the aggregate of communities and their citizens. The legitimacy of these institutions is, therefore, engendered by the trust citizens develop in them.

Trust in policing is dependent on a complex and sometimes conflicting set of interactions between the police and the state. On the one hand, police are dependent on the sponsorship of the state, and on the other, they must have independence from politics and political intervention. Policing also requires independence in the application of discretion on the one hand and conformity through oversight and control on the other and collaboration with the community but also confidentiality and secrecy. Such competing and sometimes divergent interests and expectations present major challenges to the development and maintenance of trust. These types of challenges are universal to police organizations in democratic societies and developing societies alike but are particularly difficult for police in societies emerging from long periods of conflict and civil unrest. Community participation in the established social cohesion and social order is critical for the establishment of public trust and the legitimacy ascribed to the institution of policing.

Trust and legitimacy enable police leaders to look beyond bureaucratic responses based on expert-based models of strategic management to those that are collaborative and consensual. A model of community intelligence represents one such model. The reality, however, is that, like community-based policing, it is neither new nor novel; it is simply a reframing of existing practices in a manner that realigns the importance of community collaboration for effective policing. Pseudo-justifications for presenting commonsense strategies as new models can only serve to threaten trust and legitimacy for very short-term gains in professional credibility. Instead, police leaders must simply do their level best to create meaningful and transparent partnerships with communities and stakeholders that enhance opportunities for information sharing and risk assessment.

Police leaders must continually rethink the relative value of particular strategies and responses and the community's reaction to increased or diminished levels of police intervention. How do particular responses impact local crime and disorder, as well as perceptions of fairness, misconduct, and abuses of processes? Which social cohesion indicators are relevant, and which have outlived their relevance for determining the levels of overall social cohesion in the customer community?

Zero-tolerance strategies, for instance, are generally seen as indiscriminately aggressive and can lead to a worsening of police-community relationships. Even beyond policing, the repercussions can impact a wider set of stakeholders, including, for instance, courts, correctional services, bail and parole, and those engaged in social services and public health. Zero-tolerance strategies need to be implemented with careful consideration of the target problem, a cost-benefit analysis, and assessment of both short and long-term impact on the community and stakeholders. Trust and legitimacy require sustained assessment of how well leaders and their organizations are perceived and how effectively they meet current community expectations. Police satisfaction surveys tend to be too general. Surveys are seldom specific enough to identify subtleties that might be particular to smaller segments of society and are rarely specific to the extent of determining trust and legitimacy based on offense-based assessment.[2] Surveys could also, for example, be more specific in assessing the impact of citizen-initiated versus police-initiated intervention and the resulting satisfaction or perceived legitimacy resulting from such contacts or, for example, how well services address needs where social surveys indicate poor reporting of crimes, as is the case with domestic violence and sexual assaults.

Although trust and legitimacy are theoretically distinct, it is important to understand the nexus between the two. The link that binds the two is the processes and principles that institutionalize public confidence in the governance of the social institutions, among which policing is one. In societies that are emerging from conflict, the link (conceptual distance) between trust and legitimacy is wider than in societies with defined and established institutions. What does this mean? Simply put, in established societies, the processes for governance are widely accepted and adopted, while those in emerging democracies have yet to be tested and proven. In most advanced democracies, for instance, the governance of a privately administered condominium board is very similar to that of a police service board or city council. There is a chair, a vice chair, and a treasurer, and there are rules and schedules that guide governance in a commonly understood and accountable manner. Even among tribal societies, there are common elements, such as an elder or council of elders, a tribal council, a chief, and so on. The important element is the recognition of a commonly held standard of expected governance by those being governed and those entrusted with the power to govern. The extent to which these commonly understood and accountable processes are trusted and relied upon gives systems their legitimacy.

Trust is critical for establishing social cohesion and necessary for overcoming conflict, including its causes, precursors, and catalysts.

Trust is also critical for reestablishing social cohesion following social conflict. Trust can be either *calculus-based trust* (CBT) or *identification-based trust* (IBT).[3] This classification helps to develop a framework for the understanding of the relationship between trust, legitimacy, and social cohesion. Calculus-based trust is established and maintained through a transactional type of motivation wherein individuals make a calculation of the punitive or negative consequences of actions that would undermine trust versus the benefits of engaging in actions that would reward their compliance to trust-based actions. CBT is related to deterrence-based trust because consequences can include normative sanctions (ranging from social shunning or being outcast or excommunicated) or substantive sanctions based on laws that call for monetary fines or even imprisonment.

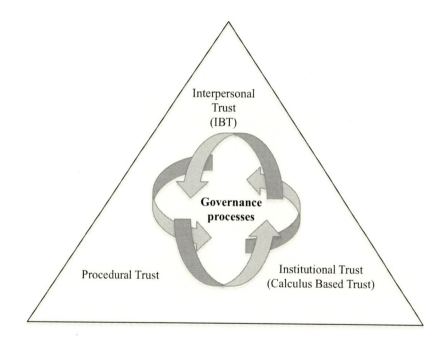

Figure 1. Legitimacy—Factors that cause citizens to subject themselves to obedience to police authority.

There is an implication that the role of norms, based on informal and consensual social contracts, among members of a society are at least as powerful as, if not even more influential than, the formal substantive laws of a society. CBT provides normative controls for maintaining trust, even where there is no substantive reason to act otherwise, in order to avoid losing one's social position, influence, or status. In other words, individuals do what they promise to do because they want to avoid the consequences of not doing what they have promised to do or are expected to do. For this reason, CBT is also sometimes referred to as *deterrence-based trust*.[4]

It is important to note that although the outcomes of choices made by two individuals might be the same—that is, two individuals might both do what is expected of them under the same circumstances—the sponsoring motivation for their actions may be very different. One might do what is right and be motivated by the intrinsic reward or value of the act itself, simply wanting to do what is right or correct. Another individual, who on the surface may not appear to be any different than the first, may base his or her choice on the fear of probable social or substantive sanctions associated with making the wrong decision. The uncertainty of motivation (sincerity of action) causes CBT to develop incrementally and cautiously. Due to the fragility of CBT, any violation of trust results in long-term damage and increasing reticence by the offended party to reestablish a trusting relationship.

Organizations and systems are subject to CBT in the same way as individuals. Stakeholders and customers will assess the sincerity of decisions made by institutions and systems in the same way as they would with individuals. Institutions may respond to a crisis with responses designed solely to mitigate liability or when compelled by recommendations of public inquiries or inquests. Responses based on such avoidance-based motivation undermine the principles of CBT. This is particularly true where decisions appear to be motivated primarily by a desire to save face rather than for redressing underlying attitudes that may have contributed to the crisis in the first place. Such perceived insincerity diminishes trust, and each subsequent breach, or perceived breach, increases the difficulty of reestablishing trust and legitimacy. Transparency and accountability provide useful processes for organizations to communicate their underlying motivation and for demonstrating their sincerity during periods of diminished goodwill.

A secondary category of trust is identification-based trust (IBT).[5] IBT is more intimate and personal in nature, having its foundation on the personal interactions among individuals that lead to the development of the appreciation for each other's desires and intentions. With IBT, "the mutual understanding is developed to the point that each person can effectively act as the other."[6] It is as research describes, a second-order learning, wherein parties are able to act for each other in ways that foster the development of mutual trust and understanding. Parties are able to predict each other's needs, respond like the other, and empathize strongly with the other, leading to the development of working relationships that become stronger, closer, and more personal.

In terms of institutional trust, it is engendered by the degree to which stakeholders and clients perceive institutions and their processes to be honest, trustworthy, and legitimate in the care of the customer communities (internal and external to the organizations) they serve. Trust results from the fairness of the laws, their social relevance, and the fairness and effectiveness with which "fair" laws are enforced. There is a normative component to the perception of fairness, in the determination of the treatment of others within the community by the authorities as being fair. Fair, however, is more than just the equitable application of the laws. Fairness is determined within the context of the normative standards of the society or customer community, supported by the procedural fairness with which laws and services are rendered. Legitimacy results when citizens perceive laws instituted by the processes of governance to be just and the institution of policing as having earned the entitlement to enforce, creating in themselves an obligation to obey—in other words, the factors that cause citizens to subject themselves to obedience to police authority and the laws they enforce.[7]

The degree of perceived fairness and legitimacy attributed to the police and other public institutions serves as the foundation for the level of general social trust within a society, among its members, and between communities—what we will explore as the concept of *social cohesion*. Intergroup and intragroup trust represents the social bond, or measure of shared norms, among members of a social network and the values they share.[8] Trust and legitimacy, therefore, are not only important from the perspective of policing; they are generally relevant in the overall development of social cohesion, contributing to other trust-based initiatives, such as volunteerism and democratic attitudes. It is for these reasons that policing requires ownership by customer communities, including the police, citizens, local governments, nonprofit organizations, and special interest groups.

The measure of the success of police leaders in providing effective solutions to crime and disorder and to removing barriers for the development of collaborative crime management is dependent on their ability to develop defensible and legitimate models for policing that contribute to the building of trust and legitimacy in their institution. Provision of policing and the mobilization of communities require social cohesion as an integral component for the maintenance of civil society. Indicators that monitor the health of communities include their capacity to form trusting partnerships within the community and with the types of groups and resources noted above. The types of policing programs intended as public relations activities, sometimes termed "promotional justice"[9] may be useful from the perspective of modeling social capital (volunteerism for instance). Promotional activities must, however, be communicated as such to avoid such activities being perceived as manipulative or as substitutes for core policing. Identification-based trust should not be used as a means of extracting calculus-based trust, although the end result of enhancement in either IBT or CBT can be the enhancement of the other.

There are underlying factors that account for the differences in the commitment to social capital. One of the most evident is the difference in the effectiveness with which governments are able to share and distribute wealth among their citizens. Fair and equitable provision of services and governance lessens, or at least mitigates, the emergence of separation between social classes. The greater the sense that wealth and services are unfairly distributed, the greater the division of classes and increased likelihood of social unrest. Societies where public services are perceived to be relatively less effective and less efficient are also likely to be perceived as less trustworthy. This contributes to suspicion and dissent, diminished legitimacy of state institutions, and expressions of civil disobedience and protest. Under such circumstances, police leaders are frequently placed in the unenviable role of contending with the widening gap between social classes and between their dual function as a mechanism of state control and their role as public servants. The police are, in this way, often thrust into the position of being a pseudo-mediator in social conflicts wherein there are unrealistic expectations of their mandate and authority to provide resolution to contentious issues. The reality is that the police have no substantive power other than to maintain the peace—as an example, the management of protests involving land claim rights of First Nations peoples.

It is a contradiction given that police are empowered by governments as the sole authority sanctioned to use force within the state and funded by the state through the revenues accrued through the taxation of its citizens. The irony is mitigated in democratic societies by a separation of policing and politics. The challenge for police services lies in maintaining trust and legitimacy while dealing with conflicts in a manner that meets with expectations of procedural fairness and remains within the normative standards of the community. This, however, will only be achieved if police leaders work preemptively to establish a standard of trust and legitimacy with state sponsors and customer communities in advance of the emergence of crisis.

The institution of policing is integral for the transition of societies from those with limited social capital to those with trusted public institutions, and the role of police leaders is critical to the type of societies that emerge from that transition. A study of the trust in police among more than a dozen countries in Europe found that if public institutions, particularly of the types that are involved in policy-implementation, including social or health-care services and police services, are perceived by citizens as being trustworthy, effective, and reliable, then they in turn contribute to the establishment and maintenance of a generally higher level of social capital among citizens.[10] The quality of democratic institutions is central in the establishment and maintenance of social capital. There is a general expectation that the relatively greater social capital in Nordic countries (Finland, Sweden, and Norway), with correspondingly higher levels of trust in their public service institutions (health, education, and social welfare) also contributes to the increased perceived legitimacy of the police.

While it is beyond the scope of this discussion to provide a complete analysis of the determinants of legitimacy, what is important here is to develop an understanding of the potential interplay between procedural justice, instrumental fairness, trust, and legitimacy and for leaders to be mindful of each of these as critical components to any strategy for responding to crime and disorder or providing community support.

Trust and legitimacy are founded on good governance and can generally be accepted to include five principles identified by the United Nations Development Program (UNDP): legitimacy and voice, direction, performance, accountability, and fairness.[11] These five principles can be readily applied to the governance of police services and in the evaluation of a balanced scorecard for policing, as a measure of the strategic vision in providing direction for the system and corporate responsiveness, along with the measure of effectiveness and efficiency in determining performance. Application of the rule of law and equity are essential for ensuring fairness, transparency and accountability and the level of consensus orientation and participation (internal and external) necessary for establishing trust and legitimacy.

Strategic vision—leaders and the public have a broad and long-term perspective on good governance and human development, along with a sense of what is needed for such development. There is also an understanding of the historical, cultural, and social complexities in which that perspective is grounded.	*Direction*
Responsiveness—institutions and processes try to serve all stakeholders. **Effectiveness and efficiency**—processes and institutions produce results that meet needs while making the best use of resources.	*Performance*
Equity—all men and women have opportunities to improve or maintain their well-being. **Rule of Law**—legal frameworks should be fair and enforced impartially, particularly the law on human rights.	*Fairness*
Transparency—transparency is built on the free flow of information. Processes, institutions, and information are directly accessible to those concerned with them, and enough information is provided for people to understand and monitor them. **Accountability**—decision-makers in government, the private sector, and civil society organizations are accountable to the public, as well as to the institutional stakeholders. This accountability differs depending on the organizations and whether the decision is internal or external.	*Accountability*
Consensus orientation—good governance mediates differing interests to reach a broad consensus on what is in the best interests of the group and, where possible, on policies and procedures. **Participation**—All men and women should have a voice in decision-making, either directly or through legitimate institutions that represent their intention. Such broad participation is built on freedom of association and speech, as well as capacities to participate constructively.	*Legitimacy and Voice*

Figure 2. Five Principles of Good Governance.

This fundamental shift in thinking from a bureaucratic model to one that is more democratic in nature does not imply a complete devolution of power or abandoning of performance measurement, oversight, control, or authority; it does imply a philosophical shift toward greater inclusiveness of a larger group of stakeholders in the organization and management of services.

These principles provide a broad framework by which police leaders can assess opportunities for establishing legitimacy based on instrumental and procedural justice. They provide a foundation for the reevaluation of how police leaders view their relationships within the internal police organization but, even more important, with the communities they serve. These principles contribute to the forging of real partnerships capable of developing solutions to address emerging social problems. The level of confidence with which police and community relationships are developed and maintained can be measured using general social surveys that can reveal the levels of social confidence indicated through charitable contributions, volunteerism, sense of belonging, and confidence with government institutions.

Inclusion of these five governing principles enhances the likelihood that individual citizens and communities develop positive perceptions of the police. It is important to note, however, that regardless of the efforts put into the establishment of legitimacy and trust, a single negative event can have damaging and lasting consequences. While most studies confirm the benefits of procedurally positive citizens' contacts with police, a single instrumentally or procedurally negative encounter can have a disproportionate negative impact on overall legitimacy. One study reported that a poor police-citizen contact, regardless of whether it was police initiated or citizen initiated, had between four and fourteen times the impact of a positive experience on citizens' confidence in police.[12] Negative experiences from citizen-initiated contact with police resulted in a significant negative attitude change about police, while a negative experience from a police-initiated contact did not alter people's attitude about police.[13]

Another study of the association of citizens' perceptions of quality of life and their neighborhood conditions found that there was only a small variation associated with the measure reflecting quality of life and citizens' perceptions of quality of life. This study indicates that police programs that target physical decay and social disorder (remedies to the broken windows and neglect) only result in a very modest impact on citizens' perceptions of their neighborhood or quality of life. Yet many police programs continue to politicize the importance and allocation of resources to these types of community programs, when in fact they have little value to police-community relations or citizens' perceptions of their neighborhoods.[14] Like promotional policing,[15] programs that have a very modest impact on citizens' perceptions of their neighborhood or their quality of life will undermine trust (IPT and CBT) and therefore the legitimacy of the service.

Regardless, it is not enough that police services focus on satisfaction alone, without also focusing on the mechanisms for the development of citizen perceptions and for strengthening relationships through an evidence-based approach. Police leaders must at all times be mindful of a balanced scorecard for assessing their services. Modern policing has been impacted by three dramatic and unexpected realities during the past two decades. The first is the emergence of terrorism, highlighted by the attack on New York in 2001. The second is the dramatic drop in crime in many countries around the world, particularly in North America but also in Europe, Australia, Latin America, Africa, and Asia.[16] The third is the new economic reality of diminishing public resources, fiscal conservatism, and public accountability—an increasingly contentious reality within which leaders must navigate for their share of public resources. These remain the dominant determinants for how police leaders advance strategic policies in assessing and responding to the emerging priorities of their communities and for designing and developing programs. At the same time, an increasingly educated public with unprecedented access to information means citizens are better informed and more engaged with policy making, resulting in greater expectations for transparency and accountability.[17]

Policing, particularly in developed economies, has tended to be examined as an independent civil institution, somewhat separate and apart from the general security sector, unencumbered by the larger challenges faced by societies undergoing postconflict transformation to democratic governance. Adherence to this perspective, however, limits our understanding of the issues of policing and law enforcement within only one component of the much larger security sector aimed at the efficient and effective provision of state and human security within a framework of democratic governance.[18] Effective and legitimate policing, like freedom of the press, forms a fundamental pillar in the development of civil societies. Under the rule of law, based on the principles of democratic governance, the legitimacy with which police represent their constituents is engendered by the social contract between governments and their citizens, including where necessary the authority to apply force against its citizens toward the preservation of the contract. This contract is not fixed or static but instead must respond to evolving social expectations and norms as, for instance, through the interpretation and application of civil rights charters, human rights, codes of conduct, and interpretation of the law by courts.

Policing has undergone a range of reformations to meet the expectation of the institution it represents and societies it serves, as reflected for instance in the advances from the reform era of policing to the more progressive practices of the professional era. Despite the remarkable gains, even in developed democratic societies, many police organizations continue to harbor dysfunctional or ineffective remnants of reform-era management practices that can hinder the continued democratization of policing.

Previous systems of police governance and practice often contributed to autocratic leadership and insular decision-making, shielded from scrutiny or criticism from within as well as outside and feared by those susceptible to intentionally or unintentionally biased law enforcement. The reform era relied on highly centralized and bureaucratic control systems to formalize authority, prescribe procedures and policy, and manage resource allocation. In contrast, the era of professional policing is expected to be characterized by a decentralization of control, better discretion, and improved responsiveness based on the principles of good governance, professionalism, transparency, and public accountability.

Despite substantive gains, observers suggest that police leaders have simply rebottled old content in new bottles. Others argue that many characteristics of modern policing are systemic indicators of a return to the very problems that contributed to the corruption, nepotism, and illegitimacy of an earlier era. Still others note that while systems and attitudes may appear to change, all that is being observed is merely an overt expression of change, even though the underlying attitudes continue to reflect longstanding systemic biases and preferences for power and control. Systems and cultures that are traditionally insular remain resistant to change, and systemic bias for self-preservation of power and authority exhibits a persistence, which, without continued perseverance and insistence, is inclined to become covert and corrosive. Such criticism, although disconcerting, deserves examination and reflection. These claims are not idle conjecture or retort but stem from the studies and observations of academics and practitioners alike and are reflected in several contemporary challenges, such as the race-based issues facing many American cities today.

It should be the responsibility of every citizen to expect the best of public institutions and to hold their officers, managers, and leaders responsible for fulfilling the obligations of their social contract. The demand for transparency and accountability has never been greater, given the demands on the security sector post-9/11, during a time of unprecedented global connectivity and increasing nationalism. On the one hand, the security sector, comprised of the judiciary and justice ministries, criminal investigation and prosecution services, prison regimes, ombudspersons, and human rights commissions, must ensure the security and interests of the population.[19] On the other hand, nonstatutory civil groups, such as the media, research institutions, nongovernmental institutions, and the public at large, must inexorably play an increasingly larger role in the oversight and accountability of the security sector.[20]

The overall focus of this work is to provide impetus for a dialogue on identifying, limiting, and replacing remnants of reform practices with more progressive strategies that enhance opportunities for the professionalism and enhancement of law enforcement as a forward-focused vocation. This work examines policing from a view of advancing a policy model founded in the recognition that policing, like health care, is a public service entrusted with public funds and state-sanctioned powers that can have a profound impact on the fabric of society and the values and principles shared by its citizens, as well as the degree and quality of social cohesion among its citizens. This idea of a relationship between democratic ideals, social cohesion, and criminality and crime is neither recent nor surprising.[21] The extent to which citizens respect one another and value their relationships influences how they care for each other and should be an important determinant for the public services that aim to maintain order, enhance safety, prevent crimes, and enhance social cohesion.

Social cohesion is a product of the social contract or collective efficacy represented by the capacity of communities to constrain citizens from violating common norms and laws, being a factor of the size, density, and breadth of social networks and the level of engagement of citizens in those networks.[22] Trust forms an important element of social cohesion, reflecting citizens' faith and reliance on one another as well as the state and its institutions and services. It includes a sense of fairness and equality based on shared values, the sense of oneness—increasingly important given the unprecedented migration of citizens, displaced persons, and refugees, whose values must have their basis in the pluralism of increasingly globalized and diverse postmodern societies, and emerging ideological grievances and conflicts.

Social cohesion can be defined as the ongoing process of developing a community of shared values, shared challenges, and equal opportunity, based on a sense of trust, hope, and reciprocity among all.[23] The challenge for policing lies in identifying the indicators of social cohesion—the types of indicators that security services can use to design policies and programs in responding to community needs. Identifying and defining indicators, qualitative and quantitative, requires an iterative process specific to the nature and needs of each community. Examples of these types of indicators include distribution of income, poverty, employment, mobility, health care, education, adequate and affordable housing, population health, economic security, and personal and family security.[24] Other indicators include urbanization, deindustrialization, population turnover, and ethnic and racial heterogeneity.[25]

While community policing works to enhance social cohesion, intelligence policies, such as those that create a community matrix of intelligence sources, serve to enhance intragroup suspicion, thereby undermining processes for social cohesion. Studies demonstrate that citizens often perceive their police as having less to do with risk and victimization and more with their judgments of social cohesion and moral consensus. In England and Wales, for instance, studies show that police may not be seen as providers of a narrow sense of personal security (crime and order) but more as the symbolic moral guardians of community values against emerging long-term change, the types of changes that are perceived to threaten ideas and emotions about nationhood, culture, and state.[26]

It has been said that "[t]he pursuit of police hegemony also works to bolster a potent sense of moral good to which officers frequently aspire. Police work is not only defined by officers as an opportunity to uphold the law or to demonstrate bravery, but as part of a wider struggle between good and evil."[27]

The influence of such symbolic interpretations, by citizens and those employed in the security mechanism, can have a profound impact on the integrity and nature of social cohesion experienced by a community and should not be underestimated—particularly for the preservation of the hard-won pluralistic values of postmodern societies that are increasingly prone to communal and nationalistic influences.

In addition to a general discussion of contemporary policing, this work attempts to advance a model for performance measurement using social cohesion as a basis for determining strategic policy decisions—a model designed for guiding decisions on the application of intelligence-led and community-policing policies, based on the concept of social cohesion and an assessment of the general impact of the two strategic policies with a view of identifying alternatives for moving beyond their present applications, which remain founded largely on quantitative outputs and outcomes.

The discussion advanced herein provides an integrative alternative for including quantitative indicators (of the type relied on by CompStat), as well as qualitative indicators of the types that determine the general health and well-being of communities (social cohesion). Even as the prominent criminologist George Kelling noted, there are increasingly critical discrepancies in the control mechanisms that presently pervade police management and the work and services they are intended to control.

> The research suggested that the control mechanisms that pervaded police organizations—especially rules and regulations, oversight, and militaristic structure and training—were incompatible with the problems that confront police officers daily and the realities of how police services are delivered. Aside from several who were scholars, few police administrators realized how "out of touch" existing practices were with day-to-day police realities.[28]

Kelling was highlighting the subtle yet critical disparity between what is popularly expected as the work police do and the work and services actually provided. It speaks to how police leaders and policy makers motivate, recognize, award, and justify performance.

> The official definition of police mandate is that of a law enforcement agency ... The internal organization and division of labour within departments reflect categories of crime control. Recognition for meritorious performance is given for feats of valor and ingenuity in crime fighting. But the day-to-day work of most officers has very little to do with all of this. These officers are engaged in what is now commonly called peacekeeping and order maintenance, activities in which arrests are extremely rare. Those arrests that do occur are for the most part peacekeeping expedients rather than measures of law enforcement of the sort employed against thieves, rapists, or perpetrators of other major crimes.[29]

Despite the recognition of such disparity by criminologists and social scientists alike, there has remained a stalled stagnation in the wait for an alternative framework for the measurement of performance in policing. Furthermore, such observations provide opportunity for mindful leadership and for a reexamination of some core concepts critical to policing, many of which have been rendered rhetorical because of their indiscriminate overuse. There is an increasing need for an examination of crime trends and performance measurement, the application of a balanced scorecard to policing, boundary belief and interactive controls, community policing, participatory and restorative justice, intelligence-led policing, social cohesion, discretion, trust, and legitimacy, all of which have a profound impact on how officers respond to their roles as peacekeepers and law enforcers. Herein we examine existing practices and draw on a wide scope of global experiences from within policing and criminology, as well as economics, philosophy, social science, law, health care, education, and alternative dispute resolution to develop a new framework for examining policing performance from a renewed perspective based on social cohesion and democratic governance.

This work will benefit anyone connected to or influenced by the security sector, whether in a public or private organization in a postmodern society, postconflict society, or transitioning democracy who is seeking to enhance awareness and understanding of the overarching issues that impact modern policing toward building strong and caring communities.

PERFORMANCE MANAGEMENT

Policymaking ought to be evidence based and motivated by a desire to foster social cohesion, encourage civic participation, and foster civic confidence in ways that strengthen communities. Confidence and trust in community and polity are manifest in many ways, perhaps none more important and evident than the policies designed for responding to crime, maintaining public safety, and ensuring civil liberty. Modern policing requires collaboration and consultation with community members, civic organizations, social services, community leaders, political parties, religious and educational institutions, and special-interest groups. Policing is highly dependent on relationships and is intended to enhance trust between law enforcement and communities, as well as social cohesion.[30]

One of the most perplexing trends over the past two decades has been the sustained decline in crime rates across the globe. The trend has been unexpected and surprising, and explanations for the decline have withstood substantiation despite criminologists' and economists' attempts to develop plausible explanations. No one hypothesis seems to provide a comprehensive explanation for the declining crime rates across North America and the world. Crime has declined even during times of so-called "bear markets," periods associated with the downturn of the global markets and increasing unemployment and fiscal constraint, periods during which there is increasing unemployment, disparity between the rich and poor, and social unrest. Analysts have attempted to account for the trend, resorting to a variety of possibilities, including improved property security, widespread adoption of closed-circuit television surveillance (CCTV), local crime-reduction initiatives, and changes in policing and the wider criminal justice system (e.g., electronic surveillance, records management, business intelligence, intelligence sharing, and minimum/mandatory prison sentences). Explanations have even included theories ranging from the impact of *Roe v. Wade*,[31] the Obama Effect,[32] the exposure of preschool children to lead,[33] and the impact of globalization on the economy attributed with job and wealth creation.

The Federal Bureau of Investigation (FBI) in the United States reported dramatic reductions in crime rates. By 2014, the FBI reported a 4.4 percent decrease in violent crimes over 2012: 12.3 percent below the 2009 level and 14.5 percent below that of 2004.[34] By 2011, homicides had fallen by 67 percent from 2008 in Minneapolis, 47 percent in Seattle, 39 percent in Charlotte, 31 percent in New York, and 17 percent in Los Angeles—a period marked with relatively low productivity and high unemployment in the country. The fact is that it remains unclear why there have been dramatic and sustained declines, some of which were even accelerated in certain jurisdictions during periods of economic decline. The United Nations Commission on Crime Prevention and Criminal Justice reported that cross-national data for common types of crime are insufficiently sensitive to identify a possible relationship between crime and economic factors.[35]

According to the Crime Survey for England and Wales, overall crime trends in England and Wales have remained at their lowest levels since the survey was introduced in 1981. The survey indicated a 10 percent decrease in 2013 from 2012, and figures are 20 percent below those reported for 2007–2008. In fact, the police-recorded crime figures are 38 percent lower than in 2002–2003, when the National Crime Reporting Standards were first established.[36] The declines in England and Wales, where there was a fall of 166,000 violent crimes recorded between 2007 and 2012, were so dramatic that they strongly affected the overall European Union (EU) crime data for the same period.[37] A number of the EU member states have also reported dramatic decreases in violent crime: Lithuania (42 percent), Croatia (33 percent), Scotland (32 percent), Latvia and Slovakia (both 30 percent), and Malta (27 percent).[38] Canada has also experienced some of its lowest crime numbers since the early 1970s.[39] The downward trend has been consistent and dramatic. In Canada, the police-reported crime rate for 2014 was the lowest since

1969 and 34 percent lower than a decade previously.[40] The crime-severity index, which measures both the volume and severity of police-reported crime in Canada, declined for the tenth consecutive year, down 9 percent in 2013 from 2012 and 36 percent lower than in 2003.

It is troubling, however, that perceptions of crime do not reflect this reality. In England and Wales, public perception of crime reported in the British Crime Survey (2010–11) indicated that the majority of people (60 percent) believed crime had risen across the country as a whole in the previous few years.[41] Despite the lowest crime rates since the 1970s, almost two-thirds (62 percent) of Canadians believed that the amount of crime in their neighborhoods was the same as five years earlier, while one-quarter (26 percent) felt that it had increased. Less than one in ten (6 percent) of Canadians perceived that crime had decreased.[42] Australian studies report similar misconceptions—a majority of the population (89.3 percent) held incorrect perceptions of the state of crime as increasing, when in fact it was either stable or had declined.[43] Australia reported, for instance, a 26 percent decrease in the number of victims of murder compared to 1999 and a 32.6 percent decline in the rate of robbery victimization between 2007 and 2012.[44] In Canada's most populous province, Ontario, where one out of three Canadians lives, nearly 80 percent of citizens felt that crime in their neighborhoods was either increasing or had remained the same, despite the fact that Ontario had one of the lowest violent and nonviolent crime rates in Canada between 2007 and 2009.[45] Similarly, the countries forming the European Union (EU), under the umbrella of Eurostat, reported 12 percent fewer crimes in 2012 than in the previous nine years, a trend that has been consistent since 2003.

If we are to have a true and reliable understanding of the impact of policing on crime, we need a comprehensive understanding of the general impacts of social policies on crime and order. Theorists have attempted to explain crime from a variety of perspectives: social disorganization, economics, rational choice, deviance and psychopathology, or environment and space. Each of these has independently enhanced our understanding of crime and deviance. While policing and the criminal justice system are often credited when crime rates decline, the reality is that these two components of civil society only respond to small elements of the antecedents of crime: poverty, lack of education, socioeconomic deficiencies, environmental deterioration and neglect, poor health, and political conflict.

The Ministry of Children and Youth Services in Canada made the following observation:

> [M]eta-analysis of several macro-level criminological perspectives, found that criminal justice system variables were consistently among the weakest predictors of crime, with the exception of incarceration, which was negatively related to crime rates. Over all, the most obvious implication of the findings is the likely futility of continued efforts to reduce crime by focusing exclusively on criminal justice system dynamics, with the exception of incarceration. The wisdom of expanded imprisonment must nonetheless be balanced against its financial costs and its questionable impact on the social vitality of inner cities. This implies that policy-makers must exercise caution when ignoring the root causes of crime and placing potentially excessive faith in criminal justice solutions to control crime.[46]

Franklin Zimring, a criminologist at Berkeley and author of *The City that Became Safe*, noted, "The crime decline of 2008 to 2010 comes at a really inconvenient time for the conventional wisdom, in two respects. One, the economy is going to hell, and two, this is the first time in forty years that we are not removing more prisoners from the streets than we're sending back."[47]

These types of observations are important for several reasons. First, while police practitioners have traditionally measured outcomes and performance based on quantitative standards and designed policies on conventional expectations of cause and effect, there is increasing urgency for looking beyond conventional methods of measuring effectiveness. Second, crime reduction is a complex process influenced by many factors, the impacts of which remain inconclusive, and leaders should be cautious in taking credit too hastily for crime reduction, thereby diminishing opportunities for learning more effective solutions. Third, despite declines in crime and increased police spending, studies indicate that citizens perceive crime as relatively higher than is the reality. The public does not appear to have derived a psychological benefit from crime reduction wherein societal norms can become more receptive to enhanced social cohesion or for including more suitable alternatives to emerging trends and challenges based on ideological grievances, extremism, and nationalism—alternatives that might include, for instance, restorative justice and therapeutic jurisprudence, which by the way also serve to divert the rhetoric of a war on crime to one that is more applicable to an ethic of care.

Another public policy challenge lies in the fact that while crime rates have been declining, police services continue to report record increases in spending. Public expenditures in the United States, for instance, quadrupled between 1982 and 2006,[48] and Canada reported a 3.5-fold increase between 1985 and 2010. Factors impacting costs include the emerging realities of the twenty-first century, such as globalization of commerce and crime, immigration, unprecedented social interconnectivity, and transnational terrorism. Costs have also been impacted by the increasing complexity of plural societies and seismic shifts in global demographics. Future impacts on policing can also be expected as developed economies continue to experience low birth rates and an aging population, while converging economies experience high birth rates and unprecedented numbers of young educated workers.

Examination of the budgets of most Western police services indicates that the bulk of police budgets are spent on salaries. How well police leaders respond to fiscal challenge has an impact on public perceptions, and perceptions influence how citizens perceive the role of police. Policing impacts how citizens feel not only about their personal safety and well-being but also about their very sense of belonging within the larger society of which they are members.[49] Anemic levels of confidence in personal and community safety may have been justifiable given the much higher levels of violent crime experienced during the 1990s. Today, however, public perception is not reflective of the reality. Today, much of the concern for public safety and crime is driven by perceptions rather than the reality of crime and antisocial behavior. Studies show that while crime is down, the impact of antisocial behavior, particularly less serious infractions, influence societal perceptions of safety with far more impact than is believed or currently measured.[50]

According to *Crime in England and Wales 2010/11*, antisocial behaviors (incidents such as begging, drunkenness, dog fouling, or littering, which are crimes in law but not of a level of severity that would result in their being recorded as a notifiable crime) are still not integrated into strategic policing or included in recorded crime data collection,[51] despite the fact that minor crimes may in fact have a disproportionate impact on citizens' perceptions of public safety and police performance. This predisposition, while reinforcing a hard-on-crime focus, neglects a fundamental premise of the broken windows theory (policy) on which much modern policing has been largely premised—that less serious antisocial infractions can often be the precursors to increasingly serious offenses. Yet most police agencies don't record or measure the impact of such offenses on perceptions of safety or the quality of life of their constituents.

Furthermore, many crimes that are not reported or those that are critically underreported too can influence a community's perception of safety and legitimacy of police. Motivation for reporting or not reporting crimes can be influenced by various reasons, including fear of retaliation, sense of duty, a desire for the arrest and punishment of the perpetrator, seriousness of the crime, fear of the criminal justice system, and the support network of the victim.[52] In Canada, sexual assault is among the least likely crimes to be reported to the police.[53] According to a 1999 survey on victimization, 78 percent of sexual assaults remained unreported.[54] According to one report, 90 percent of sexual assaults in Canada go unreported, less than half of sexual assault reports made to police in Canada resulted in criminal charges, and of those charges, only about one-quarter resulted in guilty verdicts.[55] Such marginalized or unreported victimization represents perhaps the more vulnerable and may over the long term signal a desensitization of victims, offenders, and perhaps even entire communities to certain types of crimes.[56] As one Canadian law professor stated to a national paper, even she as an expert on sexual assault would counsel someone she comes to know of having been sexually assaulted to "think very hard before calling the police."[57] Such concerns and comments present significant challenges to the legitimacy of policing and the criminal justice system at large. Unfortunately, underreporting has often been ignored in the assessment of the quality of life of communities or the assessment of legitimacy of the services provided by the criminal justice system.

Large segments of society—youth, aboriginal communities, and those suffering from mental illness, substance abuse, and alternative lifestyles—continue to be marginalized or are perceived to be marginalized by police services around the world. Despite sharp declines in the arrest of young persons under the age of eighteen, youth and children in England continue to lack trust in the services of police. A 2014 parliamentary report, written with the support of the National Children's Bureau in England, found that there is a "profound" lack of trust, "characterized by poor and unconstructive communication and lack of mutual respect."[58]

In the United States, young New Yorkers who experience "stop-and-frisk" report distrusting police and become increasingly less likely to report crimes, even when they are victims themselves. One study reported that 88 percent of young people surveyed believe that residents of their neighborhood did not trust the police, only four in ten respondents would be comfortable seeking help from police if in trouble, and only one in four respondents would report someone whom they believed had committed a crime, thereby posing a serious threat to public safety in that city.[59] Unfortunately, police leaders, for the most part, have contributed to an even more grievous public safety threat by condoning, promoting, and institutionalizing unconstitutional practices involving the subjective routine targeting of marginalized groups through practices such as the stop-and-frisk search. And even though police leaders are just now coming to recognize and limit such practices, once again, it was not their own assessment and recognition of the illegality of the practice that led to the change but rather the forced advocacy of citizens' rights groups and courts. This is another lost opportunity for leadership and for the proactive building of trust.

There is ample research dealing with the issue of relationships between police and minority and marginalized groups. Many of these studies focus on discrimination, bias, negative attitudes, and disproportionate enforcement against minorities. This work is not intended to examine or expand on this area of focus but rather only to remind us of the scope of issues that impact the experiences of citizens and the resulting levels of trust and legitimacy ascribed to their police services and the need for relevant measures of police performance and social cohesion—generally identified by networks of individuals bound by trust, reciprocity, and civic engagement. If citizens with higher levels of social capital tend to trust police more than individuals who appear to be isolated from their neighbors, then civic participation in programs, such as food banks, charitable donations, volunteer fundraising, and support for nongovernmental civic programs may provide another measure of trust, cohesiveness, and public satisfaction with society and police.[60]

Unfortunately, performance measures have not matched changes in crime trends and generally continue to rely on traditional measures, such as major crime indicators (e.g. homicides, violent crimes, assaults, charges, response times, and so on) as the primary measure of community safety and police performance. As a result, little progress is seen in the reporting of qualitative indicators that impact citizens' quality of life and well-being, and where qualitative data is measured, it tends to be limited, arbitrary, and ancillary to quantitative performance measurement. This reticence for qualitative measurement may, in part, be explained by the prevailing cultural perspective that policing is about providing protection first and care only as a derivative to protection. An ethic of care is, therefore, envisioned not entirely as secondary but perhaps better characterized as being embraced within an ethic of protection—a perspective that can limit the responsiveness of policy makers to changes in societal norms, and in crime trends, as a determinant for service provision and resource allocation. Policies based on an ethic of protection may be more appropriate during times of increasing crime or imminent threat; however, an ethic of care may become the more suitable priority during times of low crime or declining threat. The relative importance of an ethic of protection versus an ethic of care must be iterative and responsive to the state of crime and disorder.

As has been noted for sexual assaults, official crime rates do not account for unreported crimes, underreported crimes, and undetected crimes, and yet each category may have significant impact on the quality of life and well-being of citizens and communities. Legitimacy requires that the public understands what is being measured and reported. There is an expectation that what is being reported is correct and conveys the information intended. Too often, reports are based on convoluted and encapsulated measures that distort what common consumers believe is being measured and reported. Take, for instance, uniform crime reports collected from police services that include only those crimes that come to the attention of the police and are considered the most serious offenses. They are often limited to the most serious offenses recorded for each incident or offenses subject to the longest maximum sentences.[61] The remaining offenses are excluded. The point is that the public and police services too often rely on the use of statistical performance measurements with very complex limitations that are not always understood by police leaders themselves and even less by the average citizen. What does it mean when reports indicate that crime is down? Does it mean that crimes are occurring less frequently, or is it a reflection of decreased reporting of crime? And what is included in the definition of *crimes*?[62] In South Africa, prior to late 2007 and the introduction of the Sexual Offences and Related Matters Amendment Act of 2007 (SOA), the police reported separately on rape and those incidents termed *indecent assault*. However, once the act was enacted, police reports stopped providing data disaggregated by type of sexual offense and only provided figures for the total number of sexual offenses overall. As a result, from 2008 onward, it is not possible to distinguish between which of the fifty-nine sexual offenses contained in the acts of 1957 and 2007 are included within this total and which are excluded.[63] Such changes, made for whatever reason, make it difficult for the average citizen to understand what in fact is being reported or the state of improvement or decline. From a policy perspective, do these measures warrant the funding that police agencies demand, or are such demands simply being justified based on what is being measured arbitrarily? These are important questions for law enforcement officials, politicians, policy makers, and citizens. It does not make sense that on the one hand law-and-order policies and strategies are based on the broken windows theory, professing that simple misdemeanors are the antecedents for a widening array of more serious offenses and social disorder and yet police exclude less serious offenses from reported crimes measurements.

This propensity for analytics and statistical decision-making is fostered by the thought that if performance can be measured, then effort and resources can be managed more effectively and requests for new resources (including legislative and administrative) can be advanced rationally and more persuasively. In policing, as with other public services, performance measurement is complicated and extremely difficult. Police leaders face ever-increasing demands to report statistically the variables for which they are accountable or those which are likely to impact the legitimacy of their effort. These include inputs, outputs, outcomes, and costs, to name a few. Such tendencies have resulted in a culture of analytical reliance that now permeates almost all levels of police services.

Along with the increasing demand and reliance on statistical reporting, there is an increasing body of research indicating that measurement systems should be used with caution. Indiscriminate use and reliance, compounded by insufficient knowledge of the full effects and consequences of measurement systems, can lead to unintended organizational dysfunction, which in the final analysis can cost organizations more than the quantitative improvements for which the measurements were originally intended.[64] A report by the Police Executive Research Forum on community policing notes:

> Policing has yet to evolve from basic performance measures (levels of reported crime, clearance rates, operational costs, etc.) that do not inform our strategic thinking. A new focus on developing performance measures to assess the community's satisfaction with our "products," our effectiveness, and our strategies is needed.[65]

Despite this reliance on analytics, police leaders continue to struggle with performance measurement. The report *Public Security in the Americas: Challenges and Opportunities* lists the following among the issues[66]:

- There is a glaring lack of reliable and systematic information.
- There is an overemphasis on policies that control and suppress crime, such as increasing police manpower, reducing the age of criminal responsibility, and expanding the prison population, and too little attention on preventative aspects.
- Programs for monitoring, assessing, and measuring the impact of public security institutions are inadequate.
- The primary missions and functions of the police are not clearly defined.
- The police do not have modern management and transparency policies in place and rely too heavily on a reactive model for their security work.
- Existing institutions have yet to make the full transition to the new democratic, transparent, and rule-of-law perspective of public security.

Whether administrative or operational, policies need to be designed, implemented, and monitored carefully. With regard to intelligence-led policing, for instance, John Kleing notes:

> Intelligence-led policing, moreover, is premised on the value of efficiency, and though the normative importance of administrative efficiency and value for money should not be dismissed, executive virtues such as efficiency and economy need to be coupled with the values of fairness, respect, and the consideration of other's legitimate interests if they are not to be corrupted in significant ways. In addition, intelligence-led policing can easily become embedded in a performance-oriented culture whose dedication to measurement, outcomes, and fiscal parsimony can eviscerate the human

dimension of policing that, at least in liberal democratic communities, should be a pivotal consideration.[67]

Concerns are compounded by the fact that police services are, for the most part, cost-centered operations and lack the checks and balances or accountability associated with profit-centered organizations. Managers often tend to define control too narrowly, as diagnostics for measuring progress against plans for achieving quantitative goals, without the management accountability found in the for-profit world. As a result, trends can appear distorted when measures remain focused on activities that are self-serving or too narrowly focused on quantitative outcomes. For instance, studies show that much of what officers do is motivated by ambitions to demonstrate their capabilities and aptitude to be considered for specialized assignment and career advancement.[68] Activities motivated by such ambitions, particularly in hierarchical paramilitary cultures, are prone to distortion by ambition and can quickly become dysfunctional. Narrowly focused systems have a tendency to become highly authoritative and can lead to behavior predisposed to avoidance motivation (avoid being embarrassed or passed over for promotion) versus approach motivation (the compulsion to do the right thing for intrinsic values). Carefully considered performance measures are crucial given that studies demonstrate that very little of what police officers do is actually about catching criminals or enforcing crime legislation. One white paper on police reform by the Home Office in Britain (1993) noted that in a typical day, only 18 percent of the calls for service are about crime and only about 40 percent of an officer's time is spent dealing with crime.[69]

Jonathan Jackson and Ben Bradford suggest that the uniformed police serve as more than mere crime fighters.

> ... they are for many the "symbolic guardians" of social order and justice engaged in the state's struggle for legitimacy at three levels: through ceremonies of national unification; through the provision of economic or material support for the population; and through a constant process of readjustment by national leadership

in the face of different political, economic and social demands from subordinate populations at specific historical junctures.[70]

It should not be surprising, under scrutiny, that many police leaders, given their annual budgets, defer expenditures until the last quarter in order to "remain prepared for any unforeseeable exigency." This may be fair, since it is often difficult to prepare for the unexpected; however, it should be equally of concern that the same managers then rush to spend their remaining budgets in the final quarter, at any cost, regardless of a need for targeted policing, need for equipment and training, or crime. The result is often a waste of taxpayer money or, worse, overpolicing just to have the remaining budget spent.

Policies on public order and social development are intertwined, more than ever, and must be based on long-term strategies that remain committed to strengthening trust in the state and community, fostering inclusion, fighting marginalization, encouraging education, improving opportunities for employment, and creating opportunities to enhance social cohesion. And while policy makers must incorporate a comprehensive basket of social factors impacting crime, the legitimacy of policing will be increasingly dependent on the measurement indicators and fiscal policies on which police leaders base their services. Determining how agencies measure what officers do is increasingly important for justifying what the public expects from their police service and how police leaders manage and justify their services and associated costs.[71] In the following sections, we examine ways of enhancing performance measurement and accountability.

APPLYING A BALANCED SCORECARD TO POLICING

Communication is the cornerstone of police work, constituting the critical element in relaying information, collecting information, and dispatching instructions during routine patrols, answering calls for service, and establishing relationships or contact with members of the public. Communication is the tool by which officers exert social control, establish trust, and build legitimacy. And yet few police services include the effectiveness of communication as a performance measure. How many other critical areas of ubiquitous police function remain unmeasured? The following are examples of how performance measurement tends to be defined.

Performance measurement:

> A performance measurement system enables informed decisions to be made and actions to be taken because it quantifies the efficiency and effectiveness of past actions through the acquisition, collation, sorting, analysis, interpretation, and dissemination of appropriate data. Organizations measure their performance in order to check their position (as a means to establish position, compare position or benchmarking, monitor progress), communicate their position (as a means to communicate performance internally and with the regulator), confirm priorities (as a means to manage performance, cost and control, focus investment and actions), and compel progress (as a means of motivation and rewards).[72]

Performance measurement system:
> Performance measurement is the ongoing monitoring and reporting of program accomplishments, particularly progress towards preestablished goals. It is typically conducted by program or agency management. Performance measures may address the type or level of program activities conducted (process), the direct products and services delivered by a program (outputs), and/or the results of those products and services (outcomes). A "program" may be any activity, project, function, or policy that has an identifiable purpose or set of objectives.[73]

Performance measures:
> Performance measurement is the process an organization follows to objectively measure how well its stated objectives are being met. It typically involves several phases: e.g., articulating and agreeing on objectives, selecting indicators and setting targets, monitoring performance (collecting data on results), and analyzing those results vis-à-vis targets.[74]

In 1992, Robert Kaplan and David Norton introduced the balanced scorecard as a new strategic management tool for augmenting the traditional focus on financial metrics.[75] The balanced scorecard incorporates both tangible and intangible assets for linking long-term strategies with short-term actions. In part, the balanced scorecard provides opportunities to anticipate performance by including the three dimensions to the financial perspective: a customer perspective, an internal processes perspective, and a learning and growth perspective. Most important, the balanced scorecard offers a link between an organization's vision and its management strategy and, as we will note later, between what Robert Simons in "Control in an Age of Empowerment" distinguishes as diagnostic systems, boundaries for behavior and performance, beliefs, and interactive controls.[76]

Most contemporary police performance measurement systems have their basis in computer-assisted statistical management (CompStat), instituted and popularized by the New York Police Department. CompStat, a diagnostic system, introduced during William Bratton's command of the New York Police Department (NYPD), tracks crime complaints and uses crime trend mapping to identify trouble spots for holding precinct commanders responsible for the identification and resolution of those problems. The system uses major crime indicators to report on crime trends and was used by Mayor Michael Bloomberg and his predecessor, Rudolph Giuliani, to compare New York to other cities.

Our assessment of police performance measurement systems commences with a look at CompStat. This examination is not intended to be a criticism or promotion of the merits of CompStat; rather its purpose is only to provide a frame of reference for a discussion of policing policies generally and for advancing alternative and complementary frames of reference.

Computer Assisted Statistical Management— The Diagnostic Approach

CompStat's strategic and tactical approach to crime identification, response, and analysis provides a powerful diagnostic management and accountability mechanism, whereby regional commanders can be held accountable, before their peers, for their performance in an open forum. Many police leaders and researchers credit this management tool as a paradigm shift in accountability and responsiveness and for paving the way to New York's remarkable reversal of crime trends. On the other hand, a growing number of scholars and, to a lesser extent, practitioners have been divided on the usefulness of CompStat for crime management and its overall impact on modern policing practices. While some see CompStat as a new paradigm, others view it as a reversion to an older, more bureaucratic style of management.

Even though CompStat has its genesis in the broken windows theory, the two addressed very different values. CompStat was designed to get a handle on crime, to reduce crime, and to guarantee that results are measured and monitored to ensure a declining trend. Its purpose was not to be as soft on police strategy. Its purpose was simple: to hold officers and commanders responsible for delivering on crime reduction. And while perceptions of lawlessness, dereliction, and civic apathy may have been identified as factors contributing to the distortion and deterioration of civic norms and as precursors to crime and disorder, CompStat focuses primarily on crime, not its antecedents. In contrast, broken windows focuses on the antecedents of disorder and crime, those factors that act as catalysts for susceptibility and affinity to crime, the causes of crime rooted in the perceptions of the deteriorating state of physical and social integrity of the environment that contribute as factors in the predisposition to lawlessness.

Proponents support CompStat for its strengths in holding middle managers and commanders accountable for identifying crime and disorder problems and for developing effective strategies for responding to them. This strategic management ensures that operational commanders are held accountable for achieving departmental goals and objectives under the watchful eyes of executive-level commanders, who in turn are responsible for ensuring that sufficient and appropriate support and resources are provided for achieving success of operational plans developed by subordinates.[77] Proponents see CompStat as a means for ensuring systemic commitment by requiring that upper managers ensure that adequate resources and support are provided to commanders who in turn must demonstrate accountability for a four-step process: accurate and timely intelligence, rapid deployment of resources, effective tactics, and relentless follow-up and evaluation.

While celebrated and duplicated by practitioners across the globe, critics contend that CompStat is a repudiation of community policing; that it removes responsibility from frontline officers and community members and transfers power back to commanders and managers; that it is a reversion from the generalist policing, which works to make neighborhood officers and their community partners experts on community issues to expert-based specialized policing; and that it has more to do with traditional concerns about the crime and criminals than with any in-depth analysis of the root causes of crime and their impact on high-risk groups. It is noteworthy that it was only after sufficient numbers of senior officers retired from the NYPD that a relatively different impact of CompStat was exposed. A report published in the *New York Times* reported that more than a hundred retired NYPD captains and higher-ranking officers had testified to intense pressure to produce annual crime reductions, which in turn had induced many supervisors and precinct commanders to manipulate crime statistics.[78] Another study of the effectiveness of CompStat, conducted across three large cities in the United States, found that CompStat not only failed to gain widespread commitment for management's objectives, but it often conflicted with important preexisting strategic goals, such as community policing, and led to disaffection and conflict among frontline workers.[79]

Numerical or quantitative indicators don't alone always show how well an objective is being met. Several lessons should be implanted in the institution of performance measurement processes and systems. First, performance measurement diagnostic systems must be appropriate to the circumstances for reporting planned outcomes. CompStat may have been exactly what the NYPD required within the context of one of the highest crime rates in North America in the 1990s, but whether it remains relevant now, when crime rates have dropped to among the lowest in America, is a question that deserves examination. Secondly, performance measurement systems like CompStat must themselves be monitored to ensure that they do not result in dysfunctional behavior as a consequence of the incentives and disincentives built into the system. Systems and people must be monitored to ensure that they are not directly or indirectly incentivized to provide results at the cost of other beneficial activities or so strongly influence processes that their outcomes become corrupted. An example of the indirect impact of CompStat may be observed in penology. Studies indicate that under CompStat's demand for intelligence, rapid deployment, effective tactics, and relentless follow-up, the principles of problem-oriented policing (the targeted enforcement against specific problems) diminish. In the case of CompStat, the emphasis, both cultural and operational, shifted from analyzing and developing possibilities for tailored responses built in partnership with other social services to providing the quickest response, which in turn led to a renewed commitment to extricating criminals quickly, incarceration, and moving on to the next problem.[80]

Third, every performance measurement system must be appropriate to the uniqueness of specific circumstances and determined on geographic and temporal considerations. What is appropriate for New York is not necessarily appropriate for Seattle, nor is what was good for New York in 1990 necessarily appropriate for New York in 2013.

Even highly celebrated and effective systems must be subject to critical examination. Although effective as a diagnostic tool, CompStat's impacts on other levers of management control (belief systems, boundary systems, and interactive control systems) are unclear. Each is, however, an important source of feedback that would enable management to adjust inputs and processes to more closely match larger long-term goals. It is important to maintain a healthy skepticism about the sustained effectiveness and continued relevance of any performance measurement system to its particular social circumstance, as well as the potential for consequential groupthink, as in the case of policing, given that police culture and networks are prone to quickly transposing the experiences of a single jurisdiction to their counterparts around the world.[81]

Underlying Causes of Neglect, Delinquency, and Crime Causes for the Broken Windows		
Dereliction ("broken windows") and the recognition of a distortion of civic norms that contributes to desensitization to disorder and increased tolerance for antisocial norms.	}	"Broken windows" focuses a social and normative responsibility on state and social actors to remedy the antecedents of crime and disorder.
Development of antisocial behavior manifests crimes and victimization.	}	CompStat is an accountability mechanism for measuring and holding accountable managers.

Figure 3. Broken windows—underlying causes of neglect, delinquency, and crime and its normative impact.

Despite its adoption as a theoretical framework for understanding neglect and crime, broken windows falls short of focusing sufficient attention on the origin of neglect, delinquency, and crime by implying moral responsibility for the causes of neglect on affected communities, when in fact marginalized communities rarely have the capacity or control over the resources needed for addressing the causes or symptoms. A careless application of a broken windows policy, without careful and sensitive consideration of the affected community, can thereby serve to *otherize* affected neighborhoods, increasing stigmatization and further diminishing collective efficacy.

As a comparison and in contrast, during the same time that CompStat was being heralded as the new paradigm for policing, British Airways, with over sixty thousand employees, servicing more than two hundred destinations around the world, had undertaken to improve its market position by placing "superior customer service" as the focus of its strategy.[82] The Chairman of British Airways (BA), Sir Colin Marshall, recognized that employees must understand their role in delivering superior service and must have the power to deal with customer problems firsthand if BA was to achieve its strategic goals. Under Marshall's leadership, the airline undertook significant research to understand what "superior service" meant to its customers. Following some four hundred focus groups and associated interviews, the airline identified eight "moments of truth,"[83] which could potentially influence customers' perceptions of service. The airline conducted extensive data analysis and interpretation to determine statistically significant relationships between the various factors that linked customer satisfaction with financial performance. Most important, British Airways used research to examine its assumptions about performance linkages by expanding the analysis to break down traditional silos (market research, human resources, and so on) to overcome existing assumptions about performance measurement. Unlike the many police leaders and their counterparts in private industry, Marshall recognized and undertook the challenge of designing a performance measurement system suited to his own very specific requirements. British Airways ensured that the outcomes of its performance measurement actually targeted the areas important to its strategic vision and could achieve the desired results in quantitative and qualitative terms before implementing a measurement process unique to its particular needs. For policing, moments of truth might include assessment and inclusion of risk factors and protective responses, many of which are difficult to quantify but critical to therapeutic intervention—the types of interventions that enable access and enhance social cohesion: access to governmental, nongovernmental, for-profit, and nonprofit organizations; those that enhance self-esteem, self-efficacy, a sense of responsibility, tolerance, positive parental support, positive peer influences, or an awareness of the determinants of well-being.[84] Police performance systems would be well served to become more holistic. Systems like Statcom, well-intentioned and relevant as they may be during periods of increasing crime, lack the qualitative component to make the necessary adjustment when crimes begin to decline and when quality of service becomes increasingly important. Today's police performance measures must include their own moments of truth. Decisions in policing need to be developed using a wider scope of observations and based on a holistic approach to performance inputs. Diagnostic measurement should enhance monitoring, promote intellectual flexibility, and reconcile discordant information from different sources, using different methods. Once goals are established and managers have aligned performance targets with corresponding incentives and disincentives, it is expected that employees will work diligently toward meeting targets and responding to moments of truth while keeping within organizational expectations. The reality, however, is that officers will attempt to redefine their processes for maximizing personal reward, often at the cost of other organizational goals and interests. For this reason, organizations institute forms of personnel evaluation process toward ensuring that employee conduct aligns with strategic goals, outputs, and outcome.

In policing, personal evaluations generally commence from the time suitability for hire is determined as members are undertaking training at the academy and continue until retirement. The form and frequency of evaluations may change, depending on seniority, rank, and assignment, but remain fundamentally universal. The most common form of evaluation consists of an appraisal (annual or semiannual) done by a supervising officer and generally approved by a second-level supervisor or unit commander. The legitimacy of the appraisal is determined not by the appraisal itself, at least in the mind of the employee, but by perception of its impact on what is valued by the employee—reclassification in rank, selection for specialized assignment or squad, promotion, or award. Unfortunately, police evaluations, for a variety of reasons, are conducted more for the purpose of conformity to bureaucratic standards and only indirectly for the work police officers actually do.

Further, studies indicate that police officers only spend a very small proportion of their time fighting crime and a supervisory officer only ever observes a very small portion of their patrol deployment.[85] One study of the activities of patrol officers in Britain found that there is a lack of clarity of purpose, given that in a typical day, only 18 percent of the calls for service are about crime and only about 40 percent of an officer's time is spent dealing with crime.[86] The vast majority of a police officer's time is spent alone in a patrol car, with up to 85 percent of police patrol time being spent not dealing with citizen contacts.[87] And herein lies the paradox: while police performance systems tend to be quantitative-centric, personnel performance appraisals tend to rely heavily on subjective assessments by supervisors of how well they think or perceive their officers are performing. Such assessments are limited and cannot be considered relevant or reliable when assessment is centered on what officers do outside of the station and in the field, without including a method of assessing what officers do when they are alone and unsupervised. The problem is that officers are seldom observed when working alone (nearly 85 percent of the time), and assessments reflect only a limited observation of the officers' conduct. And when objective criteria are applied, they tend to be heavily weighted on quantitative assessments focused on how much is achieved as opposed to how well officers perform their functions. For these reasons, it becomes difficult to determine how well officers might be identifying and responding to those moments of truth that should be relevant to their managers and to the communities they serve.

Assessments must not become linked to organizational performance measurements that are not aligned with the specific requirements of officers' duties and functions during their day-to-day contact with diverse segments and subcultures within and external to their policing community. Misalignment often distorts the officer's activities into self-incentivization toward activities that are more likely to be detected by supervisors and recognized and evaluated as pertinent for seeking reward (reassignment or promotion) and not necessarily for doing what is right. Studies indicate that even in those cities where police managers' and patrol officers' value orientations coincided, there are challenges in winning officers' commitment to organizational goals or overcoming cynicism and resentment of what frontline officers see as contradictions between evaluations and stated values, strategies, and goals.[88] This dissonance between conflicting goals can, if not managed, lead to self-justified rationalizations for the distortions of behavior. In other words, workers begin to do what they see as needing to be done, concealing their actions from measurement, thereby compromising other measurement systems and undermining the legitimacy of management, policies, and processes. The result manifests in a form of avoidance motivation wherein workers rely on their personal value systems to do the right thing and only what is required to avoid negative consequences, as opposed to doing what is required and right for achieving recognition and self-actualization.

In other instances, particularly when officers do not seek reassignment or promotion, a culture of professional protectionism, through strong police unions, can contribute to a culture of self-protectiveness, wherein supervisors too avoid creating dissention by issuing complimentary evaluations, thereby marginalizing the importance, effectiveness, and value of performance appraisals. This adds to a predisposition for cultural insularity and can result in performance evaluations being used more as a tool for reward and punishment rather than a means for promoting development and enforcing policy. Organizations can compound marginalization of performance appraisal systems by instituting performance categories construed to evoke conformity with the paramilitary nature of policing, such as driving ability, appearance, teamwork, and impact and influence. Ineffective performance appraisals then contribute to an array of what Ericson calls "recipe" rules—rules that become part of the occupational culture and guide officers on how to get the job done in ways that are acceptable to the organization, for instance, determining which types of people to deal with in which situations and for what offenses and how to avoid unnecessary and restrictive supervision controls.[89] Narrow performance appraisals based on enforcement and compliance do not present opportunities necessary for fully encouraging, evaluating, and rewarding activities that are at the core of community policing—the bulk of what police do. Given this scope and range of potential for self-generated activities, policing offers a wide capacity of discretionary decision-making, which cannot always be controlled through codification. Discretionary tendencies underscore a need for managers to think about other levers of control available to them—belief systems, boundary systems, and interactive control systems.[90]

There is another dimension that police leaders contend with; as public concern and awareness increases, police organizations become increasingly sensitive to criticism and public complaints. Police organizations tend to respond by systemically instituting more supervisory oversight, in some cases, holding supervisors to higher standards of liability and accountability when they fail to detect and address misconduct. This in turn leads to a mode of management that stresses that every small mistake or oversight be identified, documented, and corrected. In effect, police organizations develop a cultural fear, or liability phobia, wherein competency as a supervisor or candidacy for promotion comes to be based on one's ability to demonstrate a capacity to catch employees making mistakes and holding offenders accountable. The focus becomes deterrence and as noted earlier, contributes to attitudes that may only reflect compliance. Results are then illusory expressions of conformity; all the while underlying attitudes continue to persist under the radar of what are perceived to be unfair and punitive management policies. Even small mistakes are likely to result in disciplinary action, and opportunities for learning or for exercising discretion become increasingly circumscribed.

As members cultured in this mind-set are promoted, there is a proportionate rise in a groupthink that views managers and workers as separate entities and at odds with their respective values (management versus frontline). Managers and organizational leaders come to be perceived as placing great value on the proficiency for finding deficiencies rather than rewarding employees for doing things well. Adversarial norms widen suspicion, insularity, conflict, and hostility between frontline officers. The notion that managers can be teachers, mentors, and coaches becomes secondary to the notion of managing issues.

The problem becomes compounded when external oversight is brought into the mix. There may increasing suspicion between management and frontline officers, wherein management is perceived to be willing to sacrifice frontline members for the greater good of preserving their own integrity. Public trust, both identification and calculus, affect confidence in the policing services, and incidents involving abuse of force, corruption (real and perceived), and the efficiency of the justice system (how quickly the justice system responds to dealing with resolving cases and injustice[91]) of which the police are a part become part of the mix. Consequently, civilian oversight, public opinion, media, courts, police services boards, and special interest groups all have varying degrees of influence on the disciplinary codes and professional standards of police organizations. The purpose here is not to examine the role of oversight itself but merely to acknowledge the factors that impact performance behavior. Management boards (police services boards), independent investigative bodies for police oversight, courts, special interest groups, and media too provide oversight. The difficulty with boards is that they are entities with significant political associations and often without technical understanding of policing. The boards that work best are those that have a mixed representation made up of politicians, representatives of citizens' associations and organizations, and police technicians who understand and are capable of designing policies and setting priorities, without intervening with the operational details or their implementation.[92] Under such influences, frontline officers and police generally draw insular fraternal boundaries, oftentimes stereotyped in the media as the "thin blue line," a condition that contributes to the development of police systems and cultures that can become overly insular and resistant to intervention or change, even where policies require that police include community groups in identifying problems, setting priorities, and integrating civic organizations and advisory groups as partners in the prioritization and mobilization of responses in defense of the values of the community and society at large.[93] Insularity is compounded by the fact that norms for engagement with police oversight and the criminal justice system require that relationships be framed on the adversarial nature of the democratic justice system. Under such norms, performance appraisals become an internal matter in which there is no scope for external input.

Nonetheless, courts and judges also influence police policy and procedures. In one study, Yvonne Marie Daly observes the impact of the judiciary in Ireland, England and Wales, the United States, Canada, and New Zealand, noting:

> One particularly important constituent part of the development of investigative procedures and practices is the approach of the courts to the admissibility at trial of evidence obtained in a certain manner. While a judge can only address the specifics of whatever cases are brought before him, the judiciary as a whole has a significant role to play in terms of police accountability and governance through their development and application of any exclusionary rules of criminal evidence.[94]

Judges can have other practical influences on police practice by altering administration and organization of courts practice. Richard Ericson provides three examples.[95] In one case, where night-shift officers were reluctant to issue summonses because they would have to be in court the next day, judges removed the barrier by allowing deferred appearances in court, which prompted the officers to increase their enforcement. Judges also issue concurrent sentences to offenders charged with multiple offences, thus providing police with less latitude for plea bargaining. And third, courts confer confidence or lack of confidence in police by upholding or dismissing charges, such as assault on police and cause disturbance, which rely solely on the testimony of the police. Each of these can impact the type of offenses officers choose to enforce, the manner in which officers interact with counsel and the accused, and how officers perceive their role and legitimacy within the criminal justice system.

At the same time that courts provide oversight, they can also serve to undermine oversight. Ericson notes that officers are well informed about their position within the constitutional framework that restricts the judiciary from directly interfering in operational and investigative matters. And yet there are strong "exchange relationships" formed with prosecutors, defense counsel, justices of the peace, and judges, which undermines the scope of oversight.[96] Other entities of the judiciary are seen to be beneficiaries of the services of the police and therefore as an important component in the reinforcement of police performance. Clearly, courts convey informal yet powerful oversight and influences on the performance of officers. Such relationships can become powerful detractors to the professionalization of policing by promoting a culture wherein officers are likely to feel that they are merely enforcers of the law, constrained by authority, rules, and procedures and constrained in their ability to make discretionary decisions. Frontline officers may perceive management and oversight focus as being on punishing failure rather than rewarding success. Once again, the consequences are obvious—officers do what they feel needs to be done, avoid authority, and may stop exercising otherwise thoughtful discretionary decisions. Staying out of trouble becomes the overarching goal.

Police organizations need to encourage officers to initiate process improvements and new ways of responding to customers' needs by providing the right incentives, aligned with performance standards that balance financial perspectives, customer perspectives, internal business perspectives, and innovation and learning. Everyone in the organization must be vested with the authority ownership to identify moments of truth. This requires managers not only to focus on analytics, but also to be concerned with the fundamental problem of how to exercise adequate control in systems that demand flexibility, innovation, and creativity. Modern policing is like a competitive business that must respond to declining crimes, evolving demographics, complex measurement processes, and limited financing. Competitive business with demanding and increasingly informed and connected customers, like those of British Airways, must rely on employee initiative to seek out opportunities and respond to customers' needs. This requires control systems that are integrative, continuously monitored, and aligned at all levels of performance management.

Dynamic organizations cannot afford to only conduct annual performance evaluations, with little or no feedback between evaluations. This creates appraisal systems that are unresponsive to evolving goals or prone to merely becoming a tool for rewarding or punishing conformity, rather than encouraging innovation or achieving the purpose for which they were intended—performance improvement. Measurements must also incorporate the quality of employees' working lives, which can provide a powerful and proven means for dealing with performance. One study on public productivity uses the term *quality of working life* as a component to a balanced approach to including personal job satisfaction as an important motivator, which "... goes beyond specific techniques or reaching of particular sets of goals. Rather, quality of working life involves the design of the workplace, work roles, and organizations, which build in the potential for employees to fulfill personal needs while concurrently contributing to improved organizational effectiveness."[97]

Police leaders need to continue to infuse policing with measures that go beyond efficiency-based standards to include more qualitative indicators of effectiveness for reducing fear of crime, increased livability of communities, and enhanced social capital—"understood as social networks and the associated norms of reciprocity and trustworthiness."[98] The balanced scorecard, while controversial in itself, provides managers with an important foundational framework for incorporating financial, customer, internal processes, and innovation and learning with belief systems, boundary systems, and interactive control systems that enhance both quality of working (organizational) as well as public (community) life. It offers measures that motivate and inspire officers to meet strategic goals, while identifying emerging issues, developing relationships based on trust and fairness, and encouraging a sense that policing is about serving the needs of communities and citizens more than state-based control.

Looking beyond empiricalization is neither revolutionary nor specific to policing. Other professions facing similar challenges support the emergence of new ways of looking at old performance measurement practices. One can find an increasingly wider range of professions that are expressing concerns about their overreliance on empiricism. In medicine, for instance, there is an increasing acceptance of the fact that, notwithstanding its foundations on scientific methodology, overreliance on empiricism may, under certain circumstances, be naïve and historically inaccurate. *The New Zealand Journal of Medicine* notes:

> Marshalling and comparing a sufficient number of observable or manageable facts as evidence rarely, if ever, leads to the one correct conclusion. Intellectual flexibility, tolerance of ambiguous and discordant information obtained by different methods from differing viewpoints and different conceptual levels, the judicious yet knowingly fallible, theory-derived construction, selection and interpretation of observations and empathically derived experiences typify the scientific method and is congruent with a form of clinical practice that is scientific, therapeutic and ethical.[99]

Performance measurement and effective resource allocation require policies that expand the scope of dimensions against which success can be assessed. For most public service organizations, such policies require a long-term strategic outlook but with a commitment to ensuring that today's short-term actions align with the long-term strategies and that these policies are designed with multiple dimensions in mind. This integrative approach ensures that employees are not compromised at the expense of developing customers or that financial goals do not outweigh the long-term impact on customers and stakeholders. In the following section, "Boundary, Beliefs, and Interactive Controls," we build our understanding of the effective controls of employees.

Simply put, police leaders can and must do better at determining how successfully their organizations and employees are performing by applying systematic ways of evaluating the inputs, outputs, transformation, and productivity through a quantitative and qualitative assessment that can provide a balanced and holistic indication of how well each objective is being met.

Mending broken fences and communities requires a commitment to building strong, caring communities, to investing in strategic changes that prefer social well-being, and to enhancing connectedness and trust among and between community members and for economic security and social investment.

BOUNDARY, BELIEFS, INTERACTIVE CONTROLS, AND DIAGNOSTICS

Organizations have three main assets—people, capital, and reputation. Of the three, the last is the most difficult to regain if impaired. Organizations respond by instituting clearly designed and defined codes of conduct that identify expectations for all employees and guard against harm by errant actions and damage to their reputation. In systems with structured hierarchies, such as in policing, gaining commitment to new policies becomes challenging because the outcomes or the outward appearance of compliance may not in fact be motivated by true commitment. We have already looked at how diagnostics systems, like CompStat, can impact organizational and employee behavior and outcomes. We will now look at the impact of other so-called levers of controls and influences. Compliance and commitment are two very different states, which may produce similar outward outcomes, while being entirely different in motivation and intent. The former is coercion based, intended to comply with authoritative incentives, while the latter relies on a buy-in by the agent of the intrinsic value of the desired outcome. Research on the use of control and empowerment can help organizations develop better thought-out processes and structures for maximizing productivity while mitigating risk.[100] Notwithstanding that diagnostics measurement systems, like CompStat, have become systemic to the measurement of police performance, boundaries, beliefs, and interactive control systems are critical for the effective delivery of police services, wherein discretion is an essential feature for ensuring fairness, equitability, transparency, and legitimacy. Boundaries, beliefs and interactive control systems provide additional ways for gaining commitment, maintaining compliance, and overcoming resistance to systems, policies, and expectations.

The discretion available to an officer responding to a situation (choice to charge or not charge, choice of charge, number of charges, commitment to scope of investigation, commitment to providing disclosure, commitment to quality of testimony, and so on) cannot be entirely codified and is an outcome of the cultural beliefs and controls of the organization and how employees' performance is measured. In instances where favorable performance is contingent on a quantitative assessment, such as charges filed and persons arrested, the officer is less likely to exercise discretion, particularly when he or she finds him- or herself short of an expected standard prior to an impending evaluation. Similarly, an officer is less likely to exercise discretion in circumstances when he or she finds him- or herself doubtful of the oversight process, which might challenge a discretionary decision, particularly when the officer lacks training, is unsure of organizational support, or believes that the decision may be contrary to conventional expectations. While boundaries, beliefs, and controls may be designed to deal with or avoid conflicts based on expectations of performance, role, effectiveness, or policy, conflicts can also provide motivational incentive for creativity. Conflicts may, for instance, arouse the motivation to solve problems that, without the expression of a conflict, might have gone unidentified, unaddressed, or generally unattended to.[101] Such challenges are real and can have a profound impact on the effectiveness, efficiency, and legitimacy of every organization and the trust of the community. In designing and implementing performance management, managers must ensure a balanced approach, one which includes boundary systems, belief systems, interactive controls, and diagnostics, each of which must be applied to leverage the unique outcomes that each influences and also to allow for the healthy expression of conflict. Should police leaders monitor charges laid by their officers? Officers may then only lay charges seen to be preferred under prevailing circumstances, or they may lay too many charges and only of the types that are easy to investigate and quick to complete. Should police leaders monitor conviction rates to ensure good investigations and follow through? Officers might then only resort to laying charges in circumstances where they are confident and can absolutely assure convictions and dismiss another charges, which might require more work or be prone to uncertainty of conviction. Should police leaders influence investigations at all? Should police leaders facilitate the sharing of information? Officers might then hide information or work under cover of oversight to safeguard their sources and information—after all, information is power.

The following section draws on the work of Robert Simons on maintaining "control in an age of empowerment" for the management of controls within a police structure. Today's police officers are constantly bombarded with directions on what to do—maintain traffic enforcement to ensure the free, safe, and unencumbered flow of workers and products, gather intelligence, liaise with community groups, attend to trouble spots, respond to calls for service in a timely manner, submit thorough reports, keep up on training, and on the list goes. Managers continually provide direction and focus, often without the benefit of having recent on-the-road experience or familiarity with emerging technological implementations. Further, today's officers are subject to unprecedented diagnostic surveillance to guard against misconduct or misdirected enforcement. Take, for instance, the implementation of business intelligence units that measure every facet of police work, in-car-cameras that provide managers the ability to remotely survey the actions of frontline officers, body-worn cameras that record every action an officer takes and the words he or she speaks, global positioning systems that report on the location and movements of an officer's vehicle, smart phones that record the officer's actions, and closed-circuit television cameras that report on community actions and interactions. Such advances in surveillance, combined with the propensity of policies, procedures, directives, and codes of conduct, can result in managers and supervisors feeling that their people are doing and will do the right thing, that good incentives and disincentives will help control workers to keep them doing the right thing and working toward organizational goals. However, research shows that this might not be enough. Even good people will be influenced by conflicting values, resulting in "pressures that lead to control failure—even crisis."[102]

Boundary Systems

Police leaders institute clearly defined policies, procedures, directives, and codes of conduct that set clear expectations of their employees. These boundary systems are critical for all organizations but especially so for organizations whose reputation is built on trust and for whom legitimacy is a key competitive asset. Without effective boundary systems, entrepreneurial individuals may sometimes blur or misinterpret the line between acceptable and unacceptable behavior. Creative employees motivated to increase overtime, for instance, may violate rules and short-circuit existing controls, the resulting aftermath of which may have the consequence of a public scandal, destroyed careers, or destroyed organizational legitimacy and trust. Nonetheless, studies of the effect of avoidance motivation and creativity suggest that boundary systems should be framed in a manner that encourages creativity and risk taking rather than framing behavior within defined procedural limits.[103] George Kelling notes that:

> Police administrations' limited ability to shape police street practice persists despite management's preoccupation with control—an orientation that largely grew out of efforts to minimize the kinds of corruption, especially political corruption, that plagued late 19th and early 20th century American policing. Yet, as valid as its origins were, police administrators' preoccupation with control, and the methods they adopted to maintain it, have had tragic, unanticipated consequences. Most obviously, this preoccupation has fostered a bitterly antimanagement culture in many police departments. In this culture officers are alienated from the citizens they serve, support a "stay out of trouble" (by doing nothing) mentality, and, while disapproving of abuse and corruption, nonetheless protect deviant officers in the name of occupational solidarity.[104]

Studies suggest that conscribing what employees can do by establishing standard operating procedures and rulebooks diminishes initiative and creativity that might otherwise be expressed by empowered, entrepreneurial employees. Telling them what not to do allows innovation but within clearly defined limits. Intended to guard against damage to reputation and legitimacy these control systems can also, when misguided or poorly thought out, constrain the empowerment that frontline officers require to exercise discretion. Discretion is essential for creating a sense of fairness (as opposed to zero-tolerance) and is a valued function when well intentioned and directed toward the achievement of organizational goals and within the scope of the organization's vision and mission. How an officer responds to a situation (choice to charge or not charge, choice of charge, number of charges, etc.) is impacted by the culture and belief system of the agency and how performance is measured. The framing of boundaries defined by procedures should be based not solely for conscribing unwanted behavior; procedures must also enable and encourage judicious and calculated application of discretion—an important element for legitimacy.

Boundary systems must be designed to balance both risk and integrity. Overly restrictive boundary systems designed to safeguard organizational integrity often become counterproductive, leading to a *liability phobia* wherein supervisors and managers are more concerned with preempting mistakes than creating opportunities for learning from mistakes. In such circumstances, organizations may inadvertently promote a management culture that rewards risk management (risk aversion) more than risk-taking (discretion), resulting in that culture wherein managers are promoted on their ability to catch and avoid mistakes at any cost, thereby developing a generation of supervisors and managers who are increasingly efficient in finding deficiencies rather than identifying and rewarding innovation and creativity. David Cox, the dean of studies at the Navitas College of Public Safety in Melbourne, Australia, puts it this way:

> The Core element of police work, when set against the "principles," might not have changed that dramatically since the introduction of Sir Robert Peel's Metropolitan

Police Act of 1829, but the context in which police services conduct their activity has become far more demanding. Dealing with uncertainty and ambiguity is something rules-based organizations find easy to accommodate (Cowper, 2000). With its command and control culture, the once taken-for-granted authority attached to policing is under challenge (Neyroud, 2009). Without disputing the importance of command and control regimes it is a relatively small element of operational policing (Peak & Glensor, 1996, p. 172). Yet its criticality, derived from the high cost of failure associated with situations that go awry, has come to weigh heavily—perhaps too heavily—on how police conceptualize "policing" as a whole (Raffe, 2005, pp. 86–7). "Worst case" scenario instruction still dominates in the academies. This frames and fashions how newly-inducted members come to perceive their relationship to the community. Placing the "command and control" culture alongside a "principles" regime brings into sharp relief the tension in contemporary policing.[105]

Like diagnostic control systems (which monitor critical performance outcomes) or belief systems (which communicate core values), boundary systems have a direct effect on behavior and should be stated, as much as possible, in terms of minimum standards. Richard Ericson notes:

> Rules serve as tools of power and as justification of actions taken. In the case of criminal-law rules, the police have an enabling resource to control what and whom are proceeded against and legitimate actions taken. The law provides "cover" in two senses. It provides "blanket" cover through the wide range of substantive offences available to handle any troublesome situation the officer is likely to confront. Also, the legal procedures for police actions are so enabling that there are few instances when what the officer wishes to do cannot be legitimated

legally. Beyond this, the police officer has control over the production of "facts" about a case, and this control of knowledge becomes a very potent form of power. The rules are not only taken into account, but they also form part of the account to legitimate the action taken. In sum, the normative order of rules made applicable and the meanings applied to a situation are closely related. The powerful nature of rules is not to be gleaned from "perceptible determination of behaviour", but rather in how rules constrain people to account for their rule-invocations, rule violations, and rule applications.[106]

Workers are inventive, and when presented with obstacles to their goals, temptation, or needs for recognition and reward, they will create new opportunities to construct value by overcoming the obstacle. However, people generally want to do the right thing, even in the absence of guiding rules—that is to act ethically in accordance with established moral codes. But pressures to achieve superior results sometimes collide with stricter codes of behavior. Because of temptation or pressure in the workplace, individuals may sometimes choose to bend rules. History is chock-full of managers who did not pay sufficient attention to their boundary systems until disclosure of improper behavior by a small number of employees was forced into public scrutiny. Scandals at Enron, Lehman Brothers, Bears Stern, and WorldCom are just a few such prominent cases. Effective managers anticipate the inevitable temptations and pressures that exist within their organizations, ensuring integration of rules, belief systems, and interactive controls to form a comprehensive management system. They spell out the policies, rules, and procedures based on the risks inherent in their strategy and enforce them clearly and unambiguously but fairly, transparently, and according to established guidelines and norms.

Belief Systems

In the past, an officer's mission was more narrowly defined by the norms of smaller and more heterogeneous communities and did not require published references to core values or formal beliefs. In contrast, today's police services operate on a global scale where social and normative controls are complex, social media omnipresent, communities more diverse, and public safety demands more urgent, making it challenging for employees to comprehend the ever-changing landscape of public perception, expectation, and organizational purpose and direction. Globalization increases the scope of international collaboration and partnerships available to police and public service organizations. At the same time, employees today possess higher and more diverse educational training and bring higher expectations for meaningful career experiences. Globalization has also increased economic and sociopolitical volatility, wherein unexpected events and ethical realignment can quickly shatter strongly held assumptions about the values and foundations of an organization and its leaders. Such volatility and uncertainty, if mishandled, can cause employees to become increasingly doubtful about whom to trust, and in the absence of clearly articulated core values, they can be forced into making assumptions about what constitutes acceptable behavior in the many different and unpredictable circumstances they encounter. Belief systems are integral to the ethics and principles that guide an officer's behavior and how he or she establishes priorities and justifies actions and activities. Today, police officers are subject to an increasing frequency of unexpected inputs from unpredictable social, cultural, political, and technological influences compared to their counterparts of a decade ago. This requires police leaders to better prepare their people and systems for responding to change and crisis than ever before. Police forces must become increasingly agile and responsive to competitive forces in adapting to global influences.

Furthermore, because patrol officers devote only a portion of their time (not more than 10 percent)[107] to responding to calls for service, boundary systems have limited utility. According to studies, the average uniform member rarely makes an arrest. Officers in the United States make an average of nineteen arrests a year, while in Canada, officers make an average of one arrest per month.[108] The time spent during the intervening arrests may include a variety of police-community contacts wherein officers rely on a set of guiding principles beyond those articulated in procedures, rules, regulations, and law. Of course, a police officer's duties involve much more than making arrests. Police officers today are called to do tasks spanning the vocational competence of nurses and social workers to paramilitary commandos, and although highly regulated, the officer is paradoxically alone in dealing with citizens when making emergent decisions, with very little guidance and almost no supervision.[109] No set of procedures could cover all exigencies. The remaining time, related to nonprescribed activity, must therefore be regulated through some other mechanism. Here belief systems become critical in providing employees with a clear and consistent understanding of the core values of their mission and their place within the organization and the increasingly unpredictable economic, social, and technological realities of the twenty-first century. Beliefs in the value and purpose of what and why officers do what they do becomes essential to the cultural effectiveness with which police services are able to achieve their goal of maintaining order through the use of persuasion, negotiation, and influence, particularly in the absence of guiding governance and supervision. Beliefs include how officers perceive and apply trust, accountability, fairness, and legitimacy. Formal belief systems require that organizations respond by instituting unambiguous statements of social contract (core values and mission and vision statements) that define their belief system and then effectively and consistently communicate these values and directions to employees, clients, and partners.

Robert Simons, in "Control in an Age of Empowerment,"[110] suggests that typical belief systems need to be value laden and inspirational. They should draw employees' attention to key tenets of an organization: how the organization creates value (for example: being committed to being a leader in the industry), the level of performance the organization strives for (for example: providing environmental stewardship to benefit society or a commitment to building stakeholder value), and how individuals are expected to manage both internal and external relationships (for example: measuring organizational success by the satisfaction of their customers, employees, and communities). Such belief systems become the critical ingredient for determining fairness, equity, and legitimacy when making discretionary choices, for instance between action and inaction.

Simons notes that belief systems are designed to be intentionally broad in order to appeal to different groups within an organization: managers, salespeople, production workers, and clerical personnel.[111] He notes that belief statements, which need to be broadly stated in order to appeal to a wide-ranging audience, are often ridiculed for lacking substance. But this criticism overlooks the principal purpose of such statements: to inspire and promote commitment to an organization's core values. Cynicism and ridicule must not mask the fact that only values that enhance ethical action can lead to real and substantive changes, as opposed to cultures that provide superficial appearances of change without the substantive change to underlying attitudes. Belief statements will, however, only achieve their transformative ends if managers demonstrate through their daily statements, actions, and behavior, a genuine commitment to their values and social contract. Employees who suspect that managers are only going through the motions as a corporate exercise quickly become cynical and distrustful. On the other hand, managers who rely on their value charters as living documents, as part of a system that guides patterns of acceptable behavior, discover a powerful lever for impacting and influencing others.[112] For this reason, one of the most important values to be included in any belief statement should be a commitment to the hyper-value–authenticity, which despite being the essential element for any real and substantive change is often overlooked.

The communication culture of an organization is also an important factor in the effectiveness of a belief system. Experts observe that without a sensible vision, organizational processes can easily dissolve into a set of confusing and incompatible projects that can take the organization in the wrong direction or nowhere at all.[113] Belief systems must be communicated at every opportunity, in sincere and meaningful ways. Unfortunately, too many leaders create the *smart-talk gap*, which in turn produces the *knowing-doing gap*. Pfeffer and Sutton note that many successful companies, including Xerox, Continental, and Apple, have fallen captive to the smart talk as their managers attempted to provide the solutions to their organizations' problems through the tools they were trained to use and understand.[114] Their tools had been based on cultures of criticism and complexity. Solutions were only considered legitimate when they could provide competitive advantage by delivering strategies that were complex and difficult to imitate. As Pfeffer and Sutton found: "Managers congratulated themselves and one another when they come up with ideas that were so elaborate and convoluted that they require two hours of multipart, multicolored slides and a liberal sprinkling of the latest buzzwords."[115] Worse, poorly managed processes for competition for limited opportunities for advancement or sought-after assignments can lead to the potential for undermining attitudes, attitudes that may remain hidden despite overt expressions of collaboration and harmony. These hidden attitudes can lead to insincere support between employees, departments, other organizations, and the community. Unresolved competitive dysfunctions have been identified as a contributing factor in many high-profile cases with tragic consequences, ranging from the intelligence gaps that preceded the attacks on the World Trade Center to many instances of more localized failures in the investigations of serial crimes. Performance management is clearly not just about statistical measurements and performance appraisals. Performance measurement is equally about effecting, guiding, and gauging the belief systems of every element of an organizational structure. Without a clear focus on creating synergy between diagnostics and belief systems, eloquent mission and vision statements risk becoming just another set of empty statements.

At Johnson & Johnson (J&J), senior managers meet regularly with subordinates throughout the company to review and reaffirm the beliefs recorded in J&J's value charter, to articulate clearly and passionately the company's responsibilities to its customers, employees, communities, and stockholders. Managers recognize the value that senior management will place on the exercise and respond accordingly. It was this commitment to its value charter that enabled J&J to respond the way it did, as a company and its employees, to the Tylenol crisis.[116] The engagement of employees needs to be meaningful, substantive to the growth and development of the organization, and embedded in the organizational culture at all levels. The engagement becomes even more critical in organizations like policing, wherein the reliance on diagnostics and boundaries is systemic and pervasive. Engagement provides opportunities for workers at all levels to understand and buy in to the overall mission and vision. Without meaningful engagement, employees remain embedded in a view that they serve only at the behest of the managers and supervisors and are otherwise marginal to the organizational leadership. Issues such as those involving emotionally disturbed persons, profiling, targeted policing, and stop-and-frisk searches are areas where more than performance must change; the change should also be based on a fundamental change in attitudes and beliefs about how best to respond to such issues and challenges. Effective managers must seek to inspire people throughout their organization by actively communicating core values and missions.[117] As managers rely increasingly on empowered employees to generate new ideas and competitive advantage, participants from all parts of an organization need to understand, as clearly as possible, their organization's purpose and mission. Foremost, there must be an unwavering commitment to ensuring the authenticity of stated, perceived, and believed values.

Belief systems become critical for success, because they inspire employees to create new opportunities. They can motivate individuals to search for new ways of creating value. This requires a culture wherein managers see employees as having a need to contribute—to devote time and energy to worthwhile endeavors—and they need to make it easier for employees to understand the larger purpose of their efforts and to see how each employee can add value in ways that can make a difference. Measurement processes that align with diagnostics and belief systems and are continually evaluated for relevance are vital to creating purpose and ensuring the success of organizations. Individuals want to understand the organization's purpose and how they can contribute its moments of truth, but senior managers must unleash this potential by engaging its most valuable resource, people, in meaningful ways that encourage ownership at all levels of the organization.

An organization faced with a crisis has to be able to manage internal and external audiences simultaneously. In its response to the contamination resulting in several deaths, Maple Leaf Meats, a leading Canadian food processing company, put aside convoluted legalese, choosing instead to provide a direct, sincere, and authentic response to their clients, shareholders, and victims.[118] The response was designed, measured, and targeted for addressing crisis management and customer concerns but equally for future innovation and learning. This was a crisis response, which like J&J's, relied largely on the company's belief systems over boundary systems and interactive control systems. Maple Leaf Meats responded in ways that demonstrated a genuine concern for the victims, concern for the public, and understandably, concern for the company's own reputation and bottom line, while also being careful to reassure its own employees of the values that guide their business practices.

Similarly, the police commissioner of Boston Police, Kathleen O'Toole, was presented with a difficult situation—the accidental shooting of a young female university student at a celebratory demonstration at Fenway Park following the win of the Boston Red Sox over the New York Yankees in 2004. Knowing that the victim was an innocent bystander, the commissioner immediately took responsibility for the death of the young student and met with the victim's family. The commissioner was quick to assess what was right, not convenient or safe, in making a statement that the Boson Police "firmly and emphatically" accepted responsibility for the incident. There was no awaiting legal advice, deferring to lawyers, or hiding behind process.[119]

The worst response an organization can undertake at a moment of crisis is one that appears to set aside its belief systems and abandons authenticity for self-preservation or defense against legal culpability over other higher values. Crisis presents particularly poignant moments of truth when employees are able to observe and assess the authenticity of their leaders and their own trust and commitment in the organization. Police leaders must learn to balance their legal obligations of confidentiality and secrecy and at times procedural requirements (as with police oversight) to speak to their employees and communities and to rise to the challenge of being present, up front, and genuine in their concern for affected parties, the community, and their own employees, as well as the organization itself.

Crisis management in policing is a routine occurrence. Police leaders are mindful of managing the impact on the public as well as the rank and file. Leaders must not, however, overrely on authoritarian

Mending Broken Fences Policing

control systems for appearing to keep people in line and for measuring compliance at the cost of disregarding or diminishing the value and belief systems as elements of their response. Police leaders need to be careful when responding to issues of public concern or police oversight. The way leaders respond to larger organizational challenges will have a lasting impact on how organizational values are perceived and valued and whether employees will treat organizational values as cornerstones for ethical decision-making or only as tools for achieving and preserving self-interest. Instilling and maintaining healthy belief systems becomes critical during times of change for avoiding fatigue and resistance.[120] While belief systems can augment diagnostic control systems by providing managers with enhanced control, they too only offer part of the solution. Every remark, action, or inaction, whether intentional or unintentional, will have the potential for being interpreted as a value statement. And value statements are subjective, open to interpretative application, and potentially lasting in impact. Take, for instance, a public investigation in which the mayor of Toronto became implicated for associating with gang members, using of alcohol, and engaging in other behavior verging on summary offenses, such as urination in public places, driving while texting, and being intoxicated in a public place. Although the chief of police of the city had attempted to maintain and impress on the public the police service's impartiality in the investigation in which the press had established the mayor's association, a simple expression of the chief's disappointment[121] with the situation led to sustained and widespread condemnation of his comments, the role of the police, and the chief's office for his remarks about the office of an elected official.[122] The comments reflected a value or belief system, which, while important as an internal control system, came to place the chief's office and the police service's intentions under suspicion of having deliberately targeted the mayor. Clearly, while not everyone can be convinced of one's good intentions, belief systems are important in guiding and preserving internal and external integrity, particularly during times of crisis.

Similarly, when newly elected New York Mayor Bill De Blasio made remarks about the manner in which he would have his son respond if stopped by police, following the acquittal of a New York City Police

Department police officer in the death of Eric Garner, his personal belief systems collided with those of the city's police officers, resulting in a campaign seeking his resignation as mayor. Value statements such as these, while personal and genuine, can have a profound impact on the individual, the organization, and the entire community. Beliefs and values have a powerful role in the control of organizations and must be tempered with adequate boundary and interactive controls to be effective.

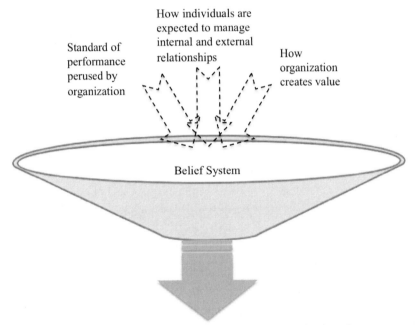

Figure 4. Belief systems—organizational goals and values, expectations, communication, and authenticity for creating circumstances that foster trust and trustworthiness.

Interactive Controls and Diagnostics

Interactive controls provide a system for measuring and responding to organizational uncertainties by integrating diagnostics with active decision-making processes. Within policing, for instance, a dashboard analysis may provide managers with an overview of the current and historical basis for assessing crime and disorder. Combined with a predictive framework, managers can make real-time decisions on how and where to deploy resources in response to emerging and anticipated contingencies. A diagnostic control system on its own is, therefore, not sufficient. Robert Simons notes:

> Instead, senior managers need sensing systems more like the ones used by the National Weather Service. Ground stations all over the country monitor temperature, barometric pressure, relative humidity, cloud cover, wind direction and velocity, and precipitation. Balloons and satellites provide additional data. These data are monitored continually from a central location in an effort to identify patterns of change.[123]

Interactive control systems provide a predictive capacity. Importantly, interactive control systems must be simple to understand and focus on constantly changing information and focus on information significant enough to demand frequent and regular attention from management. These sources of information are best interpreted and discussed at face-to-face meetings and serve as catalysts for an ongoing debate about the underlying data, assumptions, and action plans.[124] Two additional characteristics of an effective interactive control system are the capacity to merge information from multiple diagnostic control systems for facilitating decision-making between and within different levels of an organization toward a model for integrative thinking and a double-loop feedback between existing assumptions and variables.[125] Leaders must be willing to be sensitive to the characteristics in order to avoid unexpected and unintended consequences, but as Roger Martin, the dean of the Rotman School of Management, suggests, one must develop a capacity to hold diametrically opposing ideas without panicking or settling for one alternative or the other and produce a synthesis that is superior to either opposing idea.[126]

Organizations with successful interactive control systems are able to focus organizational attention on multiple issues. The discussion used to form this commentary should serve to demonstrate the need for police organizations to focus on reviewing their performance measurement initiatives. In particular, they need a focus that looks beyond diagnostics as an end in itself to include belief systems, boundary systems, and interactive control systems toward building an organizational community and providing the right incentives aligned with performance standards that balance multiple dimensions—financial, customer, business, innovation and learning parameters, and organizational knowledge.

Police leaders must be careful to avoid systems that lead to conflicting interactions between strategic aims, tactical goals, and value systems. Poorly designed police control systems not only leave officers with conflicting strategies and goals; they may even enhance public perceptions of unfairness and suspicion. Conflict is inevitable if on the one hand officers are required to collaborate with stakeholders within the criminal justice system,[127] health care, and social services toward the provision of a broader understanding and response to issues arising from crime and conflict, and on the other hand measurement systems focus exclusively on enforcement. Unaddressed, contradictions may lead to poor service delivery and public outrage at what is perceived as biased policing that unfairly targets specific constituents and fundamentally contradicts the notion that today's police officers play a far more general role and the activities that an organization measures and rewards.[128] It is not enough, for instance, for leaders of police services to conduct public satisfaction surveys that report high levels of public support as indications of successful policing. It might be surprising that survey respondents in African countries (constituting some of the most underdeveloped and contentious countries) view their local police effectiveness with remarkably similar favor as those in developed countries. According to the Economic and Social Council of the United Nations, 66 percent of respondents to UNODC Africa surveys believed that their police were doing a good or very good job controlling crime in their local areas compared with 70 percent in the thirty developed countries.[129]

Good performance management systems anticipate challenges and minimize distress. They should not simply be controls for the management of people and processes; instead, they should also, as Rupert Chisholm notes, create opportunities for employees to make meaningful contributions to their organizations, a concept that is different from simply making employees satisfied or "happy" with their jobs.[130] Policing represents a particularly insular profession, given the requirements for confidentiality, intelligence, and secrecy. There is also a level of insularity that is reinforced by the adversarial nature of the criminal justice system within which policing must operate and the oversight to which it is subject. The paramilitary hierarchy of policing adds to the inclination for conformity and groupthink. This inclination poses significant hindrances to employees in making meaningful contributions that are authentic and not filtered simply to suit what the employee thinks his or her manager wants to hear, even when the idea may be ill-conceived or even illegal as has been the case with stop-and-frisk search. Isabelle Rloyer characterizes them as cheerleading squads, the type of followership that can persist in supporting bad ideas despite mounting evidence to the contrary.[131]

Leaders should be careful to avoid cheerleaders, the types of individuals who are overoptimistic, or selecting members primarily because they share their enthusiasm for a project, including those who may only be motivated by an opportunity to make money or receive a performance bonus. Leaders should also be cautious of experts, those who have only worked on similar successful projects in the past, because such members are more likely to bring preformed expectations and be reluctant to share in the experience and enthusiasm of others. Teams formed on the basis of shared enthusiasm or previous experience among team members have their benefits; however, they also have the potential for dysfunctional influences. People who have shared previous experiences may in fact know one another too well. The danger lies in the fact that such individuals may, intentionally or unintentionally, know the drill and be able to anticipate preconceived expectations, thereby ramming through projects even when they may be incompatible, dysfunctional, or destined for failure. Often when familiar members interact, there are none of the awkward missteps or misunderstandings that can produce unexpected insights—or signs of trouble. The groupthink or common belief results in everyone rooting for something they believe in and despite present risks can result in concerns being dismissed or rationalized. This is, in fact, a state of affairs completely opposite to the type of integrative thinking that organizational and leadership experts like Roger Martin espouse as integrative thinking of opposable minds.[132]

> In the movie "World War Z" an Israeli agent presents the idea of the 10th man assigned to act as the loyal opposition assigned to counter the arguments of the other 9 members of an intelligence panel. The 10th man is assigned the role of puncturing weaknesses in the esprit de corps of the remaining 9 members, challenging misinformation, assumptions and group think, by representing the fresh eyes of a devil's advocate. Irving Janis a pioneer in the field of group-think puts it this way: "The more amiability and *esprit de corps* among the members of a policy-making in-group, the greater is the danger that independent critical thinking will be replaced by group think, which is likely to result in irrational and dehumanizing actions directed against out-groups.[133]

Oversight and control must be part of project development and be well planned, communicated, and managed to ensure that everyone understands his or her role, scope, and tenure, and the strategy must be accepted by everyone. Managers would do well to include skeptics as well as enthusiasts from the outset, paying particular attention to those who will be directly involved in making decisions. Some project management strategies even suggest changing decision makers during the course of a project in order to provide a new and independent look at the project through a set of fresh eyes. Unfortunately, most organizations only do so when forced to by circumstance—turnover for reasons unrelated to the project, like retirement, health problems, or restructuring.

Secondly, performance measurement systems must themselves be monitored to ensure that they do not result in unexpected dysfunctional behavior as a result of the incentives and disincentives built into a performance measurement system. Employees and systems subject to the measurement must be monitored to ensure that they are not directly or indirectly motivated to provide expected results at the cost of other beneficial activities or so strongly influenced by the process that their actions and outcomes become corrupted. Studies indicate that CompStat's demand for intelligence, rapid deployment of resources, effective tactics, and relentless follow-up and evaluation diminishes the principles of problem-oriented policing, wherein police response becomes the most suitable and quickest response instead of a more analytical consideration of other possibilities for a tailored reaction in partnership with other social services. This, in turn, contributes to a renewed commitment to extricating criminals quickly, incarceration, and refocus on the next problem.[134] Indicators of dysfunctional or unintended outcomes can often take months and years to become evident. Recent reports of penology in Canada indicate that that prison populations have increased notably in recent years, despite some of the lowest crime rates in decades. Some suggest that these increases may in part be due to the police policies committed to extricating criminals quickly, calls for mandatory sentencing (incarceration), and focus on problem-oriented policing with little meaningful commitment to underlying causes.[135] In the context of the Canadian experience, Canada's correctional investigator, Howard Sapers, has gone on record to note:

> [T]he growth in the custody population appears to be policy, not crime drive. After all, crime rates are down while incarceration rates grow, adding that crime rates across Canada have been declining for more than a decade, long before the current government's "tough on crime" agenda.[136]

COMMUNITY POLICING

We need to take a high-altitude look at community policing for the purposes of developing the performance management model we are working toward, but clearly, a full discussion of community policing, or for that matter intelligence-led policing, is beyond the scope of this work. It is assumed here that the reader brings some independent understanding of the two strategies.

The developments of community policing and restorative justice are interrelated ideologies similar in etiology and indicative of the level of cultural change in the criminal justice system; they are larger social changes indicative of how we view crime and conflict. Change, however, is slow, incremental, and sometimes transformative. Here we examine the two, community policing and restorative justice, to form an understanding of how transformative changes in therapeutic approaches can bring about larger transformations in the criminal justice system—an integration of participatory and restorative practices, an idea we will explore further in the next section.

Restorative justice, like community policing, despite tremendous legal and academic support, has been subject to skepticism and resistance by practitioners and the public alike. Mark Umberti writes:

> [T]here is growing evidence among both criminal justice officials and the participants themselves that victim offender mediation can be quite consistent with the community's sense of justice and fairness. Yet, there is likely to remain strong resistance by some officials and citizens to the very notion of the restorative type of justice embodied in the victim offender mediation

process. The more dominant retributive sense of justice with its emphasis on the severity of punishment, on behalf of State interests, even at the cost of addressing the direct interests of the person violated by the offence, is deeply rooted in contemporary American culture and is unlikely to be dramatically changed in the near future.[137]

Umberti's observations on the resistance to restorative justice, although intended for the criminal justice system, apply equally to those engaged in community policing, where despite the obvious advantages of policies that advocate increasing sensitivity and responsiveness to community dynamics, there remains much resistance and skepticism about *nontraditional* policing.[138]

Like the evolution of restorative justice from retributive practices, policing too has progressed from being founded primarily in public-order policing, zero tolerance, and expert-based authority to a more collaborative philosophy that emphasizes persuasion, social justice, incorporating community, and community interaction.[139] Community policing today represents a form of collaborative problem solving, which, like alternative dispute resolution (ADR) processes, aims to transform the manner in which societies view the nature and scope of crime and conflict. Community policing strategies, characterized as collaborative policing, are distinct from traditional "problem-oriented" policing. Contemporary policing has evolved to include a variety of approaches to crime and disorder management. Intelligence-led policing, problem-oriented policing, situational crime prevention, zero-tolerance policing, and broken windows policing supplement the most prominent of these approaches—community policing. Despite its prevalence and promotion, collaborative practices continue to be limited by an accompanying rhetorical extolment for collaboration, lacking in most instances the requisite substantive support and acceptance.

Bonnie Bacqueroux, the former associate director of the National Center for Community Policing at Michigan State University's School of Criminal Justice, characterizes some of this resistance to community policing in the following manner:

> For some, so massive a change implies a total rejection of their life's work. Others resist—and resent—being asked to do a job different than the one for which they were hired. Some have philosophical disagreements with a problem-solving approach that assesses success and failure on the basis of community satisfaction. Others rankle at the thought of working directly with people who live in troubled neighborhoods, often because of elitism, outright racism, or an "us versus them" attitude based on the belief that everyone who lives in such neighborhoods either commits or condones the crime and violence.[140]

Despite the resistance, there is a growing movement focused on looking for alternatives to authoritative policing as the only model for police-community relationships. Community policing aims to change the role of law enforcement by enhancing the relationships between police and citizens within the operational and organizational environments of law enforcement by including collaborative partnerships toward addressing issues of social conflict and crime management. So far, the evolution of community policing has resulted in a variety of interpretations—being "many things to many people."[141] In its simplest form, community policing can be defined as a philosophy and an organizational strategy that emphasizes effective partnerships with the community for identifying, prioritizing, and solving conflict, by drawing on the principles of community-based dispute resolution.

The rationale for advancing community-policing programs is perhaps best summarized using the principles outlined by Ray Shonholtz in "Neighbourhood Justice Systems."[142] Although Shonholtz is dealing with community justice programs, the principles he identifies are the same as those that should encourage community policing policies.

- First, diversity and the complexity of societal life directly encourages the strengthening of nonstate social entities.
- Second, peaceful expression of conflict within a community can have positive value and is necessary because the expression of

hostilities and differences within the community serve to inform and educate, which creates a base for greater understanding and mutual work between disputants.
- Third, community policing emphasizes the responsibility of the individual and neighborhoods in dealing with crime, conflict, and the underlying causes of crime. On this point, Shonholtz notes that nonstate social entities are weakened in society in large part by the state's assumption that they are incompetent and by the transferring of the problem to a state agency.
- Fourth, processes for voluntary resolution of conflict between disputants have positive value, because coerced resolutions have inherent limitations to the parties, of enforcement, of attitude, of future relations, of understanding, and of future conflict resolution modeling.[143] This point speaks to the requirement of encouraging community programs to encourage social networks and social cohesion.

In order for community policing to work, it requires collaboration with and the support of other stakeholders. Police, after all, cannot control all conditions that contribute to society's conflict, crime, and disorder. For police to respond effectively, they must be able to work with and in fact rely on other social and governmental entities—community organizations; municipal, provincial, and federal civil service agencies; the mental health system; public health; hospitals; the school system; corporate and business interests; and those engaged in alternative dispute resolution.

Community policing can only realize its potential and promise by being institutionalized as part of what has been defined as "community-oriented government," wherein community policing is made an integral part of municipal governance that delivers services across all municipal departments in an integrative manner by managing problem identification and response.[144] Institutionalization requires the formation of a city administrative department empowered with ensuring coordinated service delivery to specific areas of the community and a coordinated means for measuring effectiveness and maintaining transparent accountability. No department acting independently, including the police, would be able to abandon or neglect contribution to a coordinated response without having to account to the joint community-oriented government. Just as Statcom moved accountability downward to divisional commanders, community-oriented governance would move accountability upward in order that all government department heads would become accountable to the head of the "joint administrative department" lead. The burden of getting other departments to agree to respond to the precursors of crime and disorder would be removed from the chief of police to the city administrator, whose function it would become to ensure that all city agencies do their part toward the integrated improvement of affected neighborhoods—that is, for becoming responsible for the resolution of the underlying causes of neglect, delinquency, and crime (causes of the broken windows) and mending fences toward embedding individuals, community leaders, and social organizations for creating civic engagement whereby perceptions and conditions lead to processes for the development of communities with shared values, shared challenges, and shared hope.

INTELLIGENCE-LED POLICING

Once again, it needs to be pointed out that this is not meant to be an in-depth critique of intelligence or intelligence-led policing but rather only a quick look at the concept with the purposes of proposing an integrative performance management model.

There is no singular, universal definition of intelligence-led policing. Like community policing, *intelligence* means different things to different people.[145] To the public at large, it can suggest secret and covert activity conducted for gathering confidential information on suspects and persons of interest. To patrol officers, it's a peripheral activity that has relevance to the larger organizational goals of specialized units (antiterrorism, organized crime, antinarcotics enforcement, and police corruption as examples). To specialized units, it is the information gathered through targeted enforcement surveillance and wiretaps. A review of "Strategic Intelligence in Law Enforcement," reported in the *Journal of Policing, Intelligence and Counter Terrorism*, notes:

> For almost 50 years significant effort in intelligence studies have focused on developing a universal definition of intelligence and subsequent all-encompassing theory of intelligence (Khan 2009). To date, no universal definition of theory has been developed, instead remaining a contentious and widely debated topic (Gill, 2009). The academic discourse and theoretical positions of its various schools has important impacts on definitional work on intelligence in law enforcement—especially given the rapid change in law enforcement's operating context.[146]

To intelligence analysts, intelligence is the product of a very specific process of collection, collation, and processing; analysis; distribution; reevaluation; and planning and direction for action. Intelligence is the product of collected information that has been subject to a deliberate process of evaluation and interpretation to provide an opinion for tactical or strategic decisions. According to some, the term *intelligence-led policing*, initially called the Kent Policing Model, originated in Great Britain in response to a sharp increase in property crimes.[147] The Kent Model was designed to identify and target the relatively small number of criminals believed to be responsible for the majority of crimes.

Following the attacks on New York and Washington in 2001, the American model has evolved to include Fusion Centers, where information from various public and private databases is gathered and analyzed for information that may be useful in targeting antiterrorism or criminal threats across the United States.[148] This targeting of specific terrorism or criminal threats is an essential part of the concept of problem-oriented policing.

While intelligence is an indispensable tool for responding to terrorism, there must be a countervailing influence that works to limit its intrusion into the culture of the day-to-day policing of society. Not every criminal investigation should be directed with the cultural focus that is applied to counterterrorism. Intelligence led-policing should be employed with caution and care for its supporting evidence, purpose, and intent. John Coyne and Peter Bell note:

> Intelligence failures and strategic surprise research highlights problems associated with the relationships and communication between intelligence and policy staff as well as decision makers (Davis, 2003b). With the plethora of raw data, academic papers, and OSI [open source intelligence] available, decision makers and policy staff are increasingly undertaking their own research and analysis (Davis 2003b)—often in biased manner, preferring research and analysis that supports their own preconceived ideas. In essence, the client also becomes a competitor who is only further

supported in their approach when intelligence fails to deliver innovative and convincing products. Davis (2007) specifically argues that intelligence professionals are experiencing increasing pressure to provide tailored reports that are consistent with the client's analysis and preconceived ideas.[149]

The lack of a universally accepted definition of intelligence has also contributed to confusion over what Coyne and Bell describe as "differences between intelligence products, analytical tools, police reporting, and knowledge products."[150] Intelligence-led policing places the emphasis on police officers collecting highly subjective information for police records, which can remain as unsupported allegations indefinitely. And while intelligence-led investigations that result in the interdiction of crime and terrorism are highly celebrated, there may be large volumes of information that may never be applied to any investigative purpose and can stigmatize entire communities.

The US Department of Justice makes the following observation:

> Intelligence operations involve several levels of security: Physical, programmatic, personnel-related, and procedural. Security is paramount for intelligence operations because the materials found in intelligence files may be unproved allegations rather than facts. Protecting the public and the agency's operations require keeping information secure.[151]

The report emphasizes that even private citizens have been included in the *intelligence matrix*[152] through suspicious-activity tip lines and other similar mechanisms to collaborate on the identification of "unusual behaviour that may be related to terrorism or other criminal activities."[153] At the same time, there is an increasing reliance on open-source intelligence, which, according to some research within the American context, constitutes between 70 and 80 percent of the data held by intelligence agencies.[154]

While intelligence policing is a valuable and effective tool in the targeting of crime and terrorism and this narrative is not intended to discredit any of its valuable benefits, it creates a natural tension that must be recognized. While community policing works to enhance social cohesion, intelligence processes that incorporate a community matrix of intelligence sources serve to enhance intragroup suspicion, thereby undermining processes for social cohesion. If collecting information to target crime is the sole consideration and end goal, then this discussion is mute. If, however, the end goal is safer communities, wherein citizens become cohesive and are mobilized to withstand challenges to societal norms (crime, terrorism, and disorder), then police practitioners must be willing to engage in the larger discussion of the selection and development of appropriate long-term strategies that don't enhance suspicion, alienate segments of the community, or foster the very effects the police are attempting to deter.

The US Department of Justice's report *New Intelligence Architecture* makes the following observation:

> Empowering local officers with decision making authority and making them aware of terrorist indicators may be the key in preventing a terrorist attack. Community- and problem-oriented policing support local awareness and involvement in solving crime problems. This involvement extends to anti-terrorism efforts. However, in the wake of the September 11, 2011 terrorist attacks, some agencies shifted officers from community policing to anti-terrorism efforts, which may be counterproductive in helping to deter a terrorist attack.[155]

In many respects, intelligence-led policing leads to a form of firefighting in which officers are rushing from task to task, rarely being given, or taking, the time to completely resolve the underlying issue before being interrupted by the next fire. While many police managers admit to this strategy and many frontline officers assigned to primary uniformed response would accept this as their primary model for daily assignments, it is in fact a highly dysfunctional strategy. Reactive policing, despite its temporary effectiveness in exceptional circumstances, does not permit responders or organizations to resolve problems adequately and more critically gives up opportunities for learning and growth. A new refinement of the strategy embodied by problem-oriented (the targeted enforcement against specific problems) policing is a very different thing from problem-solving, yet the two are often confused in the urgent, primary response models espoused by systems that rely on the measurements of response times and time spent on calls. In this regard, refinements to intelligence-led policing in the form of problem-oriented policing can be useful in conveying a commitment to specific problems as compared to operations that cast a wide net on entire communities, but they remain limited in scope. Such strategies do not sufficiently contribute to a sustainable enhancement of social cohesion.[156]

Intelligence-led policing can quickly undermine the strategic aims of community policing, particularly in communities that are already marginalized or economically and socially impoverished. These communities, characteristically, consist of diverse minorities and marginalized groups with relatively poorer housing, income, and education. Such communities also tend to have poorer relationships with the police and limited experience with cooperation and collaboration and tend to have been subject to the repeated application of experimental policing strategies that have come and gone, usually with little lasting impact.

Additionally, Intelligence-led policing is complicated by the global growth of the private security sector. There are more private security apparatuses, private investigation firms, private security services, personal protection services, and in-house investigation units that gather and share information without the types of controls and oversight that guide public policing. How multinational companies, Internet-based businesses, and cross-border economies cause personal information about citizens and customers to be transferred and how that information may be shared in public-private investigations are areas of concern that have outpaced the development of privacy legislation. There are today, countless platforms for the routine collection and transfer of data on citizens' activities and movements that form an ever-increasing network of intelligence databases—public and private. This informal day-to-day policing of communities and the increasing securitization of public places have a strong impact on how citizens perceive the role of law enforcement and their relationships with police.

Studies have demonstrated that citizens often perceive their police as having less to do with risk and victimization and more with their judgments of social cohesion and moral consensus. In England and Wales, for instance, studies show that police may not be seen as providers of a narrow sense of personal security (crime and order), but more as the symbolic moral guardians of community values against emerging long-term change, the types of changes that are perceived to threaten ideas and emotions of nationhood, culture, and state.[157] As Steve Herbert puts it:

> The pursuit of police hegemony also works to bolster a potent sense of moral good to which officers frequently aspire. Police work is not only defined by officers as an opportunity to uphold the law or to demonstrate bravery, but as part of a wider struggle between good and evil.[158]

Much of the securitization resulting from the post–9/11 response to terrorism has been in the effort to identify and eliminate the threat of terrorism and threats to national security. The seepage of this securitization into daily policing activities may contribute to a larger view among police officers that they are involved in antiterrorism and antiespionage activities, contributing to an underlying cultural imperative that widens daily policing to one where every encounter comes to be seen as a struggle between good and evil.

The problem is compounded by rigid bureaucratic and procedural rules. Rules and oversight, particularly in reactive environments, leads to workers abandoning problem-solving for quick-fix responses, at the expense of creativity, commitment, and the application of discretion. This is dangerous when policing becomes overly dependent on intelligence. Such conditions can result in tragic misinterpretation of information, insufficient input of intelligence given that workers are too busy responding to the next urgency, and the lack of opportunities for advocating better analysis of the information. Such conditions also predispose organizations to an overload on information that workers become incapable of assessing, until the information becomes just too noisy to be meaningful. An example of this is the *black hole* characterization of many intelligence departments. The term refers to a place where information is sent but rarely returns for the benefit of the practitioner or the information that is returned is only an analysis of the information that was provided in the first place, no more useful than the day it was submitted for assessment.

Roger Bohn points to the importance creating the necessary cultural imperative in the following terms:

> Cultural Change requires shifts in the mind-set of the whole organization and in the behavior of senior managers. Extra work in organizations—even those that don't usually fight fires—will occasionally create pressure to begin fire fighting. At these times, the organization's problem-solving culture is critical. If managers are too far removed from the problems to see the consequences, and if the reward system favours firefighters, then the vicious cycle of fighting fires will begin. Avoiding this depends on the culture of middle and senior managers.[159]

Not only do reactive strategies diminish opportunities for effective policing, they diminish opportunities for future growth of the organization itself. Growth may become stifled over an extended period during which the organization and its members are simply too busy keeping heads above water and only react to growing concerns and criticism when they become intolerable, forcing abrupt change. Unfortunately, forced change is neither preferred—because of its perceived imposition by an external influence—nor as effective as change that results from the incremental growth of an organization. Many police organizations are therefore simply coping with stressors rather than evolving.

Clearly, there is a great need for the careful deliberation of ways for balancing intelligence-led policing, community policing, problem solving, and performance measurement through integrative and perhaps even opposable approaches.

Good policing is dependent on the assessment of each criminal threat with a specifically tailored policing response, as opposed to a general one-size-fits-all solution. Problem-oriented policing is sometimes used synonymously with the SARA model (scanning, analyzing, responding, and assessing). If not carefully defined and controlled, this collection or scanning for information places intelligence-led policing and community policing in a conflicting relationship. From an intelligence perspective, community policing places officers in an ideal position for determining community threats—the makeup of communities, their ties to other countries, their social affiliations, and their beliefs. On the other hand, engaging in community policing with the intent to conduct intelligence-led scanning, analyzing, or assessing jeopardizes public trust and the legitimacy of community policing with citizens and police officers alike. In effect, community policing comes to be seen as a means of concealing the real purpose of policing—spying on marginalized communities.

Intelligence-led policing has become the prominent policing strategy across the United States, Canada, Europe, and other modern and emerging democracies around the globe, following the attacks of September 11, 2001. This has led to a renewed tension for the protection of civil liberties and the balancing of information gathering by law enforcement and the democratic rights of individuals.[160] CompStat is not in itself a policing strategy; nonetheless, it is often regarded as a strategy in the same way as targeted policing, problem-oriented policing, and intelligence-led policing. Although police managers often employ the two prevailing strategies (intelligence led versus community policing) simultaneously and interchangeably, the underlying premise of intelligence remains that it is a covert strategy, in part because intelligence operations continue to be "plagued by a lack of policies, procedures, and training for gathering and assessing essential information"[161] and partly because police agencies mishandle the collection of information, apply poor analytics, and are challenged with the management of unprecedented sources of information.

BALANCING COMMUNITY POLICING WITH INTELLIGENCE-LED POLICING

Intelligence-led policing uses communities to provide, gather, and monitor information that may be used to prevent crime, apprehend criminals, and monitor crime trends. Intelligence-led policing by its nature is covert and perceived to be seditious to trust. The two strategies are divergent in nature; one is based on an ethic of transparency and the other in secrecy.

Whether organized crime, serial crime, or terrorism, the challenges and issues are similar. In the case of terrorism—a crime at the root of it, having both organized and serial elements—there have been notable cases of homegrown terrorism in England, Canada, Spain, and the United States by native-born citizens of immigrant families. The aftermath of each of these terrorist acts leads to an amplification of suspicion and social division among interethnic and interfaith communities. Often the ensuing security and safety responses for preventing and responding to similar incidents contribute to further escalating suspicion and tensions within the community.[162] While police services advocate for legislative changes that enhance surveillance and intelligence gathering, the response is fundamentally targeted toward the prevention of terrorism with little focus on mitigating the underlying causes that motivate homegrown terrorism.

Intelligence-led policing is focused on knowledge acquisition and contributes to the notion of a surveillance society in which information acquisition is critical for the prevention, investigation, prosecution, and reduction of crime, accomplished through strategic use of wiretapping, interrogations, covert operations, and surveillance. As John Kleinig points out in the "Ethical Perils of Knowledge Acquisition," each of these techniques threaten important social values: wiretapping threatens privacy rights, and interrogation may compromise the humane treatment of citizens, while surveillance and covert operations may jeopardize public safety.[163] In sum, intelligence-led policing is more likely to be perceived as antidemocratic.

According to some reports, there has been a tenfold increase of wiretaps in the United States since data on intercepts were first reported in 1969; with some 2,732 reported wiretaps and 1.3 million requests for data to mobile-phone companies by 2011 alone.[164] Even this is likely an underestimate given that many government agencies remain shrouded in secrecy and continue to collect intelligence on citizens without judicial authority or government sanction, as revealed by Edward Snowden. While policing apparatuses, such as the American Patriot Act, are essential to maintaining national security and public safety, there is a cost in the public's trust of law enforcement, confidence in state-based power generally, and perceptions of diminished civil rights. In fact, the cost of surveillance and the compromise of civil rights have been compounded by the disclosure of the types of National Security Administration (NSA) intercepts of communications in France and Mexico or those of the Canadian Surveillance Agency in Brazil.

As with intelligence initiatives, community-oriented initiatives too have their challenges and limitations. What the unintended adverse consequences of community policing policies are and how community policing has affected the attitudes, values, and abilities of frontline officers and their interactions with citizens remain "largely unclear."[165] A study of community policing sponsored by the Scottish Government Social Research, which examined community policing by looking at approximately 420 journal articles, book chapters, and research reports published within the previous ten years, listed the following as possible "unintended adverse consequences" of community policing: [166]

- The apparent popularity of high-visibility policing with members of the public may sometimes itself lead to the stigmatization of an area as being a high-crime neighborhood and therefore dangerous or otherwise unappealing.

- There is a risk that community policing (CP) can become a vehicle for the practical implementation of local punitive attitudes against marginalized or minority groups. CP can become problematic if it moves away from a genuine problem-solving ethos toward pseudo-problem-solving through simply appeasing public appetites for enforcement that may function as unduly exclusionary.
- The supposition that freeing up officers' time to allow them to patrol communities will somehow automatically translate into more on-the-ground community-level problem solving seems to be optimistic, without explicit coordination of community officers' time around core CP methods and a detailed understanding of what these methods can deliver.

Joseph A. Schafer, Beth M. Huebner, and Timothy S. Bynum, in a study of "Citizen Perceptions of Police Services: Race, Neighborhood Context, and Community Policing" state that:

> It is apparent that there is a need to expand current models of satisfaction with the police and police services in light of community policing. Examining only the community-policing portion of the analysis reveals the importance of dissatisfaction with police contacts in the community policing process. Perceived crime and quality of life are of less importance than is how people felt about their interactions with the police and their communities in general; the nature of police-citizen interactions is especially important in predicting perceptions within the community-policing process.[167]

A significant challenge to collaboration has its basis in the complexities of the ethnography of modern society. Given that almost all community participants in community programs do so as (unpaid) volunteers, police organizations need to remain sensitive to the conditions (cultural), both external and internal to police departments, which help to sustain community policing.[168] Policing in diverse communities requires a systematic and genuine understanding of the cultural perceptions and values of those who comprise the communities involved in a collaborative partnerships as much as those who will be subject to enforcement.

There needs to be a merger of intelligence-based and community engagement to form what has been called community intelligence or *commtel*. Commtel is defined in the following terms:

> Community intelligence is information acquired either directly or indirectly from a community, that when analyzed can be used to inform policing interventions. The information can come from a variety of sources, but it will inform police about the views, needs and expectations of a community and the risks and threats posed to it by it, either in terms of internal or external issues.[169]

Community intelligence bridges the gap between traditional crime and criminal intelligence on the one hand and community and social cohesion on the other. This change in approach requires that security services be attuned to the potential for traditional intelligence-led policing to undermine the rapport that may already have been established with marginalized and affected communities.

Policing cannot be wholly community oriented nor completely enforcement oriented. Policing represents an organic and iterative balancing of individual, community, and state interests, all of which are continually changing and straining with one another. Our focus here is on designing a model for police policy that embraces the potential for enhancing individual and community participation through enhanced police legitimacy and professionalism.

Comparisons serve to demonstrate that challenges should be expected with the use of either strategy and for highlighting the need for balancing community policing with intelligence-led policing in the design and provision of effective policies. Furthermore, these comparisons remind us of the importance of redefining how police departments measure effectiveness, equity, and accountability and that interventions must also provide an opportunity for influencing ways in which police practitioners view sociopathology, substance abuse, and issues related to mental health. The fact is that opposing ideas can be integrated into surprisingly effective strategies for dealing with longstanding challenges. What is often missing, as the catalyst for bringing about this integrative view, is a cultural shift in how we view the problem.

For our purposes of examining traditional civil policing, police leaders and decision makers require a descriptive model for making strategic decisions on the balanced use of intelligence and community-based policing and for matching the appropriate performance paradigm (qualitative versus quantitative) to the circumstance within which policing services are to be delivered.

INTEGRATION OF PARTICIPATORY AND RESTORATIVE PRACTICES

Participation is synonymous with democratization, and if policing is to change, police leaders must become the champions for that change. Furthermore, change must be explicit to the needs of their communities, with whose care police leaders have been entrusted. Police organizations must be adaptive and responsive to the social conditions: social cohesion, quality of life, and level of crime and risk to which a society may be subject at any given time. Police practitioners at all levels must become adept at balancing the principles of an adversarial criminal justice system while remaining receptive and engaged with the principles of participatory justice—the process that brings together parties and resources required to collectively resolve conflict for reintegrating and rehabilitating offenders, the offended, and all other affected parties. Furthermore, police organizations have to be representative of the communities they police, and as the ranks become increasingly trained and educated, so increase opportunities for supporting processes for resolving conflict, reducing harm, and preventing disputes through collaborative participation and a wider engagement of stakeholders able to contribute to enhancing public safety and quality of life. Participatory and restorative justice represents two areas of opportunity—enhanced, meaningful community engagement and democratization of role and function.

Participatory justice aims to restore some level of harmony among the offender, the victim, their community, and society at large and is therefore often referred to as *restorative justice*. Participatory processes include a number of emerging dispute-resolution processes, including healing circles, family circles, crime conferencing, community accountability panels, school-based restitution, reconciliation/peace-building initiatives, and extrajudicial sanctions like diversion programs. Restorative justice has been defined as "... a process for resolving crime and conflicts, one that focuses on redressing the harm to the victims, holding offenders accountable for their actions and engaging the community in a conflict resolution process."[170]

Unlike retributive justice, which prescribes sentences based primarily on the principles of specific and general deterrence, participatory justice is interested in redressing the underlying causes of conflict and restoring some level of harmony among those who are affected. Restorative justice and consensus-based justice, the civil counterpart to the restorative justice, see harm as occurring first and foremost to individuals (victim and offender) and the relationships among those affected. Harm is not merely the result of the violation of a law; instead, it is seen as arising from the circumstances underlying the act and its impact on others.

The achievement of the types of changes that can result in healing for those affected by a crime requires an integrated, multidisciplinary approach to bring about the restoration, reformation, rehabilitation, and transformation sought by the sociojustice system. Intervention, by definition, therefore must aim to do the following:

- provide a process for resolving crime and conflict
- focus attention on redressing harm to victims
- hold offenders accountable for their actions
- provide the necessary rehabilitative intervention to effected parties
- engage the community in a conflict resolution process

These goals reflect the interests of a variety of stakeholders in the prevention of crime and conflict, including police, prosecutors, correctional services, social services, public health, educators, federal/provincial/municipal governments, and, most important, communities. This is exactly where community policing, broken windows, and restorative justice intersect and where police leaders should focus policies intended for enhancing quality of life and social cohesion.

Community and stakeholder participation in the coproduction of social cohesion and social order is a critical indicator of the level of public trust and the legitimacy ascribed to the institution of policing generally.

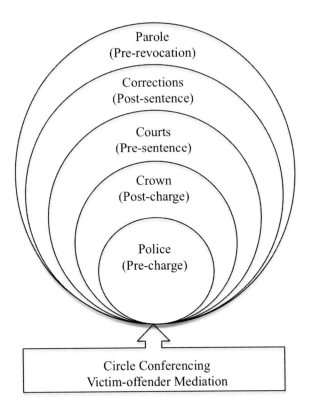

Figure 5. Five entry points into restorative processes.

Although a single consolidated definition of community policing and restorative justice remains elusive, because of the variety of responses to criminal behavior that fall under the so-called community and restorative umbrella, both are central to the notion of social cohesion.[171] Jeff Latimer and Craig Dowden group restorative justice into three categories: circles, conferences, and victim-offender mediations.[172] They describe five entry points into the criminal justice system at which offenders may be referred to a restorative justice program: police (precharge), crown (postcharge), courts (presentence), corrections (postsentence), and parole (prerevocation). These categories identify and define the roles of stakeholders whose roles and involvement are crucial to the acceptance and success of participatory processes. In addition, political and societal (public opinion) factors also represent key influences in the intervention of criminal justice. The impact of these two, while not central to the mechanics of a specific participatory process, are critical in influencing police policy and criminal justice intervention, as, for instance, with the implementation of diversion programs or therapeutic sentencing. Police leaders have an important role to play in each of the five entry points and can use these as guideposts for the assessment of their engagement with restorative justice.

This narrative on restorative practices is included herein to emphasize the importance of embracing a wider understanding of the processes that impact social cohesion. While evidence-based studies show that restorative justice has a positive impact on offender recidivism and victim satisfaction and that victims are more likely to favor face-to-face restorative justice compared to the traditional court system, police services and other criminal justice actors have been reluctant to support participatory processes.[173] A wider engagement is crucial for a participatory process if they are to be inclusive of all parts of the criminal justice system and for overcoming resistance and ambivalence to alternative practices.

Canada, Australia, and New Zealand are among a handful of jurisdictions where much has been learned from the experiences and wisdom of their First Nations peoples, and participatory processes have been received with greater openness than in other countries.[174] Sentencing reform and the legislation dealing with young offenders in Canada's Youth Criminal Justice Act, entered into force on April 1, 2003, reflects a significant change within the Canadian justice system. These changes center around a number of principles that focus on rehabilitation and restitution as opposed to retribution:[175]

- rehabilitation of offenders
- restitution to individual victims or the community
- protection of society where necessary
- remorse and acceptance of responsibility by the offenders

These changes are founded to foster participatory justice, based on twelve generally applicable principles:[176]

- early intervention
- accessibility
- voluntariness
- careful preparation
- opportunities for face-to-face dialogue
- advocacy and support
- confidentiality
- fairness
- relevant and realistic outcomes
- efficiency
- systemic impact
- flexibility and responsiveness

Although participatory processes are being increasingly accepted into the mainstream, they nevertheless continue to be perceived as marginal and inconsistent with traditional practices and political motivations. Mark Umberti, the founder of the Center for Restorative Justice and Peacemaking in the United States and a leader in the field of restorative justice and alternative dispute resolution notes that:

> There is growing evidence among both criminal justice officials and the participants themselves that victim offender mediation can be quite consistent with the community's sense of justice and fairness. Yet, there is likely to remain strong resistance by some officials and citizens to the very notion of the restorative type of justice embodied in the victim offender mediation process. The more dominant retributive sense of justice with its emphasis on the severity of punishment, on behalf of State interests, even at the cost of addressing the direct interests of the person violated by the offence, is deeply rooted in contemporary culture and is unlikely to be dramatically changed in the near future.[177]

Brandon Welsh and David Farrington, in their paper "Evidence-Based Crime Prevention Conclusion and Directions for a Safer Society," note that: "Evidence of what works best is rarely a factor in implementing new crime prevention programs. Politics and policy considerations *seemingly dominate.*"

They cite political interests and government priorities as important factors in the implementation or expansion of successful programs or even ending ineffective or harmful programs. Most important, Welsh and Farrington note that:

> Other political considerations that are germane to crime prevention include politicians' apprehension that they may be perceived as being soft on crime if they support social crime prevention efforts (see Gest 2001), and politicians' short time horizons, which make programs that show results only in the longer run less appealing to those who are trying to get elected every few years.[178]

Although there is an assumption that political agenda is driven by public opinion, this is not always the case. Often policy statements reflect popular political expectations rather than actual underlying public interests. Mark Umberti notes that despite the strong "law and order" and "get tough" political rhetoric policy, decisions are not reflective of evidence–based analysis. As noted earlier, perceptions of crime are often influenced by anecdotal experiences, media reports, and stereotypes, yet they can influence the shaping of laws and public policies and the setting of penalties. Perceptions of insecurity and feelings of being under threat of victimization are, therefore, often independent of the reality.

Research indicates that despite the "tough on crime" attitude, there is far more public interest in restitution, prevention, and the underlying social injustices that contribute to crime than in retributive justice.[179] Police leaders have a difficult challenge in reconciling the dissonance between evidence-based knowledge and popular cultural expectations and the resulting influence of the rate and level with which legislative and policy changes are implemented and accepted.

Even though studies have repeatedly shown that increasing punishment does not reduce crime, evidence-based studies are ignored in favor of addressing short-term political agendas. Take, for instance, the so-called war on crime, a phenomenon that in North America has not only resulted in sentences that are more severe than in most countries in the Western world but also resulted in the United States having the largest per capita prison population in the developed world.[180] Police services represent a tool by which politicians can express their "get-tough" policies, and frontline agencies become the focus of policy implementation. Police leaders themselves succumb to increased expectation and resort to the rhetorical arguments for enhancing job stability, and they increase demand for resources and recognition, thereby contributing to the war on crime; in so doing, they define the war-on-criminals values by which police and other enforcement agencies engage the justice process. It should not be surprising that such deeply institutionalized and politicized values result in participatory processes relegated as secondary to the daily battles of law enforcement.

What is evident is that the implementation of participatory programs that are likely to show positive results but only over a longer period of application become less appealing from a policing and political perspective and therefore less likely to be supported by politicians. Further, participatory programs continue to be stigmatized as being soft on crime, when, in fact, they are seen as harsher by offenders and at the same time are more effective in the rehabilitation of criminals. Police leaders have an opportunity to balance and base this discourse on empirical research rather than the politicization of crime and disorder.

There are additional opportunities for reframing the discourse around correction and rehabilitation, particularly around the issues of prison overcrowding and the associated costs of managing prison populations. The traditional response has been to do one of the following: build additional prisons, facilitate early release, diversion to community programs, or advocate shorter sentences. Anything outside of stiffer sentences and building more prisons is perceived as soft on crime, when studies show that offenders perceive community-based sentences as far more severe than imprisonment.[181] Studies indicate that participatory processes, while intended to be less retributive than traditional prison sentences, may in fact be more punitive than expected. Ben Crouch notes: "Theoretically, for prison to have the retributive and deterrent effect on offenders that the public desires, a fundamental assumption must be met: that offenders generally share the state's punitiveness in the ranking of criminal sanctions."[182] Crouch was able to demonstrate that two-thirds of the offenders in his study preferred a one-year prison sentence over ten years of probation. The preference was repeated even when the length of probation was reduced to three years.[183] Research shows, for instance, that when nonviolent offenders are given the choice of either serving a prison term or returning to the community to participate in a supervised release, which incorporated drug testing, mandatory employment, and frequent home visits by probation officers, about one-third elected prison. Additionally 50 percent of offenders participating in the releases have their probation revoked within the first year.[184] While one point of view might argue that sanctions are not useful unless they are perceived to be punitive by the offender and that the hierarchy of progressive sanctions should be based on this premise and reflected in the availability of sentencing options, primarily in terms of the length of a sentence available to a court, one cannot ignore the countervailing view. Studies confirm that while the majority of people view a community-based sentence to be preferable to imprisonment, this is not the case with offenders. When nonviolent offenders are given a choice between imprisonment or a community-based sentence involving drug testing, mandatory employment, and frequent home visits by probation officers, about one-third preferred prison. These offenders perceived work, drug testing, and home visits to be more punitive than incarceration in prison. According to some studies of those who participated in a community-based program, approximately half were revoked to prison within the first year.[185]

Such studies are important for three reasons. First, they demonstrate that there are equivalencies between traditional (prison sentences) and alternative participatory sanctions. Second, these alternative or intermediate sanctions, which range between imprisonment and parole, have the potential of being perceived by offenders to be more punitive than imprisonment if properly structured and therefore not just a "slap on the wrist," as is conventionally believed. Third, and perhaps most important, participatory sentencing is better able to incorporate the needs for retribution, rehabilitation, and reintegration. By maintaining the offender in a community-based program, intervention is more likely to incorporate resources that target the principles of need, risk, and responsiveness to rehabilitation. Most important, studies show that sanctions within the criminal justice system (traditional as well as participatory) are generally based on politicization and perhaps anecdotal evidence and that very little empirical research exists to substantiate the perceptions of offenders. Although studies indicate that it is important to consider offender perception when prescribing an appropriate level of punitive injunction, it is rarely, if ever, done.

Despite the importance of offender perception, stakeholders (police, educators, practitioners, legislators, and the public) have not been sufficiently informed about the effectiveness and benefits of sentences that are tailored to the offender, planned outcomes, or individual circumstances and characteristics of the crime. Without the widespread awareness and acceptance of such studies, participatory processes risk becoming a window dressing for the traditional criminal justice system, rather than a real alternative that incorporates the necessary principles of therapeutic jurisprudence in affecting meaningful social change and social cohesion.

Another area that deserves some focus of analysis is the area of psychological research that deals with sanctions for criminal behavior. Psychological research has identified risk, need, and general responsivity as clinical components associated with significant reductions in reoffending.[186] Several countries, including Canada, incorporate the developing of correctional plans for offenders.[187]

> *Risk Principle*—This represents the principle of proportionality. The intensity of the intervention program should be proportionately balanced with the risk level of the offender and must be tailored to match the offender's needs. A high-risk offender should therefore be subject a more intensive intervention program.[188]

Need Principle—This represents targeting of offender specific risk factors. In order for rehabilitation programs to be effective in reducing recidivism, they must be designed to target the dynamic risk factors of the offenders who have been linked to criminal conduct, otherwise known as criminogenic needs. These might include family and peer associations, antisocial attitudes, anger, and impulsivity control. Although targeting of noncriminogenic needs, such as emotional personal problems unrelated to criminal conduct and low self-esteem, may be important, they do not appear to be effective in recidivism reduction.[189]

Responsive Principle—This represents appropriate application. Like risk and need, responsiveness requires that intervention be appropriate to the learning style and abilities of the offender. Nonspecific intervention is unlikely to achieve offender-specific cognitive-behavioral learning.[190]

Craig Dowden and D. A. Andrews, with the Department of Psychology at Carleton University in Ottawa, have argued that the incorporation of all three principles is the most important factor associated with reductions in recidivism. Their study indicated average reductions of 26 percent to 30 percent. The concept presented by Dowden and Andrew is one of "therapeutic jurisprudence." Jo-Anne Wemmers defines *therapeutic jurisprudence* as the study of the role of law as a "therapeutic agent," which views legal rules, procedures, and the role of legal actors as social forces that often produce therapeutic or antitherapeutic effects on the people involved in legal proceedings.[191]

Participatory processes in therapeutic jurisprudence have been especially successful in the sphere of offenses related to substance abuse. Traditional responses of increased police enforcement and harsher sentences have not been particularly successful. Despite the well-publicized war on drugs, the flow of drugs and drug-related crimes continued unabated, forcing police, prosecutors, defense counsel, judges, and politicians to realize that incarceration alone couldn't solve the problem. In Canada, for instance, courts were being overwhelmed, partly because of the very large numbers of drug-related charges and partly because of high recidivism. The resulting delays led to constitutional challenges, as exemplified by *Regina vs. Ascov*.[192] This led to the institution of special drug courts. Springboard, a community-based initiative, was one such program that began providing a cannabis diversion program at its city center courts in Toronto in May of 1998. Springboard processed 284 clients in the first six months (May to November 1998), claiming a 92 percent success rate.[193]

This therapeutic approach to drug offenses did not result from the influence of progressive lobbying by police leaders or evidence-based analysis; rather it resulted in great part because of circumstantial pressures, namely overwhelming caseloads and escalating court costs. It was circumstantial pressure that brought about the changes in judicial conservatism, avoidance of costs, and divided authority, the three barriers identified by Justice Harris.[194] As a consequence, however, it influenced an essential change in attitude, primarily an acceptance that drug addiction was a treatable disease and that crimes associated with drug use could not be stemmed through police enforcement and the criminal justice system alone.

One study of the effectiveness of community-based correctional initiatives looked at recidivism rates for a number of community-based-alternative-to-prison programs, using data collected from a nonprofit community corrections agency responsible for the operation of twenty-two separate programs.[195] The study included residential and nonresidential programs (halfway houses, work release programs, day reporting, home incarceration, and drug courts) for males, females, and juveniles. The results showed that offenders who are released after successfully completing the requirements for community-based programs were reimprisoned at about the same rate (both are reported at being around 30 percent) as offenders released from correctional facilities. Of the programs examined, drug court indicates the greatest success in reducing recidivism rates.

Programs such as these demonstrate the potential for success when the criminal justice system incorporates therapeutic jurisprudence using multidisciplinary partnerships that include police as central stakeholders in the institution of a policy that treats each individual as both an offender and a potentially valued member of society.

Unfortunately, one cannot overlook the persistence of reform-era attitudes that contributed to paradoxes of policing. On the one hand, policy makers and justice officials espouse a tough-on-crime agenda, through harsher sentences and stiffer legislation, especially for violent crime. On the other, officials are confronted with a criminal justice system that is burdened with overcrowded prisons and a probation and parole system that is overworked, barely able to maintain standards, and has demonstrated little value in the rehabilitation of offenders.

Joan Petersilia, "In Perception of Punishment," explains the paradox in the following terms:

> While less than enthusiastic public support to build additional prisons, with a continuing public demand to punish criminal offenders severely, and with the unsuitability of probation as a felony sentence, policymakers find themselves facing a serious dilemma. This encourages states to consider alternative sanctions that punish but do not involve incarceration.[196]

The tough-on-crime policies, however, contradict the participatory processes, which, according to most research, are more effective in both dealing with recidivism and reducing prison populations. These challenges have led to a diversification of punishment that includes fines, community service, house arrest, electronic monitoring, and alternative justice, like diversion programs and conferences.

Research and philosophical intent are not sufficient to effect the practical changes that are required by the criminal justice system. Current participatory practices tend to underestimate the role of community as an essential component for successful therapeutic jurisprudence. Despite a widening body of research that supports community collaboration in the advancement of social cohesion, we continue to marginalize and underestimate the capacity and capital of community. Take, for instance, how offenders are brought before the courts.

At present, offenders are arrested and excised from the communities (neighborhoods) within which they commit crimes, where there is little sympathy for the police, who are perceived as an external and only marginally legitimate authority. At the same time, there is an opportunity for discretionary accommodation of the circumstances that might have contributed to the antisocial behavior, including poverty and unemployment. Offenders are taken to a court, usually located at a central location outside of the community. Other young persons who may be attracted by gangs and antisocial behavior don't see what happens to the offender once excised from the community; in fact, the process creates temporary vacuums for the advancement of other gang members. The accused may even become a symbol of a general resistance against what is perceived as an unfair and unsympathetic policy intervention.

An alternative approach might involve the decentralization of courts to high-risk neighborhoods in order to create participatory partnership with the community, thereby refocusing attention on the offender, community, and victim. The ensuing intervention (retributive or participatory) would be transparent and open to the community stakeholders for empowering local stakeholders in redefining their social contract for enhancing social cohesion. Community engagement and social stigmatization of antisocial behavior would provide effective imputes for redefining community norms. Communities become better-informed partners with the police and criminal justice system and are more capable of defining and instituting meaningful social contracts between the offenders and the communities. Other benefits would include increased employment and partnerships between the community and the various stakeholders within the criminal justice system. It also enables better representation of the social makeup of the community, a sense of ownership, the opportunity to set aside politicized institutional power dynamics, and the taking into account of the underlying causes that are central to the genesis of criminal behavior.

Traditional calls for stiffer sentences reflect a knee-jerk reaction not substantiated by evidence-based analysis and in fact may result in sanctions that are less punitive than those presented by alternative programs. Furthermore, traditional calls for stiffer sanctions fail to take into consideration the advantages presented by participatory programs that could be realized by devising sanctions based on multidisciplinary principles that go beyond temporarily excising the offender. Reactive calls for longer mandatory sentences that do not include alternative sentencing programs are not only ineffective in preventing violence but may be harmful to the individual and society.[197] An alternative approach might be enforcing stricter terms of incarceration in conjunction with participatory programs in order to tailor offender-specific sentences to maximize the need for retribution (specific and general deterrence), rehabilitation, shaming, and restitution.

The accompanying debate and controversy is a reflection of a healthy discussion over issues that are central to the evolution and development of participatory processes and the role of police within that development. While resistance and controversy are necessary prerequisites to change, there is a need to maintain a balance between the quantitative and qualitative examination of participatory processes. In the absence of such balanced evaluations, participatory processes are destined to become mere adjuncts to traditional justice practices, thereby widening the grasp of traditional justice into the community and maintaining the marginalization of opportunities for collaboration and innovation in policing.

The concept of therapeutic jurisprudence needs to be translated into structural changes that lead to practical benefits.[198] Furthermore, information from various participatory programs needs to be benchmarked in order to promote those that are useful and eliminate those that are ineffective or harmful. Traditional retributive and participatory processes should be incorporated to provide a flexible and supportive criminal justice system. Courts should be decentralized and moved into effected communities, where processes, such as traditional adjudication, circles, crime conferences, and diversion programs, can be intertwined to provide effective intervention and enhance social cohesion. The combined effects of the traditional process (general and specific deterrence) and the participatory process (therapeutic jurisprudence) should be examined within the communities affected by crime and disorder to determine the best responses for those particular communities and their circumstances.

Police leaders have an important role to play in the discussion and engagement of stakeholders for the integration of alternative and restorative policies for the criminal justice system. If these concepts are accepted and embraced by police leaders, social workers, sociologists, clinicians, corrections, courts, and politicians, participatory programs may provide a viable alternative for transforming communities and the ties that enhance social cohesion.

While police organizations promote the duty of the individual and neighborhoods in exercising responsibility for dealing with conflict, they do not transfer sufficient power to nonstate social entities. Rather, they merely invite participation within a framework that continues to retain power and authority within police departments and does not sufficiently accept or promote programs that serve to channel the expression of conflict in ways that provide positive value for understanding the underlying problems confronting communities. Furthermore, community-policing programs, despite the extolment of collaboration, continue to respond to disputes and conflict with what are perceived as "coerced resolutions with inherent limitations; to the parties, of enforcement, of attitude, of future relations, of understanding, and of future conflict resolution modeling."[199] The legitimacy of such programs is further undermined by the perception that they are implemented not so much as altruistic responses to societal needs as for economic effectiveness.[200]

Many programs designed as public relations programs provide increased police-community contact, with the aim of enhancing community awareness of policing activities and strengthening police-community relations, but fall short of substantively strengthening community and volunteer agencies. Some see these programs as "image work," sponsored by administrators, associations of chiefs of police, police associations, politicians, and media to develop public relations currency for times when police must use noncollaborative coercive strategies.

Some observers suggest that many of these public relations activities are undertaken by the police to show that they can control crime and generally keep the community safe, yet not so successfully as to suggest that they do not need more resources to fight crime.[201]

Collaborative policing, unlike enforcement-focused policing, is much more dependent on the qualitative nature of policing. Studies indicate that crime and quality of life are rated as less important than how people feel about their interaction with police. This in itself represents a significant challenge to the implementation and success of collaborative policing practices and signals how important it is that police organizations redefine their roles as members of society, how they measure success, and how they respond to the evolving diversification of their communities.[202]

SOCIAL COHESION

Thus far, we have used the term *social cohesion* frequently and without developing an applicable framework. Now, it is time to develop a better understanding of what we mean by social cohesion and to create a practical model for its application to policing. Once again, we find ourselves in an area of crime and order management where definitions are nebulous. As has been the case with community policing, intelligence, and restorative justice, social cohesion, despite wide-ranging research, has yet to be universally defined.[203]/[204] Nonetheless, one finds widespread use of the term in a range of contemporary police reports with what appears to be a generalized assumption of an applied understanding of the term. A report on the mapping of social cohesion in Canadian research notes: "With so many conversations going on simultaneously, it is not surprising that there is little consensus about the definitions and about links to a family of related concepts."[205]

At a larger level, research has attempted to relate social cohesion to levels of happiness. While this may seem just a bit too esoteric for the purposes of the security sector, it has nonetheless gained some traction, even among governments, economists, and politicians. The Office of National Statistics in the United Kingdom has, for instance, commenced an annual measure and statement of self-reported assessments of the quality of life of its citizens to parallel the measure of its economic growth.[206] A report by the Canadian Commission on the Measurement of Economic Performance and Social Progress put it in the following terms:

> These measures, while not replacing conventional economic indicators, provide an opportunity to enrich policy discussions and inform people's view of the

> conditions of the communities where they live. More importantly, the new measures now have the potential to move from research to standard practice.[207]

These conversations provide a rich source for understanding the varied views of what constitutes social cohesion, how it might be measured and evaluated, and how it might either effect or construct civil society. For our purposes, we must extract from those components of these conversations that which provides opportunities for police leaders to enhance the goals of civil societies.

It is important here to understand the role of policing as more than just protecting life and property, preventing crime, and resolving problems.[208] Policing must also serve to foster a society's notion of social order and cohesion. Fundamental discussions of the role of policing by police leaders as well as citizens at large is critical to understanding the contributions police institutions must make to the establishment of a state of social cohesion within which communities can thrive. As Jonathan Jackson and Ben Bradford note: "Policing and understanding policing are suffused with messages about the conditions of society, the position of people within it, and the relation between state and individual."

Jackson and Bradford reveal that certain, generally privileged segments of society relate to "their" police as a symbol by which a grander, cohesive national past can be recalled and a troubled, fractured present explained.

> Every stop, every search, every arrest, every group of youth moved on, every abuse of due process, every failure to respond to call or complaint, every racist ... sexist ... homophobic (comment), every diagnosis of the crime problem, every depiction of criminals—all these send small, routine authoritative signals about society's conflicts, cleavages and hierarchies about whose claims are considered legitimate within it, about whose status identity is to be affirmed or denied as part of it.[209]

The police are, therefore, themselves a component of social cohesion, as well as the providers and maintainers of it, and if this is the case, then police leaders must reframe the nature and context of policy decisions and actions within this larger framework of social cohesion and community partnerships. How police organizations govern themselves and how well they uphold the rights of citizens, employees, and stakeholders serve as key elements in earning the public's trust and contributing to the development of social cohesion.[210]

The emerging debate on the issues surrounding enforcement of immigration laws, particularly in the United States, but also throughout Europe, Australia, and Canada, provides a contemporary example of how issues not directly related to daily policing can impact the role of policing generally and their relationships and legitimacy within the communities they serve. The executive summary to a report on policing and immigration by the Police Executive Research Forum described the issue as follows:

> Local police and sheriffs' departments increasingly are being drawn into a national debate about how to enforce federal immigration laws. In many jurisdictions, local police are being pressured to take significantly larger roles in what has traditionally been federal government responsibility. … In the meantime, many local communities and police agencies are struggling to devise local policies and strategies that reflect their own values and are consistent with the federal government's efforts, which seem to ebb and flow with changing Administrations.[211]

The police are required to balance multiple expectations. There is an expectation that law enforcement officers maintain their oath to uphold all local and national laws but also create a level of trust so as not to deter victims of crimes and others who may require government services from seeking the assistance they require. Immigrants, particularly illegal immigrants, become more susceptible to victimization because they are perceived to be less likely to report crimes to the authorities.[212]

Without discretion in the enforcement of laws, social cohesion cannot be maintained, trust is diminished, and legitimacy suffers, both with prevailing and marginalized communities. Unfortunately, there is no single model that can assist communities and police agencies struggling to devise local policies and strategies in determining how best to deploy resources, institute strategies, and measure performance designed to reflect local conditions and values.

What can police leaders do to maintain trust with illegal immigrant victims of crime while enforcing immigration laws and maintaining expectations of the community at large on illegal immigration? There are no simple answers to such questions, but what one can do is create frames of reference that enable decisions that optimize social cohesion and ensure trust and legitimacy, without signaling whose claims are considered legitimate and whose status identity is to be affirmed or denied or enlarging conflicts. Police leaders must remain mindful of managing the impact of all decisions on the public as well as the rank and file. Policing cannot simply rely on authoritarian control systems for keeping people and issues in line and for measuring compliance, while disregarding or diminishing value and belief systems as elements of their response.

Our perspective of the emergence and development of modern policing is based on the fundamental recognition that police cannot control crime and disorder on their own, that crime is best identified and controlled through collaborative problem solving with communities and by mobilizing and empowering communities through processes that are collaborative, fair, transparent, and accountable. Healthy, appealing communities are those in which citizens themselves are enfranchised with the networks, authority, and resources to collaborate in the identification, prioritization, and resolution of local issues.

The extent to which citizens respect one another and value their relationships influences how they care for each other and should be an important determinant of police policy, service design, and response. This focus on relationships and social cohesion should remain fundamental to any community-oriented approach to policing and be accepted and promoted widely across policing. To borrow from the

Commission on the Measurement of Economic Performance and Social Progress, social cohesion can be described in the following terms:

> Socially cohesive areas can be defined as areas with relatively high levels of interaction between residents and a strong sense of community. By contrast, areas lacking in cohesion, or socially disorganized or disintegrated areas, do not have such well defined social networks and it is often the case that the residents of these areas share very few common interests.[213]

Existing research identifies two general constructs of social cohesion, as proposed in a report of the multidimensional assessment of social cohesion in 47 European countries.[214]

> Social cohesion is an attribute of social groups or of societies and not of individuals who composed them. It concerns relationships among individuals, between individuals and groups/organizations and between individuals and society/state.[215]

> Social cohesion is a multidimensional construct: on the one hand, it measures social connectedness in different life domains, such as political and sociocultural spheres. On the other hand, it covers subjective representations (attitude) as well as behavioral outcomes (involvement).[216]

In the same way, the Canadian Policy Research Network identifies five dimensions of social cohesion:[217]

- belonging versus isolation
- inclusion versus exclusion
- participation versus noninvolvement
- recognition versus rejection
- legitimacy versus illegitimacy

These two, the constructs combined with the five dimensions, provide an integrative basis for understanding the application of social cohesion within the framework of the preceding and ensuing work. Social cohesion should be perceived as a barometer for the health of communities to the extent that it indicates the well-being of communities—the willingness of neighbors to trust and collaborate on supporting one another. A sense of trust and collaboration enhances the social contract among members by holding everyone responsible for the personal dignity, respect, and attachments of each member and his or her individual values within the social community. High levels of social cohesion lead to a stronger sense of social contract wherein harm to others in that network results in a greater sense of obligation to remedy that harm. Weak social cohesion diminishes this sense of connectedness and obligation, wherein members more readily otherize those who are perceived not to belong to their own personal network. And while it is concerned with relationships among individuals, between individuals and groups or organizations, and between individuals and society or the state, it is how these relationships serve to improve the quality of lives of citizens and how both (organizations and individual citizens) entrust the other for their personal and collective well-being that matters most.

The Canadian Council on Social Development defines social cohesion in the following terms:

> Social cohesion is the ongoing process of developing a community of shared values, shared challenges and equal opportunity within Canada, based on a sense of trust, hope and reciprocity amongst all ...[218]

While I have selected these two particular constructs and five principles to frame social cohesion for the purposes of our analysis, the absence of a single consolidated definition should be seen, as with community policing, intelligence, and restorative justice, as increasing opportunities for interpretative and contextual application of policies rather than providing a single rigid framework for universal application. The resulting diversity can only contribute to enhancing our ability to design prescriptive frameworks, with qualitative and quantitative dimensions, without limiting the utility of social cohesion. From a participatory perspective, social cohesion represents the capacity of a community to regulate the behavior of its members. It is the social contract or collective efficacy represented by the capacity of communities to constrain citizens from violating common norms and laws and is dependent on the size, density, and breadth of social networks and the level of engagement of citizens in those networks.[219] Attachment to one's neighborhood fosters cohesion, while conditions that impede cohesion foster dissonance and disorder.

How young adults, minority groups, and marginalized members of society feel about their police service can have a direct impact on the development of a community with shared values, shared challenges, and equal opportunity based on a sense of trust, hope, and reciprocity within and among communities. Recall that for some police work is not only about upholding the law but a larger struggle between right and wrong.[220] How effectively and responsibly communities work to engage and reintegrate effected members of their social group as accepted and productive members is a representation of social cohesion. Aboriginal societies across the world have traditionally been far more effective than modern democratic societies in defining and employing social cohesion as a measure of their success as healthy communities. As noted, some countries now routinely include measures of social well-being as part of their national reports of economic and social development. The Canadian Centre for Justice Statistics (CCJS), for instance, now includes social control as a dimension for assessing the factors that influence crime. The CCJS notes that the urban nature of neighborhoods can be linked to a particular way of life wherein people come together, for various reasons, within neighborhoods where neighbors may or may not know each other. Any impediment of conditions that foster the development of bonds among the residents and their attachment to the neighborhood can lead to circumstances that foster crime.[221]

It is equally important to note, however, that simply establishing social cohesion is not by itself a positive outcome in all circumstances. At the other extreme, social cohesion can potentially result in the otherization of members outside of one's group, leading to significant negative consequences. Kelly Koonce argues that cohesion in itself is not enough.[222] There needs also be an emphasis on *all*. Social cohesion must include what Koonce describes as social capital, comprised of *bonding capital* and *bridging capital*. Bonding capital represents the strength of the ties between the social actors of a group, or intragroup ties. Bridging capital represents the capacity for intergroup ties, or ties that look outward to other diverse groups, leading to what Koonce describes as "broader networks that [provide] a wider range of interactions."[223]

Police leaders must ask themselves how they can better contribute to achieve such desired levels of social cohesion. In some instances, police organizations must themselves transform their own traditional cultures, many presently characterized by reactive policing, to cultures that value and deliver on social cohesion as a measurable outcome of their proactive, preventative crime-management policies. In the following pages, we develop a model, based on social cohesion and crime levels and trends, that provides a framework for determining the type of policing intervention that is most appropriate and for instituting the types of performance measurement that identify the most effective policing policy. This model provides a framework for determining which of the two general approaches to policing (intelligence led versus community based) is appropriate for the level of social cohesion and crime levels of a customer community and for the selection of an appropriate category of performance measure (quantitative versus qualitative).

Communities that exhibit low social cohesion also tend to have lower levels of trust among neighbors, institutions, and systems. There are correspondingly lower attributions of police legitimacy and a generally diminished trust of civil institutions.[224] The results are manifest in superficial relationships between members of the community and police, as well as inferior outcomes and outputs from the provision of policing services. Under such conditions, community collaboration is limited and police must rely, relatively more, on strategies based on intelligence-led processes for identifying, solving, and facilitating prosecution of criminals. Police organizations must work harder to solicit cooperation or access information about crime and victimization.[225] Relationships must be built through a demonstration of trust between the parties involved (effected communities, community at large, individuals, social institutions, governments, and police), with patience, time, and commitment. Nonetheless, security services and policing must continue to be provided in the interim. Crime and order must be maintained, even under conditions of poor community cooperation and low social cohesion.

The application of intelligence-led strategies provides one means of targeting criminals, disorder, and public safety issues but only if carefully circumspect so as not to cast too wide a net or carelessly stigmatize entire communities. Police must be mindful that intelligence-led investigations by their nature generally only come to the notice of a community when arrests are effected at the conclusion of a covert project, often accompanied by dramatic media attention and postevent photo opportunities for communicating the intent and results of the initiative. This sudden attention on a community and its issues, compounded by the lack of community consultation or awareness, may heighten police-community mistrust and tension. This, despite the success of the intervention itself, at least from an enforcement perspective, can lead to the police being perceived as biased and insincere in their partnerships and initiatives. Such feelings can enhance mistrust and suspicion, thereby undermining collaboration. Communities become increasingly suspicious of other suspected covert investigations that may be occurring within the their neighborhood, further undermining the legitimacy and relationships that neighborhood/community officers are working hard to build or, worse, leading to the otherization of neighborhood officers, members within the community perceived to be too close to the authorities, or segments of the community characterized as troublemakers.

Community officers, who themselves might have been unaware of the investigations, too may become cynical of the community initiatives to which they are assigned, worked hard to establish, and for which they may have been stigmatized as doing what their colleagues perceive as "soft policing." Such outcomes threaten social cohesion and can undermine the very principles and values that were being advocated by police leaders themselves in the first place. Leaders cannot simply be reactive to such challenges but must preplan to meet such moments of truth by recognizing and undertaking the challenge of designing responses suited for such very specific requirements. Police planners and leaders must institute systems that predict and provide interventions that mitigate harm and enhance social cohesion through, for instance, access to governmental, nongovernmental, for-profit, and nonprofit organizations and the types of services that enhance self-esteem, self-efficacy, a sense of responsibility, tolerance, positive support, and positive neighborhood influences.

Continued success, and demonstrated commitment to fairness, trust and legitimacy may help to reestablish community relationships. If communities continue to experience cycles of intelligence-led operations followed by what are perceived as tokenistic promotional public relations community policing initiatives, the barriers to reestablishing trust (procedural or instrumental) will become increasingly difficult, even if intelligence/information and cooperation become more forthcoming and even in cases where intelligence is initiated by the communities themselves. Citizens will be fearful of being perceived as informants against their own communities or as collaborators with outsiders whose policies are unfair, insensitive, and oppressive. Take, for instance, present challenges with policing against the radicalization of terrorists or policing in communities in the United States were racial tensions following the shootings of black suspects by white officers have sparked nationwide protests. Some of the issues that give rise to community dissonance, lack of social cohesion, and police legitimacy have roots in a variety of social causes; however, police must do their part in meaningful community engagement before such incidents become the catalyst for larger, more corrosive public order challenges or become embedded as systemic issues.

Despite the challenges and given the unique characteristics of each community, police leaders must continually strive toward improving legitimacy, while being reminded that police cannot be the sole agents responsible for social cohesion or responding to crime and disorder. Crime and social justice challenges are best identified and controlled through collaborative problem solving with communities and by mobilizing and empowering communities themselves to produce conditions under which citizens themselves are enfranchised to take leadership for seeking and implementing solutions to local issues. In order to be able to achieve this, police organizations must be prepared to transform traditional approaches, characterized by reactive policing, to approaches that emphasize proactive, preventative crime, disorder, and social injustice management. Police leaders must remain focused on sustained commitment to relationship building and to ensuring that frontline officers do not yield to burnout from what can appear to be a never-ending process of relationship building and rebuilding, only to be followed by yet another intelligence-led initiative of which even frontline officers are not likely to have been aware. Trust building and community mobilization requires unrelenting focus and commitment on the attitudes and culture of organizational members as much as on customer communities.

Lack of self-efficacy, particularly in deeply divided communities where there is no sense of common community, makes it difficult for people to deliberate or reflect on a common problem, because there is no sense of "we."[226] Collaborative policing programs attempt to respond to the need for mobilizing both inter- as well as intracultural attachments, through a process of "neighboring" or "bonding," which amounts to a willingness of community members to share in the more mundane activities of daily life.[227] Although difficult to measure, the degree to which these inter- and intragroup bonding occurs (among both those who belong to the dominant cultural group as well as between less dominant groups) may provide a good measure of a community's capacity for mobilization.

Consider Switzerland for instance. Swiss society, a highly cohesive society, has developed extremely effective and trusted institutions. Breaches of social norms are likely to result in the ostracization of the offender by members within this highly cohesive society and to the unsolicited notification of authorities of any obvious and existent threats against the community. Such communities represent mobilized communities wherein citizens themselves identify and prioritize issues and advocate and target state resources. Proactive intelligence-led policing becomes secondary to community-based policing in which communities become partners in the sustaining of a civil society.

In China's rural villages, where family and community ties are strong, beliefs are shared, and values and practices open to scrutiny, villagers perform self-governance tasks, including public security, with little or no state intervention or support. Policing in rural China is achieved through what is characterized as informal social control wherein enforcement is achieved mainly through informal social management through education, persuasion, moral values, and discipline.[228] Community policing in China "takes the form of social prevention rather than enforcement."[229] Community policing is a social function.

The Pashtoon, an ethnic group in Afghanistan, hold a ceremony called the *Nanate*, described as a ceremony during which an accused brings flour and kills a sheep for a community feast. It is often held at the victim's house, where the victim participates in cooking the food the offender brings. During the event, the offender is not told that he or she is bad or in need of reform, but rather socially convinced to accept that he or she has done an injustice to the victim. At the same time, the offender is assured that she or he is one of the community and accepted back among them. The success of the ceremony is directly related to two principles: use of shaming to induce conformity with social norms (social contract) and personal remorse leading to the reestablishment of personal bonds between the offender, the victim, and their community. There is also a third dynamic, which is present within rural and aboriginal communities, one that involves the responsibility of an individual to avoid inviting stigmatization and shame on one's own family and community.[230]

Much more is expected of police leadership today than merely providing effective and efficient law enforcement. Policing policies must represent iterative processes that continually adapt to emerging social, economic, and political realities. Police agencies must mobilize communities, inform social norms, empower citizens, and educate citizens among their many other functions. The US Department of Justice lists the following as examples of alternatives for responding to issues of law enforcement and public safety:[231]

- mobilizing the community (as witnesses, to patrol the community, for advocacy)
- requesting that citizens exercise informal social control over one another (e.g., parents over children, employers over employees,

coaches over athletes, teachers over students, military commanders over soldiers, lenders over borrowers, landlords over tenants)
- using mediation and negotiation skills to resolve disputes
- conveying information (e.g., to reduce exaggerated fear, to generate public awareness, to elicit conformity with laws that are not known or understood, to show citizens how they contribute to problems and ways to avoid doing so, to educate the public about the limits of police authority, to build support for new approaches)
- altering the physical environment to reduce opportunities for problems to occur
- enforcing civil laws (e.g., nuisance abatement, injunctions, asset forfeiture)
- recommending and enforcing special conditions of bail, probation, or parole
- intervening short of arrest (e.g., issuing warnings, placing people in protective custody, temporarily seizing weapons, issuing dispersal orders)
- advocating enactment of new laws or regulations to control conditions that create problems
- concentrating attention on those people and circumstances that account for a disproportionate share of a problem (e.g., repeat offenders, repeat victims, repeat locations)
- coordinating with other government and private services (e.g., drug treatment, youth recreation, social services)

While studies tend to focus on social cohesion as by-products of some process, they remain unclear on the universal drivers that result in the outcome that can be called social cohesion. Whether happiness is derived as a consequence of access to education, a narrowing of income inequality, a sense of belonging to a society, or simply a sense of well-being studies concur with the finding that the public, private, and nonprofit sector all play a role in the management of conflicts and enhancing social capital.[232]

Our aim is to introduce social cohesion as an indicator for informing policing policy development and to institute social cohesion as part of the modern lexicon of policing generally. The Intelligence Led Policing/ Community Policing (IP/CP) Model, developed herein, provides a framework for determining policing policy in relation to the existing levels of crime and social cohesion. The first step involves determining what constitutes the community and the boundaries between the various constituent parties and developing an inventory and assessment of the overriding sources of conflict—religion, class, language, nationality, or ethnicity. The second step involves determining the ability and capacity of the constituent social actors, both as organized groups as well as independent members, to undertake collective action, including the actors' capacity to develop a sense of community, shared vision, knowledge, skills and abilities, resources (physical and financial), leadership and participation of a broad and representative range of community members, willingness and motivation, infrastructure (supportive institutions, physical resources), and enabling policies and systems.[233] This is the actors' capacity for collective self-efficacy in the same way that community justice aims to mobilize communities to institute restorative and participatory processes based on concepts such as *social contract* and *public shaming*.[234]

The third step involves gauging the relative strength of the cohesion between the constituent social actors, what is called the *bridging capital*. The fourth step is determining the relative openness or permeability of the social actors between different groups to recognize and accept legitimate differences.[235] In other terms, *permeability* represents the willingness of social actors to form bonding and bridging capital toward a wider range of interactions.[236]

The gauging and classification of the relative strengths or weaknesses of the capacities (bonding and bridging) and permeability of the cohesion will be subjective and relative to the needs of each society and social circumstance. There is no single universal criterion, nor should there be, for determining the strength of the social ties; instead, what is important is that police, civic leaders, social agencies, and special interest groups all work together to assess their present position relative to where they would like to be and to determine realistic and achievable goals under the prevailing conditions, resources, and limitations.

Consider Figure 6, a model for social cohesion and police intervention, which provides a graphic illustration of the framework.

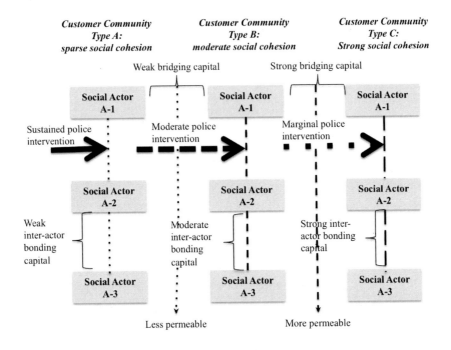

Figure 6. A model for social cohesion and police intervention.

Permeability refers to the openness of actor customer communities (groups) to other customer communities and to recognizing and accepting legitimate differences. It represents the willingness of the social actors to form bonding and/or bridging capital toward other groups/outsiders.

Bonding capital refers to the strength between members of a customer community, the sharing of values and trust among individuals; the social contract among members of a customer community.

Bridging capital refers to the strength of the bonds between customer communities.

Social networks include groups with associated norms of reciprocity and trustworthiness.

Figure 6 illustrates a three-step representation of a model for social cohesion and police intervention. In the figure, under column A, the network connections between various social actors are sparse (weak interactor bonding capital); there is little social cohesion (illustrated by a dotted line). Social actors lack a shared vision and the knowledge, skills, and ability to leverage resources or undertake collective action. Under such conditions, citizens are unable to access or lack the resources and ability to mobilize on behalf of their own self-interest. Furthermore, external intervention is perceived as the imposition of external norms and resisted by individual actors toward the preservation of their individual self-interests. Such communities are more likely to be insular and more prone to otherize outsiders, resulting in weaker bridging capital with other groups. They exhibit greater need for sustained support from external sources. The deficit of trust among actors and the capacity for self-efficacy, however, create heightened reliance for impetus for start-up support from state-sponsored institutions and nonprofit agents. Self-efficacy is dependent on sponsorship by outside agents for bridging gaps between and among actors. Outside agents provide the essential catalytic impetus for the development and enhancement of positive social modeling and for providing social persuasion toward increased cohesion.

Even though outside intervention is likely to be viewed with suspicion, it is important to leverage opportunities for establishing presence and acceptance wherever possible. Under such conditions, police will initially lack legitimacy and trust; however, they are also seen as authoritative and therefore empowered to impact the actions and behavior of other actors within the community. Police are perceived to have the power, if not the legitimacy, to impose compliance and conformity where individuals cannot or are not willing to intervene on their own behalf. Such instances, despite limited scope, can offer opportunities for grounding policing within the community. The police are able to provide access to a range of other supportive services, institutions, and physical resources, thereby leveraging a collective legitimacy through collaboration with other agents, such as social services, public health, schools, religious organizations, and volunteer services.[237] The relative reliance on outside intervention for bridging internal community gaps and for building capacity is relatively high. Low social cohesion, characterized by sparse social networks, results in low capacity and a relatively sustained requirement for external intervention.

Under column B, network connections between social agents are improved to a moderate level of interactor bonding capital (illustrated by a denser line). Under such conditions, individual social actors develop a better understanding of their relationship with state actors, but not to the extent of collaborating with other social actors to leverage state resources collectively. There are better connections with state resources and actors toward meeting their own group interests. Each social actor group or customer community is focused on its own group's relationships with state actors and does not necessarily advocate on behalf of other customer community groups. Here, state agencies are able to established some legitimacy, but it is limited to their specific relationships with distinct social actor groups. As a result, intervention by state actors, including police, requires less direct (moderate) intervention than under scenario A. While bonding capital increases, it does not necessarily follow that bridging capital also increases or that there is increased permeability for intercustomer group interaction. Under such conditions, police, as with any other external intervention, require less advocacy than under Scenario A. Intervention may be classified as moderate.

Under column C, network connections between interactor groups, or bonding capital, is strong (illustrated by a solid line). There is a strong sense of common interest among social actors (a social contract). Under such conditions, unaffected social actor groups will mobilize in support of another social actor group when norms are breached or a group member exhibits a need. Social cohesion, including trust and support among and between various social actor groups improves. The customer community acts collectively, mobilizing local resources and leveraging state support for the collective as much as for the support of individual members. Under such conditions, the need for external intervention becomes marginal; there is, for instance, less need for direct, sustained police intervention. Instead, the group itself will access and demand appropriate external support. These stages are somewhat arbitrary; in reality, social cohesion and community mobilization develop along a continuum without distinct phases. However, identifying and understanding these stages is useful for the provision of thoughtfully formulated and appropriately applied intervention.

Under scenario A, state intervention is supported by a tiered response, including a variety of support services working together to address the substantive issues and sponsoring causes. This approach provides advantages over isolated social service policies. First, a collective response draws on the marginal legitimacy of each responding agency to strengthen acceptance by affected communities. If, for instance, the community lacks trust in the police, they may become more likely to accept intervention if another accompanying service (education, health services, social services, and so on) that enjoys a relatively better relationship is part of the response. In effect, collective efficacy creates an economy of scale toward building trust and legitimacy. Secondly, the chances of issues being accurately diagnosed and resources being allocated and responded to in a timely and effective manner increase with the participation of multiple agencies. Building stronger, better communities and societies requires a concerted effort by responding agencies, each working simultaneously to redress the causes that create harm and diminish the quality of lives of citizens.

Under scenario C, the state and communities have done their work. Communities are mobilized and capable of advocating services and resources required in strengthening their communities; intervention becomes more targeted, applied by specific state actors as required. These are communities with strong social cohesion and strong network ties, with members and actors having individually and collectively developed social capital and the capacity to advocate and respond to their own issues.

The heart of the challenge arises in the identification and application of indicators of social cohesion, their measurement, and appropriate responses to social issues. Indicators must include both objective and subjective data.[238] Subjective information gathered through opinion surveys includes information about activities, perceptions, and beliefs that contribute to social cohesion—willingness to cooperate, levels of trust in people, confidence in institutions, respect for diversity, understanding reciprocity, and a sense of belonging. Community participation is central to cohesiveness and includes participation in networks and groups, voluntarism, and political participation. The processes and institutions that contribute to the enhancement of social cohesion are those that create social networks, promote norms, and provide support and opportunities for civil interaction. The work of organizations, such as business associations, religious organizations, libraries, sports clubs, schools, and community organizations and community events provide critical opportunities for citizens to interact in ways that contribute to the development of cooperation, tolerance, understanding, and ownership of their communities.

Good policing provides the safety and security within which these processes can germinate and develop and therefore represents a crucial and complex institution in the advancement and sustaining of civil society. Police provide security and order for the development of the conditions in which civil processes can be initiated and at the same time represent an obstacle for the expression of civil processes. Public protests serve as an example of community mobilization for the expression of popular dissatisfaction with government and public institutions. While protesters undertake civil disobedience as a strategy for impacting policy and awareness, the tolerance for protests and associated occupations across various jurisdictions is dependent on the capacity of police to safeguard democratic expressions of public protest while upholding civil processes for government accountability and public safety and security. Many protests, such as those of the civil rights movement of the 1960s or the Equal Rights Amendment protests of the 1970s, were also an expression of the bonding and bridging capital among and between fractured groups and interests across many cities and countries. Many such issues that give to social unrest will remain outside of the realm of police authority; nonetheless, it is incumbent on managers to look for indicators that give context and provide meaningful understanding of the scope of the social issues to which they must respond as well as the underlying causes to which they might be able to make positive contributions, at least in the longer term.

Some of the types of indicators might include distribution of income, poverty, employment, mobility, health care, education, adequate and affordable housing, public health, economic security, and personal and family security.²³⁹ Other indicators may include urbanization, deindustrialization, population turnover, and ethnic and racial heterogeneity.²⁴⁰ How police respond to larger issues of social cohesion in rapidly changing societies, particularly those that are likely to experience accelerated diversification in a rapidly globalized era, is critical to how residents, immigrants, and visitors perceive the health of communities.

Identifying and defining indicators, qualitative and quantitative, should be an iterative process specific to the nature and needs of each community. These indicators should also serve as a standard for the tailoring of multistakeholder responses to community needs. The iterative processes for determining social cohesion are beyond the scope of policing alone and should rightly remain beyond the scope of policing alone. The emphasis requires developing collaboration with subject matter experts across a range of disciplines, agencies, and institutions.

Leaders in policing require processes for identifying indicators of social cohesion through careful observation of needs-based assessment for specific communities for which services are designed. The types of processes that go beyond developing legislated requirements for providing social services to include programs that enrich and elevate sponsoring values, attitudes, and social norms. They can be for specific neighborhoods, larger communities, or even an entire city or region, depending on the indicators and the scope and scale of the bonding and bridging required. Take, for instance, the issue of the sense of belonging of children of immigrant families born in France and Great Britain who continue to feel otherized and marginalized. The unemployment data for youth across Europe indicated unemployment levels as high as 54.9 percent for Spain, 57.3 percent for Greece, 41.8 percent in Italy, and 48.5 percent in Croatia.²⁴¹ The problems are self-evident and aptly described in a recent editorial titled "Creating Capabilities for Socially Vulnerable in Europe," which advocates for a "capability approach, an approach that provides a conceptually innovative foundation for analyzing the complex processes through which policies create or thwart opportunities for young people ..."²⁴²

It primarily endeavours to promote social justice and equity in order to build societies that empower individuals to "choose to live the life they have the reason to value." Another of its aims is the assessment of social progress not only in terms of economic productivity, but more broadly as human development, i.e. in terms of beings and doings that people are able to realize. When used for the interpretation of real human conditions or in the evaluation of policies, the CA makes it possible to have a deeper and more comprehensive perspective on the obstacles that hinder the matching of personal choice with structural opportunities in the context of social justice.[243]

Failure to provide opportunities that go beyond the simply legislated requirements of, for instance, compulsory schooling or essential medical care, minimal housing, and social assistance compounds opportunities for ghettoization and radicalization. Problems arising from such issues might have been anticipated and better addressed had the focus of previous assessments included indicators for social cohesion and programs to enrich and elevate sponsoring values, attitudes, and social norms.

Progressive policing requires genuine and sustained stewardship by communities, police, citizens, local governments, nonprofit organizations, and special interest groups. Any model for the provision of policing and the mobilization of communities must include social cohesion as an integral component for the maintenance of civil society. Indicators that monitor the health of communities—their capacity to form trusting partnerships within the community and with the types of groups and resources that strengthen a sense of belonging and build networks within and outside the community and among its citizens and institutions. Performance measures for effective policing should include the ability of police officers, programs, and services to provide solutions for reducing barriers to social cohesion and for advancing collaborative crime management. This can only be accomplished if police managers develop defensible and legitimate models for policing and contribute to the building of trust and legitimacy inside and external to their institutions.

DEVELOPING THE INTELLIGENCE-LED/ COMMUNITY-BASED POLICING MODEL (IP-CP) AND QUALITY/ QUANTITY/CRIME (QQC) MODEL

Intelligence-led policies/strategies can provide an alternative to collaboration during times of high crime and low social cohesion. However, state-sponsored initiatives for intervention through intelligence-led initiatives can become counterproductive, particularly if continued within communities that begin to transition to a more collaborative culture. Police strategists must always remain sensitive and responsive to cultural changes within their customer communities—sensitivity being founded on performance measures appropriate for the conditions within which the services are being rendered and for the desired outcome of the services provided. Intelligence-led initiatives, coupled with emphasis on quantitative performance measurement, is more effective for responding to crime during times of increasing crime and low social cohesion (designed for resetting norms and enhancing public safety). Community programs based on collaborative policing, on the other hand, is more suitable for establishing trust and transparency essential for community mobilization and capacity building. The *Intelligence-Led/Community Based Policing Model (IP-CP)* provides a framework for selecting the appropriate strategy, dominated either by intelligence-led policies or community-based policies. Selecting the appropriate strategy by itself, however, is insufficient. It is equally important to develop an understanding of how emphatically those strategies must be implemented, enforced, and sustained. The *model for social cohesion and police intervention* provided three levels of intervention—maintained, moderate, or marginal. Effective strategies also require application of appropriate performance measurement systems—qualitative versus quantitative. The *Intelligence-Led/ Community-Based Policing Model (IP-CP)*, combined with the *Quality/ Quantity/Crime (QQC) Model*, provides a framework for doing both.

In the following section, we determine how to frame the societal context for which a policing policy is intended and offer a way to determine the most appropriate strategy. Second, IP-CP and QQC will enable us to incorporate both qualitative and quantitative performance measures for determining the most suitable strategy for the specific customer community. Together, IP-CP and QQC enable us to determine which of the two, quantitative or qualitative, provides the most effective measurement framework for the specific conditions of a customer community based on its specific level of social cohesion and crime.

It is important to understand from the onset that neither intelligence nor community strategies are wholly qualitative or wholly quantitative; both have elements that are qualitative and quantitative, despite fundamental differences. Community policing strategies are founded on collaboration, empowerment, crime prevention, and social well-being and represent a trust-based strategy. Community-based strategies see healthy relationships as goals in themselves. In contrast, intelligence-based strategies use relationships to achieve secondary goals—the gathering of intelligence information. This predisposes community-based strategies to being more qualitative in nature as compared to intelligence-led strategies. Strategies based on relationships are more reliant on qualitative elements, while results-based strategies based on intelligence are more contingent on analytical analysis and therefore more quantitative in nature. Nonetheless, both can be equally subject to either qualitative or quantitative measurements.

While both have qualitative and quantitative elements, the Quality/ Quantity/Crime (QQC) Model provides a framework for assessing, in relative terms, the appropriateness of the measure (qualitative or quantitative) based on the state of crime (increasing versus decreasing). The QQC Model provides a framework for determining the appropriate performance strategy. It suggests that quantitative-based performance measurements and consequently, quantitative outcomes are more relevant during times of increasing crime as opposed to declining crime. When crime indicators are increasing, quantitative strategies should receive greater emphasis for reducing crime and targeting enforcement. On the other hand, when crime is decreasing, as has been the trend during the past decade, qualitative strategies aimed at increasing appreciation of safety, embedding legitimacy, mobilizing communities, and empowering stakeholders should take precedence—the types of programs that contribute to the achievement of policing outcomes through the enhancement of social cohesion.

Together, the IP-CP/QQC Model provides a framework for determining the types of societal concerns, security issues, perceptions, and intelligence that contribute to decisions on how communities are policed. It provides a framework for understanding when strategies, such as community-based policing, intelligence-led policing, and problem-oriented policing (like broken windows), can be combined with environmental design, diversion programs, restorative justice, and therapeutic jurisprudence to impact quality-of-life issues that impede social cohesion. And it provides a framework that supports a balanced scorecard approach to assessing needs, providing services, and measuring success.

It is unfortunate that politicization of contemporary policing (justification for funding, lengthier and mandatory sentences, increased powers of search and surveillance, and so on) has continued to sustain a rhetorical justification based on the argument that reductions in crime are the exclusive result of effective policing—primarily traditional quantitative intelligence-based policing. Such rhetorical arguments result partly from a lack of understanding of how to frame policing policies during times of sustained crime reduction. It is simply easier to revert to tried and tested arguments for maintaining and sustaining police resources, funding, and power even if they may not always be true.

The US Department of Justice notes:

> ... common local government responses to crime and disorder, such as hiring more police officers and deploying them in conventional patrol and investigative modes, having police respond rapidly to all incidents, having police patrol the streets in random patterns, and assigning all criminal cases for follow-up investigation by detectives are of far less certain value than commonly believed.[244]

Police leaders should be cautious not to remain anchored in a view that the best response, the most efficient response, and the most effective response to crime and disorder is more policing. Such justifications claim credit for that which cannot be measured (crime prevention), when it would be far more useful to use conditions of low crime to better target the precursors of crimes—poverty, lack of housing, lack of education, lack of trust in institutions, and acceptance of social norms. Present conditions of historically low, and still decreasing, global crime trends in fact provide the perfect opportunity to design new and innovative policies that create opportunities for harm reduction, integration, and enhancing sustainable civil communities. Police leaders must fully and sincerely embrace, in principle and in spirit, the notion that policing forms but only a small part of an ongoing process for developing communities with shared values, shared challenges, and equal opportunities, based on a sense of trust, hope, and reciprocity among all citizens within a society.

Recall from the model for social cohesion and police intervention (Figure 6) that social actors within a community can have relatively strong or weak bonds (bonding capital) and that two or more customer communities might, similarly, enjoy relatively strong or weak bonds among one another (bridging capital). Also recall that police intervention focused on issues within these communities is impacted by the strength of these bonds and may need to be in the form of a maintained intervention, marginal intervention, or minimal intervention. Communities with weaker social cohesion require a maintained or sustained response, while those with strong social cohesion require minimal intervention.

We now add crime and crime trends to what we have learned about the social cohesion of a community to develop an understanding of whether the predominant police response should be intelligence-led or community-based. Figure 7 illustrates the IP-CP Model (intelligence-led/community-based). Now we add crime level and trends and intelligence-led versus community-focused intervention for determining the best response to a variety of community types, based on their specific crime trends and degree of suggested police intervention.

The shaded cubes (darker for stronger cohesion and lighter for weaker cohesion) represent the three types of customer communities represented in figure 6 (those with sparse, moderate, or strong social cohesion). Crime levels are represented on the left side of the vertical axis and social cohesion on the horizontal axis. Crime trends are interpreted as movements from point to point on any part of the matrix. This framework provides suggestions for positioning policing services in such a way as to best respond to crime trends and social cohesion. For instance, in communities with sparse social networks, and therefore sparse social cohesion and high crime rates, policing policies should prefer intelligence-led initiatives to community-based, represented on the model as IP-CP. As crime falls to lower levels (low crime), even while social cohesion remains low, policing policies should be developed toward giving preference to community-based policing over intelligence-led, represented on the model as CP-IP.

When crime increases, and social cohesion is negatively impacted—for instance a community transitioning from moderate crime and high social cohesion toward one with high crime and moderate social cohesion, that is, the community is moving toward a state of high crime and weaker cohesion—police initiatives changes focus from Community based preferred (CP-IP) to intelligence-led preferred (IP-CP). Communities with high levels of crime, even those exhibiting strong social cohesion, require greater emphasis on intelligence versus community policing. As crime drops and cohesion remains high, police initiatives shift from intelligence focused to community based, encouraging greater nonstate intervention.

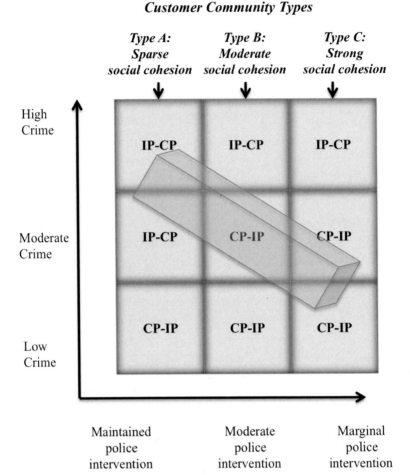

Figure 7. IP-CP Model (Intelligence Led/Community Based).

This model provides suggestions for position policing services in such a way as to provide an articulable means for responding to crime trends and social cohesion. We also, as a next step, revert back to the model for social cohesion and police intervention (Figure 6) to determine the intensity focus of the *type of intervention that is appropriate, as either maintained, marginal, or minimum*. Recall that police intervention should be based on the strength of the bonds and may need to be a maintained intervention, marginal intervention, or minimal intervention. Communities with weaker social cohesion require a maintained or sustained response, while strong social cohesion requires minimal intervention.

For instance, in communities with sparse social networks and therefore sparse social cohesion, and high crime rates, policing policies should prefer intelligence-led initiatives to community-based. As crime falls to lower levels (low crime), even while social cohesion remains low, policing policies should be developed with preference for community-based policing over intelligence-led, while maintaining the degree of intervention. As crime increases and social cohesion is negatively impacted—that is, the community moves for example from a low to a high state of crime, and from sparse to moderate cohesion—police initiatives refocus from community-based policies towards a preference for intelligence-based initiatives. Even though stronger in terms of social cohesion the community requires greater emphasis on intelligence versus community policing. The level of police intervention may also be reduced from maintained to moderate. As crime drops to low, and cohesion strengthens to strong, police initiatives begin to shift from intelligence-focused to community-based. Police intervention has gone from maintained to moderate to marginal, encouraging greater nonstate intervention.

We can now combine and apply the IP-CP Model (Intelligence Lead/Community Based) in conjunction with the model for social cohesion and police intervention (Figure 8) to establish the relative strength or weakness of a community, its bridging and bonding capital, and the position of that community relative to crime and social cohesion to determine the predominant policing strategy (intelligence-led versus community-based) and whether the police intervention should be maintained, moderate, or minimal.

The following are examples of the application of the IP-CP Model in conjunction with the model for social cohesion and police intervention.

Scenario: A community with strong social cohesion is experiencing high crime, indicating a deterioration of cohesion levels from high toward moderate.

High crime, even under strong social cohesion, calls for policing with greater emphasis on intelligence versus community policing.

A community with strong social cohesion requires marginal police intervention because its nonstate agencies are well established, and community actors are encouraged and supported in collaborating to identify, prioritize, and solve problems. Marginal intervention also implies officers have greater freedom to exercise discretion. As community cohesion deteriorates to moderate police intervention must increase to moderate levels. Moderate intervention implies a withdrawing of some discretionary tolerances previously extended under a state of high social cohesion.

Scenario: A community with high social cohesion is experiencing a reduction in crime from high to low.

Communities with high levels of crime regardless of their strong social cohesion require greater emphasis on intelligence versus community policing. As crime drops and cohesion remains high, police initiatives shift from intelligence-focused to community-based, which encourage greater nonstate intervention. However, because the community remains highly cohesive, there is no need to change the intensity of the intervention; it remains marginal.

Scenario: A community with high crime and sparse social cohesion transitions to a community with moderate crime and moderate social cohesion.

As a community with high crime and sparse social cohesion progresses to moderate crime and moderate social cohesion, preference shifts more rapidly from intelligence-based to community-based. At the same time, police intervention may be reduced from maintained to moderate. In the reverse, if a community with strong social cohesion and low crime suddenly experiences a rise in crime from low to moderate, and deterioration in social cohesion from strong to moderate, community-based policies remain preferred over intelligence-led. However, the intensity of police intervention shifts from marginal to moderate.

Scenario: A community continues to experience moderate crime but strengthens social cohesion from moderate to high.

Under conditions of moderate cohesion and moderate crime, a community is subject to services with greater focus on community-based policies and moderate police intervention (some discretionary tolerance). As the community progresses to high social cohesion but continues to experience moderate crime, the police focus remains on community-based policies versus intelligence-based. The degree of police intervention, however, is adjusted from moderate intervention to marginal intervention and increased discretionary tolerance.

The IP-CP Model, in conjunction with the model for social cohesion and police intervention framework, incorporates tolerances for fluctuations in crime and social cohesion to minimize the rate of shift in preferred policy postures. In communities where crime and social cohesion are moderate but there is a subsequent change to higher levels of crime, greater emphasis should be placed on intelligence, whereas if crime falls, there should be increased emphasis on community programs. Where crime in communities with moderate social cohesion trends from low to moderate, the community-intelligence focus remains unchanged. What does change is the level of police focus on either quantitative or qualitative outcomes. The IP-CP framework provides justification for measured policing and appropriately targeting resources and policies, with emphasis on each community's specific circumstances. We now need to add the quality/quantity dimension.

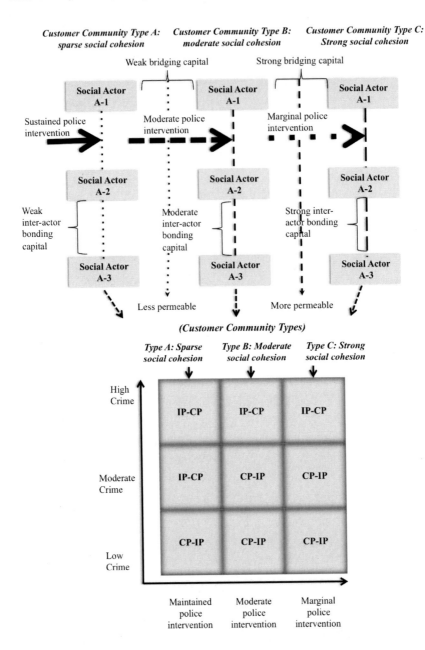

Figure 8. Combining the IP-CP Model (intelligence-led/community-based) with the model for social cohesion and police intervention.

Mending Broken Fences Policing

Our model is incomplete without adding a dimension for qualitative versus quantitative performance assessment—that is, determining whether qualitative or quantitative performance should have preferred focus given the previous assessment based on the IP-CP and social cohesion framework.

The *Quality/Quantity Model (QQC)* combines crime, performance measures, and time, for determining the suitability of the appropriate performance measure (quantitative versus qualitative) based on the prevalent conditions. The transparent box represents the range of normative trends that based on societal tolerances and social development, as well as resources and capacity defined over time.

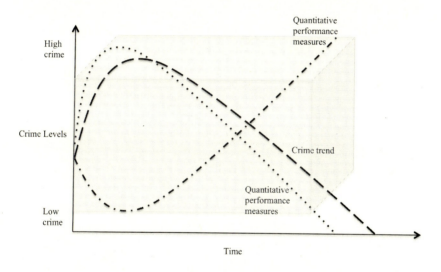

Figure 9. QQC Model (Quality/Quantity/Crime).

According to the QQC Model, periods where crime is on the decline provide opportunities for communities to reset or redefine collective norms. During these periods, enforcement should not be primarily about catching as many offenders as identifiable, but rather about taking the time to focus on identifying the antecedents of crime and disorder, education, and information, and for strengthening social cohesion, mitigating the factors that contribute to the violation of societal norms and developing strategies for removing incentives and causes for the continued violation of laws. Continued emphasis on the quantitative assessment of services (numbers of arrests, charges, tickets, lengths of sentences, and other similar quantitative measures) is more likely to be perceived as targeted or quota-based enforcement, which can diminish opportunities for strengthening relationships.

Recognizing the importance of officers' discretionary authority is critical during periods where crime is decreasing. Prudent discretionary decisions are dependent on the policies that determine performance measurement, performance evaluation, culture, and the nature and scope of oversight. Increasing levels of crime require policies to be adjusted accordingly. Times of high crime represent periods when norms and societal tolerance are exceeded, and emphasis shifts to quantitative performance measures with enforcement focused on managing crime to keep it from spiraling out of control. During periods where crime is increasing, the emphasis shifts to deterrence and enforcement-based policies. While qualitative measures cannot be excluded, their relative importance is outweighed by the need to quantitatively control escalating crime and disorder.

As crime begins to come under control, discretion can be extended to enhance community collaboration, legitimacy, and building trust, with increasing emphasis being shifted to resources that enhance the quality of interactions between police and community. Emphasis shifts to the quality of the services and outcomes. Police services can use these periods for reassessing their policies with increased emphasis on the quality of services (decreased dropout rates from school, decreased recidivism, improved collaboration and information sharing, reduced complaints against police, and so on) rather than the quantity of services. Discretion becomes increasingly important to the officers' daily assessment of when to enforce and when to advise and caution. Indiscriminate enforcement will do more harm in alienating police services and forgoing opportunities for strengthening the social contact between the police and the community.

As crime is reduced to acceptable levels, the emphasis of qualitative and quantitative measures becomes interchanged. Now the norm for police performance measurement can shift from qualitative to quantitative measurement, with greater reliance on community relationships and focus on the collaborative management of the underlying causes of crime. In the accompanying diagrammatic representation, the apex of the quantitative

Mending Broken Fences Policing

curve and trough of the qualitative curve are positioned so that qualitative measures only begin to outweigh quantitative measures after crime trends start to indicate a decline. Quantitative and crime curves are more synchronized than the qualitative curve, which lags behind slightly.

Now, if we revisit the scenarios noted above we can combine our analysis of Quality/Quantity/Crime (QQC) Model with the model for social cohesion and police intervention, and Intelligence-Led/Community Based Policing:

Scenario: A community with strong social cohesion is experiencing high crime, indicating a deterioration of cohesion levels from high toward moderate.

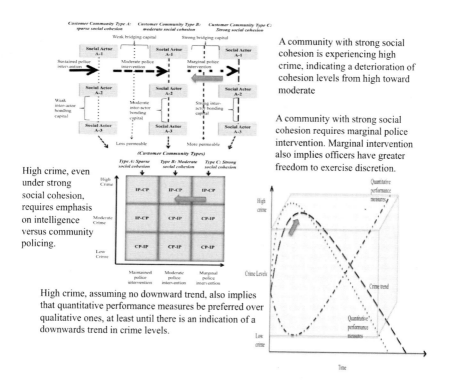

Figure 10. *Scenario: A community with strong social cohesion is experiencing high crime, indicating a deterioration of cohesion levels from high toward moderate*

High crime, even under strong social cohesion, calls for policing with greater emphasis on intelligence versus community policing.

A community with strong social cohesion requires marginal police intervention because its nonstate agencies are well established, and community actors are encouraged and supported in collaborating to identify, prioritize, and solve problems. Marginal intervention also implies officers have greater freedom to exercise discretion. As community cohesion deteriorates to moderate police intervention must increase to moderate levels. Moderate intervention implies a withdrawing of some discretionary tolerances previously extended under a state of high social cohesion. High crime, assuming no downward trend, also implies that quantitative performance measures be preferred over qualitative ones, at least until there is an indication of a downwards trend in crime levels.

Scenario: A community with high social cohesion is experiencing a reduction in crime from high to low.

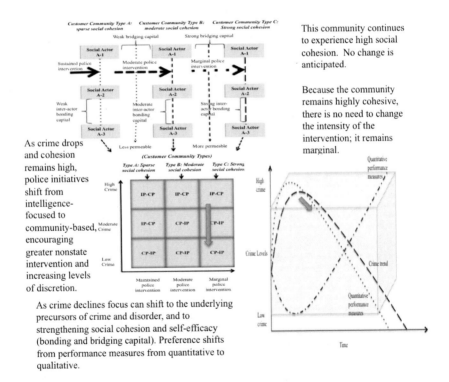

Figure 11. *Scenario: A community with high social cohesion is experiencing a reduction in crime from high to low.*

Mending Broken Fences Policing

Communities with high levels of crime regardless of their strong social cohesion require greater emphasis on intelligence versus community policing. As crime drops and cohesion remains high, police initiatives shift from intelligence-focused to community-based, which encourage greater nonstate intervention. However, because the community remains highly cohesive, there is no need to change the intensity of the intervention; it remains marginal. What does change is the preference of performance measures from quantitative to qualitative. As crime levels decline and there is greater control over crime, greater focus can be shifter to the underlying precursors of crime and disorder, and for creating conditions that strengthen social cohesion and self-efficacy for bonding and bridging capital.

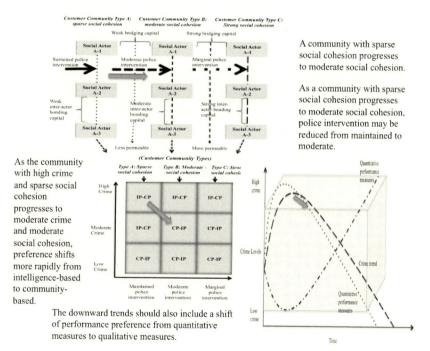

Figure 12. *Scenario: A community with high crime and sparse social cohesion transitions to a community with moderate crime and moderate social cohesion.*

As a community with high crime and sparse social cohesion progresses to moderate crime and moderate social cohesion, preference shifts more rapidly from intelligence-based to community-based. At the same time, police intervention may be reduced from maintained to moderate. The downward trends should also include a shift of performance preference from quantitative measures to qualitative measures. In the reverse, if a community with strong social cohesion and low crime suddenly experiences a rise in crime from low to moderate, and deterioration in social cohesion from strong to moderate, community-based policies remain preferred over intelligence-led. However, the intensity of police intervention shifts from marginal to moderate, and a refocusing of performance measures from qualitative to quantitative.

Scenario: A community continues to experience moderate crime but strengthens social cohesion from moderate to high.

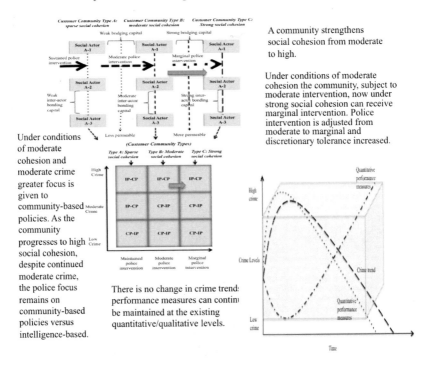

Figure 13. *Scenario: A community continues to experience moderate crime but strengthens social cohesion from moderate to high.*

Mending Broken Fences Policing

Under conditions of moderate cohesion and moderate crime, a community is subject to services with greater focus on community-based policies and moderate police intervention (some discretionary tolerance). As the community progresses to high social cohesion but continues to experience moderate crime, the police focus remains on community-based policies versus intelligence-based. The degree of police intervention, however, is adjusted from moderate intervention to marginal intervention and increased discretionary tolerance. There is no change in crime trends and performance measures can continue to be maintained at the existing quantitative/qualitative levels.

Jointly, the Model for Social Cohesion and Police Intervention and the Intelligence-Led/Community-Based Policing Model (IP-CP), combined with the Quality/Quantity/Crime (QQC) Model, provide a four-step process for developing an articulable police intervention policy.

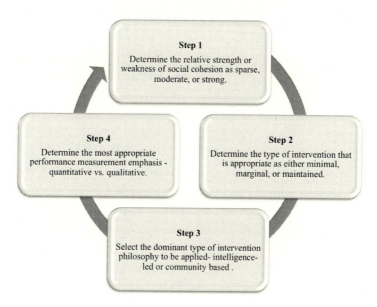

Figure 14. Four steps to applying the model for social cohesion and police intervention, Intelligence-Led/Community Based Policing Model (IP-CP), and Quality/Quantity/Crime (QQC) Model.

DISCRETION

A 1999 report for the National Institute of Justice tried to grapple with why, given the pervasiveness of discretion in daily police work, its importance had not been raised by legal scholars, criminal justice academics, and practitioners.[245] The answer was framed in the following terms:

> The answer is that phenomena which are self-evident to one generation are not necessarily evident to others. This high-lights the role of paradigms in scientific research. Paradigms describe observed phenomena, define problems, and guide research. Phenomena that fall outside the prevailing paradigm either are not noticed at all or are dismissed as unimportant and not worthy of investigation. So it was with discretion for early crime commissions.[246]

We have alluded to the notion of discretion throughout the previous sections and should take pause to better understand exactly what discretion means. We have stated that discretion is essential for unleashing creativity, which is valued when well-intentioned and directed toward the achievement of organizational goals and within the scope of the stated vision and mission. Without the application of discretion in the enforcement of laws, social cohesion could not be maintained, trust would be diminished, and legitimacy would suffer. We have also noted that discretion is determined by policies, performance measurement, performance evaluation, culture, and the nature and scope of oversight. Despite the centrality of discretion to policing, the concept of police discretion remains contentious and only relatively recently subject to the scrutiny it deserves. It has been noted, for instance, that "[t]he discovery of discretion as a topic of scholarly attention came relatively late. A mere thirty years ago, Superintendent G. Fryer, in charge of the New South Wales Police Department's prosecuting branch, opined in his forward to the published proceedings of a seminar on Police Discretion in the Criminal Process, held at the Institute of Criminology of Sydney, that the seminar "provided a forum for [police discretion] to be fully ventilated in New South Wales for the first time."[247]

At the same time, courts have upheld that discretion is an essential feature of police work, noting that eliminating discretion would render a system unworkably complex and rigid.

> Discretion is an essential feature of the criminal justice system. A system that attempted to eliminate discretion would be unworkably complex and rigid. Police necessarily exercise discretion in deciding when to lay charges, to arrest and to conduct incidental searches, as prosecutors do in deciding whether or not to withdraw a charge, enter a stay, consent to an adjournment, proceed by way of indictment or summary conviction, launch an appeal and so on. The criminal Code provides no guidelines for the exercise of discretion in any of these areas. The day to day operation of law enforcement and the criminal justice system nonetheless depends upon the exercise of that discretion.[248]

The success of policing, generally, requires accommodation and encouragement of well-intentioned risk-taking by frontline officers, which in turn requires recognition for flexible action and accommodation for the well-applied use of discretionary powers. This starts with boundaries, beliefs, and interactive controls, having regard for the framing of job descriptions and performance measurement that accounts for the activities that involve discretion, trust, legitimacy, collaboration, and quality-of-life parameters central to the well-being of cohesive communities.

All decision-making involves some level of subjectivity, and it is impossible to divorce decision-making processes from subjectivity "... as subjectivity (for example the development of personalized policing expertise) is at the heart of much good police work."[249] Discretion is a vital part of good police work, without which officers are left with zero-tolerance and no subjectivity. A state that does not allow discretion is one that lacks compassion or an ethic of care for its citizens. Like Javert, the policeman in Victor Hugo's *Les Miserables*, a police officer unable or unwilling to use discretion and judgment is one who may be proficient at applying the letter of the law but who has no understanding of the spirit of the law or the social consequences of such a policy.

Democratization of policing necessitates that decision-making be transferred downward to allow grassroots initiatives, choices, and decision-making whereby communities, stakeholders, and frontline officers can identify and prioritize problems and develop solutions and strategies for responding to local issues but also decide on the measures for success. The US Department of Justice, Office of Community Oriented Policing Services, notes the centrality of discretion in the following terms:

> In trying to achieve their objective, police have at their disposal a wide variety of tactics and strategies. Although many people think that the main way police achieve their public safety objectives is to enforce law. In most interactions with the public, police do not issue a citation or make an arrest. Indeed, even were it possible for police to fully enforce the law—which it is not—it is unlikely that most communities would tolerate such a thing. Sometimes it is counterproductive to public safety, as, for instance, when it provokes such widespread public hostility as to engender even more widespread disorder and lawlessness.[250]

The state of law enforcement depicted in *Les Miserables* is not what a civil society aspires to have or expects from its police. On the contrary, there is an expectation that police have discretion and use such discretion wisely. Civil societies recognize the importance of discretionary decisions to good police work, allowing for wide latitude in discretion in all areas, ranging from whether to investigate, to question, to search, to arrest, to caution, to charge, or to negotiate a plea. Courts have upheld that police officers exercise an essential discretion in relation to the discharge of their duties to enforce laws and investigate crime.

> Applying the letter of the law to the practical, real-life situations faced by police officers in performing their everyday duties requires that certain adjustments be made. Although these adjustments may sometimes appear to deviate from the letter of the law, they are crucial and are part of the very essence of the proper administration of the criminal justice system, or to use the words of s. 139(2), are perfectly consistent with the "course of justice." The ability—indeed the duty—to use one's judgment to adapt the process of law enforcement to individual circumstances and to the real-life demands of justice is in fact the basis of police discretion.[251]

At the same time, there remain underlying concerns about the abuse of discretionary powers that lead to further abuses, such as arbitrary detention, racial profiling, and corrupt practices. Absent appropriate safeguards against discriminatory actions (deliberate or unintentional), discretion can quickly cross the bounds of suspicion and reasonable grounds. How then should discretionary empowerment be balanced with how officers alone determine reasonable suspicion or the exercise of equitable, fair, and appropriate application of discretionary powers? The decision notes:

> The required justification is essentially two-fold. First, the exercise of the discretion must be justified subjectively, that is, the discretion must have been exercised honestly and transparently, and on the basis of valid and reasonable grounds (reasons of

> Chamberland J.A., at para. 41). Thus, a decision based on favouritism, or on cultural, social or racial stereotypes, cannot constitute a proper exercise of police discretion. However, the officer's sincere belief that he properly exercised his discretion is not sufficient to justify his decision.[252]

The decision further states:

> First, it is self-evident that the material circumstances are an important factor in the assessment of a police officer's decision: the discretion will certainly not be exercised in the same way in a case of shoplifting by a teenager as one involving a robbery. In the first case, the interests of justice may very well be served if the officer gives the young offender a stern warning and alerts his or her parents. However, this does not mean that the police have no discretion left when the degree of seriousness reaches a certain level. In the case of a robbery, or an even more serious offence, the discretion can be exercised to decide not to arrest a suspect or not to pursue an investigation. However, the justification offered must be proportionate to the seriousness of the conduct and it must be clear that the discretion was exercised in the public interest. Thus, while some exercises of discretion are almost routine and are clearly justified, others are truly exceptional and will require that the police officer explain his or her decision in greater detail.[253]

Discretion is a crucial part of police work and police authority, and yet, in my experience, very little time is spent in formally discussing or teaching the concept to police recruits or, for that matter, frontline officers and police leaders.

The traditional response to controlling discretion has involved two approaches. The first is increasing procedural controls, and the second is instituting mandatory administrative policies. The first includes, for example, the range of policies that make investigations of domestic violence and child abuse mandatory, changes that generally stem from developments in social attitudes and expectations that reset social norms. The second represents the more traditional responses to managing performance for ensuring that discretion is applied in appropriate measure and with appropriate intent and effectiveness.

The institution of policies and procedural controls cannot, however, alone suffice for ensuring the appropriate and justifiable exercise of discretion in an honest and transparent manner. George Kelling puts it this way:

> Pushing harder and more stridently with current control mechanisms that exert little real control over substantive work will not lead the way out of this quandary. Such specious thinking has been in place since the 1950s (e.g., just a little more inservice training, a slightly tighter span of control, a few more general orders or rules, more militant internal affairs units, improved rewards and punishment, improved or more representative recruitment, greater militarization of recruit training). Instead, police officials need to focus on the substantive control of police work morally, legally, skillfully, and effectively; then structure and administer departments on the basis of this literal work and not a fictionalized view of police work. In other words, a clear definition and description of quality policing is needed around which appropriate organizations and administrations can be developed.[254]

The quandary to which Kelling is referring is the challenge of enabling and empowering frontline officers with discretionary authority, while at the same time attempting to control the associated risks, but, most important, also to impact the subjective decision-making process or assessment on which individuals determine to exercise discretion.

Recall that there is a lack of clarity of purpose given that in a typical day, only 18 percent of the calls for service are about crime and only about 40 percent of an officer's time is spent dealing with crime.[255] Our quandary is complicated by the fact that discretion remains an intrinsic quality of policing that is extremely difficult to regulate, supervise, and control, because it pervades almost everything that a police officer does. As Darren Ellis notes, there exists a "Lack of consideration for informal working practices during street-level policing and lack of clarity regarding the criteria for reasonable suspicion."[256] Further, Ellis notes that "[I]t is the officer alone who determines, at street level, reasonable suspicion which is a concept that has eluded academics and lawyers in more reflective surroundings."[257]

Discretion is central to policing; it is applied by all officers who routinely find themselves confronting complex crime and social issues, alone, at street level and having to make difficult decisions to undertake immediate courses of action or inaction without opportunity for consultation or deliberation. Poor control mechanisms and management's limited ability to control officers' activities, the majority of which remain out of sight of supervision, make discretion impossible to manage.[258] Behavior cannot be managed through mechanistic responses (tighter oversight, regulation, and enforcement) alone. Discretion needs to be a core concept in the training of new officers and should be a part of the ongoing development of organizational and social values that include belief systems. Contrary to the expectations of police managers, simply instituting more boundaries or interactive controls can worsen the problem by diminishing substantive control or access to the decision-making factors that motivate officers' discretionary activities.

There are many instances, as in the case of crackdowns, in which officers are motivated to suspend discretion when they may otherwise have exercised an alternative resolution in lieu of prescribed enforcement. Officers responding to a crackdown might, for instance, issue tickets even when there are available alternatives for issuing caution. Officers may decide to remand offenders in custody instead of offering a conditional release, or the officer may choose to enforce all identifiable offenses instead of discretionarily pursuing only some of the violations and choosing to overlook others. One might even consider such policies as amounting to an abdication of responsibility, discretion, and fairness. Discretionary decisions can be overt and operational, as noted above, or subtle and invisible, for instance, an investigator's commitment to the investigation, the quality of the interview, the extent of support extended to victims and witnesses, the commitment to documenting evidence, collaboration with the prosecutor, and even giving full, frank, and fair evidence at a trial. Each of these is difficult to discern but weighs heavily on the impact on the effectiveness, efficiency, and impartiality with which each officer responds to his or her vocation.

Kelling notes at least two limits to negative policies—the things officers may not do:

> First, they leave untouched a large area of necessary discretion and second, they are perceived as irrelevant and unhelpful restrictions—as rules that "tell us what we shouldn't do" and thus: give the brass plenty of rope with which to hang us," but that "don't tell us what we should do."[259]

Police leaders must make explicit what has been implicit in police performance expectations about discretion. By police management not directing the necessary focus and attention that discretion demands, managers leave large areas of performance unrecognized and unregulated. Further, frontline workers may perceive this as evidence that they are managed by rules and directives and that belief systems are simply a fanciful extolment of core values without the substantive support of the risks that frontline officers take to achieve organizational goals. This is exemplified by a study at the University of East London on the impact of legislated controls of stop-and-search practices. The introduction of a more limited standard of "reasonable suspicion" to replace discretionary decisions resulted in an unexpected finding. The study reported:

> What appears to have occurred through the introduction of the concept of "reasonable suspicion" into the stop and search context is a shift of focus from rooting out racism

> to rooting out subjectivity. This is both impossible, as decision-making processes cannot be divorced from subjectivity, and simply futile, as subjectivity (for example the development of personalized policing expertise) is at the heart of much good policing work.[260]

In effect, officers continued to apply discretion in the form of reasonable suspicion but became better adept at justifying their decisions through a process of "creative accounting"—the postdecision design of a justification of the reasoning behind the decision that would justify a disinterested third party.[261]

Kelling correctly notes that mechanistic responses by police managers, driven by what I call a "liability phobia," contributes to a cover-your-ass culture, which places officers in a defensive posture, oversimplifies management of complex issues, and creates suspicion and separation between management and the front line. Messages about what is right and wrong become further complicated by the oversimplification of policing as law enforcement, which overlooks the complexities of modern-day policing. Kelling cautions that there is an emergent need for the thoughtful "consideration of new policies and models for dealing with 'active political and community control of police discretion and development of new police guidelines."[262] Discretion is also impacted by strategic policy direction that communicates the latitude and scope of the acceptable application of discretion, for example, those inferred by the rhetoric on the "war on crime" as reflected in the abandonment of discretion and enforcement of zero-tolerance. Additionally, discretion is also influenced by corporate performance policies, the measurements applied, the cultural expectations, and professional oversight. A study by the Police Foundation in the United States looked at the impact of CompStat in three American cities—Lowell, Minneapolis, and Newark—specifically, noting the differences between community policing and CompStat in the following terms:

> ... issues have converged in the interaction between community policing and CompStat, as they set forth competing ideals of law enforcement. CompStat, as we

have seen, gives command staff most of the responsibility for reducing crime, largely excludes patrol officers from the decision-making process, and has a relentless focus on crime reduction. Community policing, on the other hand, devolves decision making to the level of the street, envisions police and citizens as partners in problem solving, and makes officers responsible for responding to a broad spectrum of community concerns. At stake here are two vastly different conceptions of the officer's role in modern society. In one, they simply follow their superiors' orders, while the other grants them considerable discretion as the guardians of their individual beat. Given the gap between the two models of policing, CompStat naturally tends to encounter the greatest resistance in departments that are most committed to community policing.[263]

Discretion is an essential part of modern policing and a critical element in the determination of the success of collaboration and democratization. The quality of discretion is dependent on a variety of factors, the full examination of which is beyond the scope of this narrative but requires some comment on the essential elements applicable to the IP-CP and QQC Model. As noted in the preceding scenarios, there are instances wherein the IP-CP matrix prescribes identical policing strategies, with the difference residing solely in the type of intervention prescribed on the level of social cohesion among the actors constituting the customer communities—the level of intervention being prescribed as sustained, moderate, or marginal and the accompanying level of discretion aligned with the application of the IP-CP and QQC Model.

Good policies for defining boundaries for the application of discretionary decision-making require much more than one-dimensional performance-measurement processes. Discretion cannot, for instance, be measured by quantitative performance measures alone, and while discretionary outcomes may be identified and counted, quantitative measures alone fail to account for the sponsoring processes that lead to the discretionary outcome.

While increased intervention and diminished discretion may be appropriate during times of high crime and disorder, perhaps even zero-tolerance, the same approach may not be effective or appropriate during times of low crime. Community-based initiatives require higher standards of discretionary decision-making as compared with intelligence-based initiatives. Communities subject to community-based policies are more likely to be collaborative and therefore ready for enhanced discretionary interaction and stakeholder engagement. Customer communities with low social cohesion are more likely to perceive unsolicited police contact as targeted enforcement. Such perceptions are exasperated where officers are unintentionally incentivized by misaligned performance systems that emphasize unnecessary contact or contact that is inappropriate to the circumstances. The policing strategy and performance measurement must, therefore, be aligned to achieve a coordinated result. The Police Research Forum describes this challenge in the following terms:

> The problem-solving component of community policing shifts the unit of work from individual incidents to clustered problems, and those are harder to count. It is also hard to evaluate whether problem solving is effective and whether individual officers are doing a good or a bad job at it. The public often wants action on things that department information systems do not count at all. As a result, both individual and unit performance is hard to measure or reward. However, the thrust of CompStat and other new "accountability processes" in police departments is that measured activities get attention and unmeasured accomplishments do not, even if the measured activities do not matter very much.

As implied by the Police Research Forum, services must be adaptive to the outcomes that are required and create the incentives that reward activities and behavior that reflect appropriate responses for the situation. Discretion must be an integral component of the overall performance management system for a balanced scorecard that aligns with an organization's vision, strategic direction, and internal and external communication. Performance measurement and oversight must be balanced with discretion in enforcement, engagement, and conflict resolution. Discretion is an important element of the IP-CP/QQC Model. So far, the IP-CP/QQC Model provides a framework for an assessment of the social cohesion between and among the social actors that constitute a customer community, a gauge for the intensity of the police intervention, and an assessment of the balance between community-oriented and intelligence-led policing strategies. Now we develop our model further by adding discretion as an element in our framework. We can now enhance the IP-CP/QQC Model as a framework for determining the balance between qualitative and quantitative performance measurement by the application of discretion in the provision of policing services. In order to do this, we first need to understand how discretion fits into our model for understanding conflict and responding with the application of suitable levels of discretion.

The following model aids in the understanding of the explicit nature of objective expectations and the subjective application of those expectations in setting acceptable and unacceptable norms. The following illustration is an adaptation of how changing norms can affect boundaries and how boundaries determine acceptable discretionary norms.

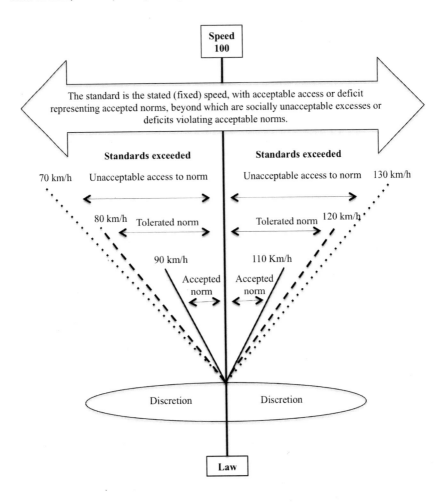

Figure 15. Boundaries and discretion.

In this model, we use speed limits as an example for how boundaries are established and tested, norms set, and expectations reset. Take a roadway on which the speed limit is set at 100 kilometers per hour (km/hr). This limit is established in law; however, in practice, drivers will travel at a range of speeds both above and below the posted 100 km/hr. How authorities tolerate these variances and enforce violations to the 100 km/hr represent exercise of discretionary tolerance. Tolerance will also become dependent on normative trends. For instance, if the majority of drivers travel at 110 km/hr, 110 km/hr becomes the norm. In fact, those travelling at the set speed limit of 110 km/hr might become outliers, making 100 km/hr the accepted norm. As the norm is tested, pushing the speeds in excess of 100 km/hr, the authorities might tolerate violations to reasonable excess. However, as individual drivers exceed tolerated norms, authorities may enforce ticketing against individuals, and if the accepted norm begins to trend to a higher speed level, then authorities might attempt to reset the norm by withdrawing discretion through, for instance, engaging in a publicized antispeeding campaign or undertaking a zero-tolerance approach to ticketing speeders.

Tolerances range from acceptance of discretionary norms in variances from a stated boundary to acceptance of some excesses to stated boundaries or norms to unacceptable variances where discretion becomes counterproductive. Note that, as far as speed limits are concerned, standards can be exceeded on either side of the stated boundary (100 km/hr) either by exceeding limits or driving so slow as to interfere with the normal flow of traffic.

Exceeding boundaries and norms can damage the legitimacy of the system and must be reset before the integrity of the system is permanently damaged. If norms are distorted for long enough, the distorted limits may establish new norms. Applying this to the broken windows theory, if communities that were once thriving are allowed to deteriorate without revitalization, over time, the new dereliction itself may become the accepted norm.

Discretion is the exercise of tolerance and is itself subject to a process of checks and balances. As an example of how discretion plays out in practical terms, compare for instance driving in Chicago with driving in Bangkok. Both jurisdictions have legislated and posted traffic rules with specified speed limits. One way of examining what differentiates the traffic in the two cities is by comparing the societal tolerances for divergences from the defined norms. Traffic volumes, road conditions, cultural influences, and vehicular diversity might be factors that cause norms to be distorted more in Bangkok than in Chicago. Despite differences (adherence to speed limits, right of way, driving within marked lanes, and so on), there are socially defined limits to the tolerance, which, when violated, result in the general societal call for action by the authorities. The range-of-norm distortion may therefore be greater in Bangkok than in Chicago, thereby influencing the application of discretionary enforcement, but the principles remain the same.

In considering discretion within the context of social cohesion, customer communities with strong social cohesion will exhibit stronger social contracts among their actors. These communities exhibit a stronger sense of belonging and a greater sensitivity to potential for social shamming, thereby creating greater influences for conformity. Such communities are more likely to be self-regulating and advocate for resources and state support. These communities, therefore, become better candidates for increased discretionary tolerance and less police intervention. In contrast, customer communities with weak social cohesion consist of social actors who have weaker social ties and less inter- and intragroup self-regulation. Norms may be divergent and less defined. Individual actors have not as yet identified sufficiently defined community norms, and violation of existing norms does not carry the same significance as compared to the violation of norms in a community with strong collective norms. Consequently, individual actors and groups become less obliged to intervene in the affairs of others. Under such conditions, even though external influence may be resented, external authoritative intervention forms an important source for defining and maintaining collective standards for social cohesion.

Discretion is dependent on at least four factors—rules and regulations, oversight, performance evaluation, and culture—which are bounded by the three distinct but interdependent systems: belief systems, boundary systems, and interactive control systems. Each of these systems and factors contributes to the application of discretion, but discretion itself also contributes to each of the four factors and systems—oversight, rules and regulations, culture, and performance evaluation. The system is interactive and iterative over time, place, and circumstance.

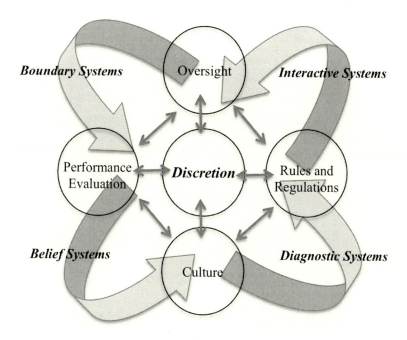

Figure 16. Factors contributing to the application of discretion.

One more point needs to be made here. It is not sufficient to empower citizens; several other components must also be included for strengthening the value of police-community partnerships.[264] Community collaboration is dependent on extending trust and discretion for the development of "meaningful partnerships." Police leaders have to embrace, in principle as well as spirit, the notion that policing must be part of an ongoing process for developing communities with shared values, shared challenges, and equal opportunities, based on trust, hope, and reciprocity among all citizens. Partnerships must be substantive and meaningful. Sherri Arnstein characterized partnerships in terms of a "ladder of participation."[265] The ladder consists of three rungs or three categories: *nonparticipation, tokenism,* and *citizen power.* At the lowest level, nonparticipation relationships are *manipulative,* wherein those in power select participants and control the process and resources. At the next level, partnerships become tokenistic. Services are provided in a one-way direction without asking others what they need. Tokenistic partnerships can be *informing* partnerships wherein the other is given real information, although only in a one-way transfer of authority, information, and control. Tokenistic partnerships can also be *consulting* partnerships where people—through surveys and neighborhood and public meetings—determine common practices but where the power continues to reside with the consulter. *Citizen power* represents the highest level of partnering in which relationships involve genuine negotiations about power. Parties develop appropriate balances that empower and delegate control to all partners on their *joint endeavor.*

It is through "meaningful partnerships" that customer communities and stakeholders ascribe police legitimacy. Police leaders should be careful not to take on processes that unnecessarily exceed their vocational bounds by needlessly expanding their role into the realms of other disciplines—public health, corrections, psychology, sociology, business, and politics, to name a few. Role expansion in itself may result in intervocational tensions that diminish opportunities for stakeholder engagement and collaboration. Take, for instance, harm reduction and decriminalization. Despite evidence that safe injection sites serve to control the spread of infectious disease and increase awareness of health risks, police leaders have resisted and thereby shaped public discourse on health care. Such unconstrained overextensions into the areas of expertise of other stakeholders have constrained and limited what may otherwise have provided positive and productive alternatives to the *war on drugs*.

Arnstein's taxonomy provides a good framework for understanding the type of partnerships being sought, understanding limitations and intent, and being honest with the participants about what is actually being offered in return for their participation. Still there are other limitations that must also be considered. How will community partners be selected and incorporated? Will partners be invited to participate and share power, and to what degree will partners be provided the sustainability required to access human, social, or spiritual capital? Community partnerships are seldom accorded the degree of participation wherein police delegate substantive authority or empower citizens.[266] Police leaders can improve partnerships by being sensitive to the fact that police are answerable to the public even if not accountable to the public. Take, for instance, advisory groups; even with the most well-intentioned partnership, the impact of the direction and assistance of an advisory group remain hidden from public scrutiny. It is never clear or transparent just how much of the direction and counsel of an advisory group actually impacts substantive decisions or if they are merely constituted to be a support group, having been selected for their congruence with existing policies and views. The makeup of advisory groups can in itself present challenges in determining just how representative the advisors are of the community they supposedly represent.

As the dean of studies at the Navitas College of Public Safety in Australia puts it:

> One hundred and eighty years ago Sir Robert Peel sketched out a normative framework for policing. He understood that police would learn the majority of their skills on the streets. By issuing the nine principles to his constables, Peel also understood that no training could ever equip an officer with all the skills to meet every situation they might encounter. They would, Peel knew intuitively, have to exercise judgement and discretion as a matter of routine. Somewhere along the way policing forgot that central tenet.[267]

So what should all this mean? The forgoing is intended to, in the least, highlight the importance of discretion as a concept and application for policing, as well as the importance of understanding partnerships and their nature and understanding that rules and norms are equally important in the day-to-day role of frontline officers. Therefore, much more time should be dedicated to the training and education of police officers in the application of discretion; organizations should better define their normative boundaries so as to make discretionary decision-making a meaningful, assessable, and core concept for the effective practice of day-to-day policing; and police leaders should use rules and regulations, oversight, performance evaluations, culture, belief systems, boundary systems, and interactive control systems together when defining boundaries, norms, and expectations for the performance of their members and organizations.

SELECTING PERFORMANCE INDICATORS

Every one of us, even during our most routine tasks, conducts our activities to meet some performance goal or indicator. This can be as simple as managing our personal budgets to meet short- and long-term goals or as complex as determining the performance of bonds, futures, and stocks. Performance indicators can be implicit or explicit, approached deliberately or through routine, and under supervised direction or based on personal commitment. In all cases, performance can only be evaluated if one establishes standards and indicators against which to compare change. As identified in the previous chapters, police use a complex set of performance indicators. Many of the functions of policing, such as crime prevention, order maintenance, and crime rates, are difficult to assess. In the case of crime data, it is unreliable because not all crimes are reported to the police, clearance rates are limited because they depend on public cooperation and on the type of crime, and prevention is difficult to quantify because one cannot measure what did not occur. Also measures of what police do in response to crime and calls for service are very different from those that involve crime prevention. The difficulty is complicated even further since, as we have learned, there may not even be the expected correlation between the numbers of police officers and crime rates and that the tactics used by police may not be effective in reducing crimes.[268]

Despite the importance of the topic, the identification of performance indicators remains a contentious issue. Here we examines how police can enhance performance measurement within the context of what police actually do or should be doing—facilitating social cohesion, crime prevention, order maintenance, intelligence gathering, and law enforcement. Researchers continue to draw attention to the fact that most police practices are not systematically evaluated and too little is known about what works and under what conditions. Peter Fahy, chief constable for the Greater Manchester Police, for instance, questioned the ability of police leaders to account for what their officers actually spend time doing, the numbers of situations where officers actually deal with a crime, and the percentage of crimes that are investigated.[269] Peter Fahy points to the fact that today's management requires a very different way of looking at policing than the culture to which most leaders have become accustomed. The issue is aggravated by three other factors: the establishment of a performance systems industry that is analytics driven, an extremely aggressive and competitively promotion-oriented police culture within which there are increasingly limited opportunities, and governance systems that limit discretion and judgment. In addition to the competition within police departments and among their various subunits, there is at present too much competition for scarce tax-based resources.

These challenges should be seen as providing opportunities for police leaders to reevaluate how they define and measure what they do and how well they do what they are doing. For instance, it is clear that responding to crime and social disorder in discrete units separated by departmental compartments is not an effective means of redressing the underlying issues or assessing the usefulness of programs or their effectiveness. If we agree that policing entails more than merely enforcing laws and apprehending criminals, then collaborative partnerships provide important opportunities for looking past the internal indicators on which police generally rely for determining measures of performance effectiveness. A collaborative model enables police to identify and include factors outside of their direct control, such as housing and public health, and to identify indicators that can be incorporated in predicting crime trends but equally to predict how performance by other stakeholders will impact police resources. Together, collaborative partnerships with joint performance measurements systems may provide a better, more holistic, and deeper understanding for developing and evaluating strategies aimed at resolving the issues that plague well-established hot spots, be they crime, disorder, homelessness, substance abuse, environmental degradation, early school dropout, or any other social issue. Such partnerships can greatly enhance the identification of unseen and underreported crimes and public safety/well-being issues. For instance, public health can identify resources and alternatives to the criminal justice system by leveraging mental health professionals in the case of emotionally disturbed persons. Hospital emergency centers can help in the identification of victimization associated to domestic and other violent crimes that would otherwise go unreported. The trends in the use of drug treatment programs may provide an indication of the success of the antinarcotics unit, and engagement with school-police-liaison programs might provide insight into the levels of cohesion among youth from various immigrant communities, potential for conflict, and specific social needs. What is essential are better ways to enhance performance measurements based on collaboration between stakeholder agencies. The success of the drug treatment clinics may be dependent on enforcement by the antinarcotics units, but unless the two collaborate, there can be no coordination of information or predictive analysis. Better partnerships would also provide for better understanding of the benefits that each stakeholder provides, more empathy for the work and intervention by the other, and for less interagency competition and antagonism, a reality that has already resulted in far too many inquiries and inquests. The collaborative model should in fact be enhanced to include public-private partnerships. As an example, airlines may be held better involved and accountable for the interdiction of drug couriers and shipments of narcotics concealed in luggage. Better sharing of information related to the trafficking of narcotics from source regions, partnerships for the enhancement of private security, and enhanced public-private interaction may provide better alternatives to a state-based interdiction model. Measuring performance of then overall impact of social spending measured in silos of social services cannot lead to effectively dealing with crime and disorder, let alone the larger antecedents of poverty, homelessness, poor health, and poor education.

More specific to policing, even the day-to-day measurement of patrol duties and frontline performance faces significant challenges. As established earlier, most patrol officers only spend a very small proportion of their time actually engaged in activities related to crime fighting or law enforcement.[270] Given such findings and given declining crime rates, it becomes difficult for police managers to defend staffing levels, particularly during times when crime trends have been on the decline. This problem has, however, in great part, been brought on by the historical inability—and in some instances failure—of police leaders to define what their officers do. It is not sufficient to try to justify police patrol staffing based on simplistic models that, for instance, compare staffing levels and workload analysis based on a relationship between the numbers of police officers available to the numbers of calls for service. There are a number of deficiencies in this type of analysis. First, not all calls for service are the same. Some, like suspicious persons, might only entail a drive-by from a patrol car, while a call for a shooting or sexual assault may require a lengthy investigation involving a crime scene, numerous witnesses, victims' statements, and other investigative and public safety activities. Relying on a variable like calls for service requires a deeper analysis of the calls themselves. What was the nature of the call? How are similar calls for service grouped with other similar calls for service? What are the common issues and benchmarks for responding to such calls? Can the response be improved through an integrative approach to service provision? And what constitutes the variances in responses between calls within the group of calls for service? These are just a small sampling of the types of questions one might ask toward conducting a deeper analysis of the calls themselves.

Second, using calls for service requires a comparative analysis to establish trends or a baseline on which the initial staffing levels might be agreed upon. Unfortunately, many agencies have simply grown in manpower over time, without a clear articulation of how that growth occurred, how increases in manpower and resources were justified, or if those levels are justifiable under present conditions. Generally speaking, most civil services are protected by contractual obligations and cannot simply hire and fire personnel to meet short-term requirements. This, however, is no reason for neglecting the requisite analysis or an ongoing commitment to determining a transparent and justifiable staffing model. Too often, police executives find themselves defending budgets to protect contractual agreements with police unions, morale of general membership, and public support. Private sector companies often undergo large-scale downsizing during times of fiscal constraint and economic downturn. This is not the case with public service agencies. The public sector security provides for stability in managing human resources and capital budgets but can also make police leaders complacent to the accountability their private sector counterparts endure routinely. Responsible and accountable police leadership requires that transparent processes be established for justifying taxpayer-supported funding for public services. This includes establishing baselines, guidelines, and measures that are predetermined, adjustable, and communicated in a meaningful way. Police leaders must become more adept at defining the social services that their organizations provide, including a broad range of services that may be preventative and outside quantitative measures, and communicate such services in a transparent, legitimate, and ethical manner.

And third, variables like calls for service are in themselves a reflection of the public's confidence in the police and may change over time. Certain offenses, such as domestic violence, elder abuse, and sexual assaults, continue to be underreported. Others, particularly crimes in marginalized neighborhoods, may be underreported because of fears of reprisals or a lack of confidence in police. Calls for service are good indicators of the neither the level of crime in the community nor of the staffing requirements. Furthermore, calls for service only focus on the times that an officer is engaged in an assigned activity. There are many other activities that a patrol officer might engage in that are preventative and self-generated, which are neither related to crime prevention or law enforcement but nonetheless an important part of what police officers are expected to do by and for their communities. Similarly, the use of reported crime too is a weak performance measure. Citizens make the decision of whether to report or not to report a crime. These decisions are based on a number of factors, including for instance:

- the public's trust in their police service
- the cost-benefit analysis of whether engaging the criminal justice system is more beneficial than forgoing a police report—These might include personal stigmatization, potential for reprisal

from the accused, or simply not feeling the matter worth the bother of going to court.
- cultural and community norms.

Alternative indicators of police performance should therefore include the measure of public trust in the police, the inclination to engage the services of the police, the utilization of alternative services to calling police, or the measures of nonenforcement contacts. For instance, even though calls service and reported crimes may provide an indication of the trends of engagement, a true performance indicator should include other avenues of crime occurrence identification. Hospitals, for instance, treat victims of domestic violence, assaults, robberies, or elder abuse, as examples, that are not necessarily reported to the police. Similarly, homeless shelters, food banks, or private nursing homes may observe indicators of crimes that remain unreported because they are not responsible, sufficiently informed to engage with police, or feel that it is a private matter. Because these crimes are not recorded in a police report does not mean they did not occur. Many break-enters and damage to property also remain unreported because victims determine that the damage or loss does not exceed the limits of their insurance policy deductible or the matter does not deserve the time and effort it would take to report the incident to police. Capturing such unreported criminal occurrences may provide a better measure of the state of overall crime as well as the effectiveness of the police in developing and maintaining legitimacy and trust within the communities they serve. Needless to say, once again, such types of measures require collaboration with stakeholders and partner agencies and cannot be achieved in isolation.

As another example, police investigative units are generally assessed by the numbers of cases processed, charges laid, clearance rates, and cases proceeded to court, but not subject to an assessment on the basis of their impact on the communities. The indicators, therefore, only measure internal workload at best but not the impact of the crime on the community. According to some studies, investigators in the United States submit less than a quarter (22 percent) of cases investigated to the courts. A better measure might include the willingness of witnesses to participate and support investigations, the rate of successful convictions, the satisfaction of victims and witnesses with the criminal justice system, and the commitment of police and victims to engage in support services. The fact that only 22 percent of the cases are submitted may be due to a complex set of factors but is statistically significant given that studies have demonstrated a relationship between the numbers of crimes in an area and the total offenses cleared and public perceptions of whether police were doing a "good" or "excellent job."[271]

How police services define clearance rates is itself problematic. There are no universally applied definitions of clearance. In some jurisdictions, clearance is based on charges being filed or, where there is insufficient evidence, the accused being identified. In others, clearance is based on the accused being identified, while in others, it is restricted to charges being filed or cases being submitted to court. Such ambiguity makes it difficult to compare clearance rates between jurisdictions. While this might seem a minor point, clearance depends on public cooperation and on the ability of police to meet the legal requirements of building sufficient grounds and evidence to submit their case for prosecution. While it may be difficult to specify the appropriate amount of time an investigator spends on building a case, there should be better means to monitor the trends in time spent on the investigation of various crimes that are successfully submitted to court. This might include tracking the impact of various forms of administrative and investigative work that goes into preparing a case: initial response time, initial investigation, time spent on witness interviews, time spent on forensic analysis, time spent on warrants, meetings with crown counsel, trial, and so forth. While none of these measures is ideal or simple, such indicators are increasingly important in identifying the type and scope of resources that are required and for estimating how much and where expenditures are allocated and the efficiency with which they are spent. Such activity measurements can provide reliable methodologies for determining the allocation of inputs, like time and resources, to various activities to determine the links between the two and for determining the impact of inputs and outputs on achieving the intended goals.

Many police services have also persisted in developing hotspot analyses to assist with the deployment of resources. And while hotspot analysis is certainly valuable in determining the location and intensity of crimes and other occurrences when their distribution is unknown or unclear, most police officers have well-established personal knowledge of their hotspots. Once such hotspots have been mapped, there is rarely any variation from year to year on their location or the intensity of their occurrence. Yet police forces continue to apply significant importance on identifying these hotspots, seemingly failing to ask why these hotspots have continued to persist after decades of mapping. The Centre for Program Evaluation and Performance Measurement in a report on what has been learned from evaluations of place-based policing strategies notes that although problem-oriented policing in response to targeted hotspots does generally appear to have an impact on crime, it is certainly not uniformly so.[272] Further, it remains unclear which strategies are effective and to what degree and how much of the success is due to the temporary displacement of crime. The study also points to a lack of understanding of how problem-oriented policing impacts police community relations within the targeted hotspots.[273] It is important that police executives use hotspot analysis carefully within short, specified periods and in conjunction with enforcement strategies targeted at dealing with the issues within the hotspot and then conduct careful analysis of strategic inputs' impact. It is only through such controlled and iterative application that appropriate strategies can be identified and justified. There is ample evidence to demonstrate, both anecdotally and empirically, that crime is distributed unevenly across cities and neighborhoods and that the best use of police resources is achieved by targeting the limited resources to areas where the problems are reported. And while as many as seven in ten police services may be using crime mapping to target problems, there is a lack of analysis and coordination of interagency response to the underlying characteristics of the hotspot that lead to the elevated levels of crime in the first place.

Crime and disorder hotspots require a coordinated effort by more than just the police. Thoughtful and committed application of police and other social services is critical. It is not enough to simply throw resources at such persistent problem areas. It is critical to determine just how those resources are being applied and how to improve the application of resources toward effective policing that results in demonstrable changes to existing hotspots. There needs to be a coordinated effort between police and other stakeholders to determine which social service—policing, health care, social, education, and environmental design for instance—has the most significant and lasting impact on providing a sustainable remedy to the underlying issues that contribute to crime and disorder within a selected hotspot.

The Australian Institute of Criminology, for instance, suggests that the conventional measures of drug enforcement focus too narrowly on seizures, arrests, charges, and search warrants executed. These measures do not reflect the effectiveness of enforcement in reducing drug addiction, trafficking, and clandestine manufacturing. They simply provide an indication of the extent to which police resources are applied and the resulting contacts from the application of those resources. Illicit drug activities are detected because of police contact, not self-reported calls for service. Therefore, when enforcement increases, so do arrests, seizures, and searches. The results are more an indication of the application of drug interdiction efforts than of the impact on the underlying drug problem itself. On the other hand, if there is an associated reduction in addicts seeking treatment in rehabilitative institutions, fewer drug-related deaths, enhanced perceptions of public safety, and lower rates of recidivism, then these indicators reflect the impact and effectiveness of the enforcement on the drug problem generally. According to this perspective, measures for the effectiveness of drug enforcement should include indicators that encompass other stakeholders who share responsibility for the management of substance abuse, like hospitals, social services, addiction recovery centers, and those working at safe injection sites. Each of these only see a portion of the elephant, blinded by their own frames of reference.

It is important for leaders to use a multidisciplinary approach to determining the indicators of crime management and community safety and well-being. In Canada, the city of Toronto has developed a set of indices that measure well-being based on health, housing, economics, environment, safety, culture, recreation, civics, transportation, and education.[274] This program brings together a range of municipal departments and experts, including public works, licensing, shelter and housing, employment and social services, transportation, parks and forestry, emergency management services and police, public health, city managers, and economic development, just to name a few.[275] Stakeholders include hospitals, universities, religious organizations, and nonprofit organizations. This initiative serves as an excellent example of creating a culture of shared ownership for the well-being of the citizens of Toronto and consolidating the measurements of success by recognizing that no single agency can by itself effect public safety and well-being.

Figure 17. Collaborative engagement for social well-being and social cohesion.

In order to get a comprehensive indication of the challenge and the impact of their response, each stakeholder must share in performance indicators that measure combined input, output, and impact. This type of multidisciplinary approach to performance measurement requires the inclusion of indicators based on information from a wider spectrum of stakeholders, including public health and social services, for the design of a more valid performance measure of the effectiveness of the application of police resources. This principle is not limited to enforcement and is equally applicable to a variety services (community mobilization, domestic violence, holdups, and youth crime, as examples).

Managers must be able to balance accounting and economic considerations when designing performance indicators. Every decision has an accounting, economic, and human cost. While accounting costs are based on an assessment of the difference between the benefit (profit) and cost of the decision or investment, economic assessments are based on benefit minus opportunity costs. Human costs are more general, reflecting impact on the human condition. Good analysis takes into account all three areas. Opportunity costs are the differences between a selected option and the potential benefits that another competing decision might have netted. An economic model forces managers to be accountable for the measurements of the outcomes of their selected strategies and for justifying exclusion of alternatives. While accounting decisions might favor best-practice models for decision-making, economic models force a broader accountability that involves a careful consideration of all options.

Take, for instance, a decision to invest in additional officers. The financial (accounting) perspective is based on the costs associated with the hiring, training, equipping, and salaries of officers, compared to their impact on the crime levels and their performance output. What exactly determines cost-effectiveness for jurisdiction to jurisdiction or even from a policy perspective? Generally, if their impact on crime can be cost calculated and their performance output determined to outweigh the initial and sustaining costs, then the decision is profitable. On the other hand, an economic perspective asks the question: what impact would the same inputs (personnel, salaries, equipment, and so on), applied to an alternate strategy involving alternative policies, such as partnering with public health on drug diversion programs for instance, have on crime. If the benefits of a drug diversion program provide the desired outcomes of reducing crime and improving community well-being and are calculated to be more effective and beneficial than the former, then these benefits should be factored into the analysis and the benefits of the enhanced deployment of officers in the former consideration adjusted down accordingly.

The economics of opportunity costs work to encourage decision makers to consider the impact of options and to ensure decisions include collaboration, consideration of a broader set of options, and a transparent, and accountable, consideration of alternatives. Taking into consideration opportunity costs enhances the likelihood of achieving the potential of what the broken windows theory philosophically and practically intended—the opportunity for bringing together a range of interested parties and stakeholders toward collaboratively addressing underlying problems and holding stakeholders accountable through a joint social contract.

To focus the point a little further, take for instance policies on drug enforcement. Enforcement has targeted both supply and demand for drugs. It is generally agreed that both the supply and demand should be targeted, giving rise to both the war on drugs as well as an increasingly wider array of diversion and therapeutic interventions for addicts. The results for policing are generally measured on the basis of the numbers of accused arrested, charges filed, quantity of narcotics seized, and seizures of proceeds of crime. An economist perspective would provide a broader analysis. Addicts are addicts and will seek supplies, by hook or crook, with little sensitivity to the cost of their daily hit. That is, drug demand, particularly by addicts and habitual users, is relatively inelastic. Despite the cost or threat of arrest, addicts are compelled to seek a supply to fulfill their addictive dependence. This means that the demand curve is steep and that the quantity demanded by addicts will vary little with fluctuations in price, compared, for instance, to other commodities like carbonated drinks, which are very elastic, meaning that if the price of pop were to rise, consumers would simply shift to using an alternative, like juice, water, coffee, or tea. With an elastic demand, a small change in price leads to a notable change in the quantity of carbonated drinks demanded and consumed. With addicts, interdicting the amount of narcotics reaching the streets may decrease the supply and number of transactions, however the resulting shortage, as with any other commodity, drives up the equilibrium price – the reduction in quantity results in an increase in price. Due to the inelastic nature of drug demand the increase in price will more than make up for the cut in supply.

The war on drugs, has predominantly, targeted the supply side of narcotics. There has been a far greater emphasis on the interdiction of supply, importation, and distribution of narcotics as compared on the addiction itself. As enforcement interdicts supply, the supply curve is moved to the left—that is, the supply of narcotics is diminished. In a hypothetical supply-and-demand curve (Figure 14), as supply is diminished and the equilibrium of supply and demand shifts to the left, it results in higher prices for the remaining supply. The cost of a similar quantity of the narcotic rises from the previous equilibrium of $50 to a new price point of $60. Dealers have been arrested, charges laid, and the acquisition of drugs made more dangerous because of the increased likelihood of arrest. Most drug enforcement efforts are likely to stop at this point, noting success from the impact of enforcement raising prices and lowering supply. At first glance, the war on supply might appear to be effective; however, a closer look at the economic consequences might lead policy makers to reconsider their focus.

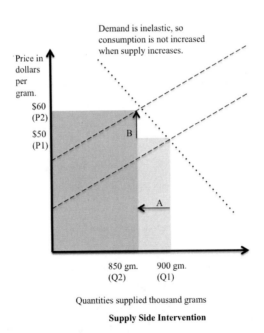

Figure 18. Supply side intervention.

The enforcement on the supply side does reduce supply and raise demand, but it also increases profits for remaining traffickers. As the profits increase, potential dealers who were not willing to join the trade at $50 now become willing to enter the market. New traffickers are encouraged to accept the increased risks for this enhanced potential for profits. Given that drug demand is relatively inelastic, interdiction on supply causes the supply curve to shift to the left—meaning that there is a shortage in supply and traffickers raise their prices at all levels of demand, but demand remains relatively unaffected. New traffickers who might not have been willing to undertake the risk at the $60 per gram level are now willing to take the risk, given a higher profit margin.

At the original price of $60 per gram, traffickers were willing to supply 90,000 grams, but interdiction shifted the supply curve so that traffickers are only willing to supply 85,000 grams at the price of $50 per gram. Supply side enforcement results in increases in profits for traffickers. The increase in profits to traffickers is due to the rise in price from $50 per gram to $60 per gram but for a smaller overall supply of only 85,000 grams. Total profits increase from $50 per gram for a total of 90,000 grams, or $4,5000,000 to $60 per gram for 85,000 grams for a total of $5,100,000 or an increase to traffickers of $600,000. Supply side enforcement simply made the industry more profitable and enticed more traffickers to the market.

The alternative model focuses resources on the demand side of the equation—programs like drug treatment clinics, drug diversion programs, therapeutic jurisprudence, and harm reduction. The second figure demonstrates how a demand-based policy might unfold. Demand side interventions cause the demand curve to shift to the left (reduce demand at any given price level). In this scenario, demand drops from 90,000 grams to 85,000 grams, exactly the same reduction as in our supply scenario but not because supply has been interdicted but rather because of fewer consumers.

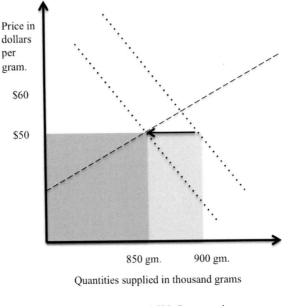

Demand Side Intervention

Figure 19. Demand side intervention.

This result is a surplus of unwanted narcotics. The resulting excess causes suppliers to compete for customers by dropping their prices from $60 per gram to $50 per gram. Under this scenario, the monetary gains for traffickers drops from $4,500,000, calculated at $50 per gram for a total of 90,000 grams, to $50 per gram for a total of 85,000 grams, or $4,250,000. Traffickers' profits decline by $250,000, which leads to an opting out of traffickers who are no longer willing to take the risk at the lower profits. Results mean fewer users, fewer traffickers, a less profitable industry, and a healthier society. Intervention results in a positive outcome. Most significant, under this scenario, even if nothing were to be done, the problem is at least not aggravated. There is no incentive for new traffickers to enter the market, and profit margins are reduced for existing traffickers. This is a simple demonstration of how two different approaches to the same problem can result in dramatically different outcomes. Further stakeholder collaboration and alternative policies can produce even larger and longer-term shifts in crime than singular enforcement-centered responses. Regardless of the strategy or intervention, there is ample evidence that confirms that altering the characteristics and dynamics of crime-prone areas through collaborative intervention produces larger and longer-term shifts in the quality of life and social cohesion of communities than singular enforcement-centered responses.

DIVERSITY

A wider discourse, beyond the narrower concerns for diversifying the ranks of police to reflect community-based programs, is essential if police leaders are to make the contributions toward building better, safer, and more cohesive societies. It is not sufficient for police leaders, for instance, to be content with the fact that there is no crime in a given neighborhood without also the knowledge and confidence that all residents also feel safe and welcome to engage in the use of their properties, streets, parks, and malls. Does everyone feel equally welcome and equally safe to engage in the full scope of social activities that their society offers? It is this next step that defines success, the stage at which not only do people feel safe from the experience of petty and violent crimes, but they also feel welcome and fully integrated as equal members of society. In effect, this is the difference wherein otherwise marginalized members of society move beyond simply being the beneficiaries of society's compliance to laws (just knowing that they are safe from violence and harassment because of their neighbors' fear of the application of legislated controls) to enjoying the commitment of their neighbors to including everyone in the full scale and scope of the fabric of society not because of laws and codes but despite the law.

For us to achieve such a state of social cohesion, the lens through which diversity is framed too must form part of a move away from reform-era practices in policing. One must not underestimate the importance of the role of police in conveying tacit messages to members of society on their roles and social acceptance that affect their sense of belonging and acceptance. *The British Journal of Sociology*, in an article on crime, policing, and social order, noted the following:

Just as the police lie at the heart of state legitimization process, policing may also act to produce and communicate contested meanings: order/disorder, justice/injustice, normality/deviance. Policing mediates collective identity, and as an institution relays messages of recognition and belonging or, conversely, misrecognition and exclusion. The police are not only representatives of the nation/state and servants of the people who comprise it, they are also in some ways constructive of the diverse social groups through which modern polity is constituted. Policing and understandings of policing are suffused with messages about the condition of society, the position of people within it, and the relation between state and individual.[276]

Global ethnocultural diversity has evolved remarkably since the early 1960s and will continue to evolve even more dramatically in the coming decades. In Canada, for instance, according to Statistics Canada ("Projections of the Diversity of the Canadian Population, 2006–2031") approximately three Canadians in ten could be members of a visible minority group by 2031. According to the same study, the proportion of persons who are foreign-born could reach between 25 percent and 28 percent by 2031, and nearly 55 percent of persons living in census metropolitan areas by 2031 may be either immigrants or the Canadian-born children of immigrants. The study notes that in Toronto and Vancouver, two of Canada's largest metropolitan centers, these proportions could be as high as 78 percent and 70 percent respectively.

Today immigrants differ dramatically from those of earlier periods. Today's immigrants have ready access to credit, travel, the ability to frequently reunite with family, and strongly maintained connections and ties to their origins. There is a strong presence of other members of their community in their new places of settlement—those who have preceded them—fluid access of media and entertainment programming from various parts of the world, and a firm expectation of the benefits and rights entitled to them, for instance, in the enactment of the Universal Declaration of Human Rights.

For many who migrated to new homes in the late 1960s and early 1970s, migration impacted their lives in ways that are very different than the impact felt by more recent émigrés. Immigration prior to the 1960s and 70s embodied a major decision to leave the homeland at substantial cost, an expectation that relocation would sever family ties for extended periods (years, decades, and in some cases permanently), acceptance of being a minority in a foreign culture, and a commitment to hard work in forging a better life for their children. With the exception of very early pioneers, who were promised parcels of land, seed money, and travel allowance, immigrants in the 1960s and '70s had little or no formal entitlements. Success in their new home depended on their commitment to hard work and a vision for a better future than the one they had left behind.

While many Western economies, like Canada, rely on immigration for foreign-trained professionals and offer values of freedom, equality, and democracy enshrined in the Human Rights Charter, current trends present challenges to how democracies evolve to redefine new norms and values on diversity and inclusiveness. Modern societies are increasingly compelled to reassess the principle on which this diversity is based. Take, for instance, the competing and opposing principles of inclusivity and diversity. On the one hand, immigrants are attracted to countries like Italy, Germany, France, Great Britain, Canada, Australia, and Brazil, for the fact that pluralism and multiculturalism allows all people to maintain and practice their cultures within a new milieu, a principle that eases the shock of integration and safeguards the commitment to equality. On the other hand, immigrants of previous eras who have become naturalized over generations, as well as those who arrived in the '60s and '70s and are now integrated within the majority, may feel the repercussions of contemporary conflicts despite the fact that they see themselves as part of the mainstream, not some exclusionary or exclusive subgroup. This is particularly poignant among those who have worked hard to integrate themselves into mainstream society and may yet continue to be subject to colloquial groupings, such as South Asian, East Asian, Middle Eastern, and the like.

While well-intentioned and useful during the '60s and '70s (earlier stages of multicultural), these categorizations are no longer appropriate or accurate. Not only do groupings perpetuate traditional stereotyping; they are in fact a form of soft segregation of peoples into convenient groupings that are not capable or effective of reflecting the larger heterogeneity of the cultures, ethnicities, and beliefs encompassed within such generalized groupings. Stereotyping, by any name, cultural or multiculturalism, serves to sustain marginalization and otherization of entire groups based on broad generalizations that are simplistic and opportunistic categorizations for framing explanations of why members of categorized groups do what they do, rather than placing the individual at the core of the examination.

For some, multiculturalism is part of a larger human rights movement, for the inclusion of diversity represents an *essentialism* for a just society. For others, multiculturalism, despite its egalitarian ideal, has come to form a constricting force that limits inclusiveness and confines minorities into manageable packages for the commoditization of political goals. Let's be clear, however, that while I use the term *multiculturalism* here, it is intended to be interpreted as a much larger, all-encompassing term that includes microcultures, like those based on place of origin, belief, race, ethnicity, creed, religion, color, and even disability, sexual orientation, sex, age, education, income, and social status.

This emerging reexamination of multiculturalism and diversity is likely to become increasingly contentious with increasing globalization, if a sober and open-minded discussion of diversity is not undertaken as part of a larger societal discourse in postdemocratic societies on all continents. The place of immigrants and economic and political migrants, refugees, and displaced peoples will all impact how this discourse is undertaken and unfolds.

A study by the International Centre for Intercultural Studies notes that the issue of belonging is central to any notion of social cohesion, and terminology can be the difference between creating inclusivity and maintaining exclusivity. The study focuses attention on issues of how long a migrant or immigrant remains an immigrant. Do children of immigrants born in an adopted country see themselves living in a *host* country? The answers to these questions are at the core of how increasingly larger numbers of members of a global community become enfranchised in the process of civil society. While countries like Canada, Australia, Britain, France, and the United States serve as good examples of societies that apply universally accepted norms of inclusivity based on social justice, even these jurisdictions are struggling with the titanic influences of globalization, nationalism, and sectarian conflicts across the globe, all of which have direct impact on the security services and how they respond in mitigating influences that work to disrupt social cohesion.

Interpreting diversity and multiculturalism as a promotion of group-based identities may serve to depreciate self-realization in lieu of what the dominant group sees as a justification for rights-based justice. In fact, institutionalized categorizations, despite their well-intentioned aims, serve to profile individuals, promote group enclaving, obscure struggles within institutionalized groups, and foster an environment for internal struggles for authority. Institutionalization of groups can therefore lead to misrecognition or nonrecognition of individuals' self-identity or forcing the interpretation of individual identity through a distorted subjectivity of an arbitrary institutional perspective. Understanding this nuanced argument on the role and scope of multicultural policies is crucial in the management of state-sponsored institutions. This is particularly important in societies where individuals may self-identify with multiple cultures and multiple racial and ethnic identities.

Police officers at are at the tip of the spear when dealing with diversity. Incidents reported as racial profiling, police bias, and targeted policing fill headlines, replete with accounts of the failure of police agencies and police leaders to train, educate, and sensitize their members to the importance of fair and impartial policing. And despite the titanic strides made toward the training and education of police officers in dealing with diverse communities; the status of illegal immigrants, refugees, and migrant workers; persons suffering from mental health issues; domestic violence; special needs; and cultural sensitivities, the challenges are not about to subside anytime soon. Cultures and identities are after all growing and changing concepts, the perceptions of which evolve as societies and citizens grow and change, demographic shifts occur, and regional conflicts impact relationships and geopolitics.

According to *The Annual Report on the Operations of the Canadian Multiculturalism Act*, 86 percent of respondents to a Focus Canada poll in 2010 viewed multiculturalism as important to Canada's national identity. The report also notes, however, that Canadians are concerned about the issues related to immigrants and the long-term integration of ethnic and religious communities, including the adoption of Canadian values. The fundamental values of multiculturalism are too important to be weakened by failing to embed everyone within the discourse of larger social and civic development. One cannot ignore that while 86 percent of Canadians value multiculturalism, there are significant signs of intolerance. According to the "Evaluation of Canada's Action Plan against Racism" (2010), nearly one-half of blacks and one-third of South Asian and Chinese respondents reported having been victims of discrimination and unfair treatment in the previous five years. The same report found that 46 percent of Aboriginal people living off the reserve felt that they had been a victim of racism or discrimination over the previous two years. This apparent divergence is an indication of a deeper dissonance in the meaning of multiculturalism within the Canadian context, a view that is reflective of similar tensions in many other parts of the world.

From a policing perspective, this requires that police leaders understand and address their own contributions to the state of social cohesion within the communities they service. There is sufficient research to show that the role of police itself is critical to a society's notion of social order and cohesion. Jonathan Jackson and Ben Bradford note: "Policing and understanding policing are suffused with messages about the conditions of society, the position of people within it, and the relation between state and individual."[277]

Jackson and Bradford use their qualitative study to demonstrate how certain, generally privileged, segments of British society relate to their police as a symbol by which a grander, cohesive national past can be recalled and a troubled, fractured present explained.

> Every stop, every search, every arrest, every group of youth moved on, every abuse of due process, every failure to respond to call or complaint, every racist …

> sexist ... homophobic (comment), every diagnosis of the crime problem, every depiction of criminals—all these send small, routine authoritative signals about societies' conflicts, cleavages and hierarchies about whose claims are considered legitimate within it, about whose status identity is to be affirmed or denied as part of it.[278]

The police themselves are a component of social cohesion, not merely the providers or maintainers of it. And if this is the case, then police leaders must reframe the nature and context of every decision and action taken in response to community needs for creating inclusivity of a higher order. There has been a subtle yet profound shift in the way nations are defining their identities based on core liberal (tolerant) values of freedom, equality, and democracy, the cornerstone of which is often based on the contentious, but persistent, ideal of diversity, inclusion, and multiculturalism that forms the fabric of global society. The shift is reflected in the reexamination of how multiculturalism impacts what national identities should and could be and how it might affect the notion of social cohesion.

Consider for instance a preference for a society described as "difference friendly" wherein assimilation to majority or dominant cultural norms is no longer the price of equal respect. In such societies, peoples of different backgrounds come together to understand and respect their differences as well as commonalities that then facilitate their interactions and relationships, especially when presented with a problem or dispute.

Identity-based initiatives, represented in for instance, the internal support networks (special interest support groups) diminishes recognition of individuals, substituted instead by arbitrary group identification. Instead, individuals should be seen as equal partners wherein recognition is not based on group-specific identification but rather on the status of the individual as a full partner in the larger social/group interaction. Fraser notes: "... institutionalized patterns of cultural value can be vehicles of subordination, it seeks to de-institutionalize patterns that impede parity of participation and to replace them with patterns that foster it."[279]

The growing application of alternative dispute resolution, particularly the type that is grassroots oriented as opposed to the programs run by lawyers as an expansion of the adversarial judicial system, offers much potential for deinstitutionalizing power and empowering communities to use the positive potential of conflict. Community mediation programs that deal with neighborhood disputes, school bullying, quarrels between workers and customers, and elder mediation are examples of disputes that might be resolved through alternative processes.

This recognition of social and cultural differences is essential to ensuring the flexibility required of successful participatory processes. In recognizing the dominance of the adversarial system in law as "an expression of our commitment to principled and just outcomes," we must recognizes that the justice systems must be committed to being flexible in responding to diverse social relationships and cultures in a changing sociodemographic context. The increasing diversity of societies around the world presents unique opportunities for examining participatory processes, not only as a means of resolving individual disputes and differences but also for creating better societies.

Most studies tend to measure the success of participatory programs on the basis of four outcomes—recidivism, victim satisfaction, offender satisfaction, and restitution compliance. These outcomes reflect what is referred to as the "satisfaction story," or a measure of the satisfaction achieved by the fulfillment of the participants' needs. While these outcomes represent quantifiable variables, they fail to take into account the *transformative story*, which emphasizes the importance of individual moral growth in transforming not only situations but also individuals and societies as a whole. Many social conflicts arise from what social constructionists see as the differences by which individuals and groups give meaning and interpretation to actions and events. The transformation, however, must have its basis in a commitment of all social actors to bring about a difference-friendly society on the basis of an intrinsic commitment to its benefits and not simply through some form of induced compliance.

How police services work toward integrating their efforts to provide fair, equitable, and just services is critical to the forging and maintenance of social cohesion within a civil society. Police-community relationships are indicative of the health of a civil community and are an essential ingredient in the development of models for egalitarian and just societies. Communities and their constituent citizens are the markets for police services; these are your clients, and it is who you are as a reflection of the communities you serve. How you as a police leader diversify your organization and, more important, how you define the cultural inclusion of a diverse workforce, not only determines the success and effectiveness of your service; it defines you as the custodian of one-half of the two most important pillars of democratic society and sets an example for the future of the societies you will help to build and safeguard. In other words, understanding the role of diversity and its application within the context of policing defines the legitimacy of law enforcement. Processes, such as restorative and participatory justice, diversion programs, and inclusion of alternative dispute resolution, can offer opportunities for exploring new paradigms for policing, rather than simply looking for improvements to existing views and strategies.

Narrower, arcane views of cultural diversity and multiculturalism, bolstered by individualism, hold multicultural categorizations as a misrecognition of a sense of self or a misrecognition consisting of a depreciation of identity by the dominant culture with the consequent damage to group members' sense of self. The reexamination of the importance of recognizing diversity should, therefore, not be seen as a repudiation of its values but rather as an effort to refashion the discourse about the collective identity of a cohesive society and its politics, while reaffirming the importance of the sense of oneself. *The British Journal of Epidemiology and Health*, for instance, notes: "It is easy to forget that categories are merely labels, and no more than a first step to understanding and defining a person's ethnicity or race. Such labels need to be recognized as shorthand for potentially important information." That study goes on to note that self-definition is gaining favor as a concept because groupings hide massive differences within group heterogeneity.[280]

Multiculturalism and diversity issues are being reassessed from both the left and right. On the right, many view multiculturalism, correctly or incorrectly, as a misguided policy that diminishes standards and promotes preferential identification based on politics. At the same time, many cultural experts are sounding the alarm against singular views of multiculturalism, citing examples of the reversal of multicultural policies in countries like the United States and Australia. As a case in point, Australia's declaration of the National Agenda for a Multicultural Society has been followed by regressive policies and statements aimed at safeguarding so-called mainstream values against the influx of new immigrants, particularly from Southeast Asia, resulting in a sharp retreat from the promotion of multiculturalism.

While observers point to Australia as an example for reversals in multiculturalism prompted from the right, a reflection of the retreat by the dominant culture from the policies put into place for the inclusivity of minority groups, what is even more notable is the retreat, not by the dominant group, but by the minority groups themselves from the notion of multiculturalism. Policies on multiculturalism are, therefore, being challenged from both the left and the right. The message should be clear—multiculturalism must not be used as a tool for the management and appeasement of egalitarian expectations through politicization. Instead, multiculturalism must become even more inclusive by enlarging the account of individualism, with its attendant uniqueness, and self-definition as a new standard for justice, ethics, and social morality.

Understanding cultural diversity, the geopolitical factors impacting human migration, and the resulting social impacts should be of growing importance to police leaders. How police and security services enforce laws and maintain order and cohesion in the face of large waves of migrants sailing to the southern borders of Europe, South American migrants illegally crossing the borders into the United States, or Rohinga refugees fleeing to Thailand, Malaysia, and Indonesia are just small examples of the impact human migration will have on the security policies of entire regions for decades to come. Beyond the initial impact of the arrival of refugees and migrants, there are the longer-term issues of inclusivity, engagement, and socialization that police leaders must prepare for and deal with successfully. Failure to get ahead of the challenges from the onset will likely result in the types of conflict manifest with the Ethiopian-Israeli Jewish refugees of the 1980s and '90s and the mainstream Israeli population in recent years, the antagonism and otherization of Roma populations throughout Europe, or disturbing numbers of youth from North America and Europe who continue to travelled to Syria, Iraq, and Afghanistan to joined ISIS/ISIL. Such manifestations of cultural discontent may be issues that could have been averted or at least mitigated with greater focus on policies that emphasize inclusion, participation, and cohesion.

CONCLUSION

Policing is an evolving profession, one that must straddle many worlds. Police leaders must be progressive and forward thinking and anticipate new and emerging challenges and yet remain founded in the types of principles articulated by Sir Robert Peel. This too then is a paradox that defines policing—know the future but remain founded in the past; serve the community and be efficient at intelligence-led policing; circumscribe rules, policies, and directives while also demanding discretionary freedoms and choices; train for diversity and yet demand conformity; and be accountable to the democratic institution of governance but demand police independence. There is perhaps no other profession wherein the demands are more complex, the job functions more diverse, the oversight more all-encompassing, and public scrutiny greater.

Despite the challenges, policing and police leadership have come a long way from the forms of rudimentary intimidation and cohesion that dominated the early days of policing. Policing today requires a level of legitimacy that demands its leaders to be well-trained, responsive, accountable, and capable of dealing with security, social management, and community leadership in ways that could not have been anticipated just a few decades back. Today's police leaders are among the most competent civil servants without whose commitment and dedication modern commerce, political stability, and social cohesion could not be maintained. Yet, despite the advances, there remains much work to be done, much to be learned, and much to be changed.

The future of policing should be a progressive journey from identifying broken windows, measuring and ensuring that police leaders and resources are focused at the issues of relevance, and producing effective outcomes to a world in which policing becomes as much about mending broken fences and building good neighbors and cohesive and caring, protective and productive citizens—*mending broken fences policing.*

Good luck, and God bless!

BIBLIOGRAPHY

"Boston Police Accept 'Full Responsibility' in Death of Red Sox Fan." CNN. October 22, 2004. www.cnn.com/2004/us/10/22/fan.death/.

"Community Policing: The Past, Present, and Future." The Police Executive Research Forum, 2004.

"Crime in the United States," Table 1, FBI Uniform Crime Reports, www.fbi.gov/about-us/cjis/ucr/crime-in-the-u.s.-2011/table/table-1.

"Crime Policing and Social Order: On the Expressive Nature of Public Confidence in Policing." *The British Journal of Sociology* 60, no. 3 (2009).

"Extending Social Disorganization Theory: Modeling the Relationships between Cohesion, Disorder, and Fear." *Criminology* 39, no. 2 (2001).

"Trust in the Police in 16 European Countries: A Multilevel Analysis." *European Journal of Criminology* (2008).

All-Party Parliamentary Report Says that Many Under-18s Have Negative Experience of Police." *Guardian*, October 28, 2014.

Arnstein, Sherry R. "A Ladder of Citizen Participation." *Journal of the American Institute of Planners* 35, no. 4 (1969).

Australian Institute of Criminology. "Australian Crime: Facts & Figures," 2013.

Bacqueroux, Bonnie. "Community Criminal Justice: What Community Policing Teaches." On Restorative Justice. http://www.restorativejustice.org/articlesdb/articles/257.

Baker, Al, and William K. Rashbaum. "New York City to Examine Reliability of Its Crime Reports." *New York Times*, January 5, 2011.

Bhopal, Raj. "Glossary of Terms Relating to Ethnicity and Race: For Reflection and Debate." *Journal of Epidemiology and Community Health* 58, no. 6 (2004).

Binnendijk, Annette. "Results Based Management in the Development Cooperation Agencies: A Review of Experience." *Background Report*, 2000.

Bissoondath, Neil. *Selling Illusions: The Cult of Multiculturalism in Canada*.

Bittner, Egon. "Florence Nightingale in Pursuit of Willie Sutton: A Theory of the Police," 1993.

Black, Conrad. "Conrad Black: The Salvation of Rob Ford." *National Post*, November 13, 2013. http://fullcomment.nationalpost.com/2013/11/23/conrad-black-salvation-of-rob-ford/.

Bohn, Roger. "Stop Fighting Fires." *Harvard Business Review*.

Bollard, John, and Deborah McCallum. "Neighboring and Community Mobilization in High-Poverty Inner-City Neighborhoods." *Urban Affairs Review* 38, no. 1 (September 2002).

Botterman, Sarah, Marc Hooghe, and Tim Reeskens. "'One Size Fits All'? An Empirical Study into the Multidimensionality of Social Cohesion Indicators in Belgian Local Communities." *Urban Studies Journal Limited* 49, no. 1 (2012).

Boyce, Jillian, Adam Cotter, and Samuel Perreault. Canadian Centre for Justice Statistics, "Police-Reported Crime Statistics in Canada," *Juristat*, 34 no. 1 (2014).

Braga, Anthony, Andrew Papachristos, and David Hureau. "Hot Spots Policing Effects on Crime." *Campbell Systematic Reviews* 8, no. 8 (2012).

Braithwaite, John. "Restorative Justice and Social Justice." *Saskatchewan Law Review* 63 (2000).

Braithwaite, John. *Crime, Shame and Reintegration*. Cambridge University Press, 1989.

Brennan, Shannon, and Mia Dauvergne. *Police-Reported Crime Statistics in Canada, 2010*. Statistics Canada.

Bronitt, Simon, and Philip Stenning. "Understanding Discretion in Modern Policing." *Criminal Law Journal* 35, no. 6 (2011).

Brosnahan, Maureen. "Canada's Prison Population at All-Time High." CBC News. November 25, 2013. http://www.cbc.ca/news/canada-s-prison-population-at-all-time-high-1.2440039.

Canadian Supreme Court Case. Regina vs. Beare [1988] 2SCR 387 at 410.

Cardarelli, Albert, Jack McDevitt, and Katrina Baum. "The Rhetoric and Reality of Community Policing in Small and Medium-Sized Cities and Towns." *Policing: An International Journal of Police Strategies & Management* 21, no. 3 (1998).

Carter, Tom, Chesya Polevychok, Anita Friesen, and John Obsorne. "Different Groups' Perception of Panhandling in Winnipeg." The Institute of Urban Studies. The University of Winnipeg.

CBC News. "Police Chief Bill Blair on the Rob Ford Video." October 31, 2013.

Cebulla, Andreas, and Mike Stephens. "Public Perceptions of the Police: Effects of Police Investigations and Police Resources." *Internet Journal of Criminology* (2010).

Chaplin, Rupert, John Flatley, and Kevin Smith. *Crime in England and Wales 2010/11, Findings from the British Crime Survey and Police Recorded Crime* (2nd Edition). Home Office Statistics Bulletin, UK, 2010. HOSB:10/11.

Charron, Mathieu. "Neighbourhood Characteristics and the Distribution of Crime in Toronto: Additional Analysis on Youth Crime." Canadian Centre for Justice Statistics. Catalogue no. 85-561-M, no. 22. December 2011.

Chen, Chao C., Patrick Saparito, and Liuba Belkin. "Responding to Trust Breaches: The Domain Specificity of Trust and the Role of Affect." *Journal of Trust Research* 1, no. 1 (2011).

Chisholm, Rupert F. "Quality of Working Life: Critical Issue for the 80s." *Public Productivity Review* (1983): 10–25.

Citizenship and Immigration Canada. "Evaluation of Canada's Action Plan against Racism." December 2010.

Citizenship and Immigration Canada. *The Annual Report on the Operations of the Canadian Multiculturalism Act 2010–2011*. www.cic.gc.ca.

City of Toronto. "Wellbeing Toronto." City of Toronto, 2012.

Cox, David. "Educating Police for Uncertain Times: The Australian Experience and Case for 'Normative' Approach." *Journal of Police Intelligence and Counter Terrorism* 6, no. 1 (April 2011): 3–22.

Coyne, John William, and Peter Bell. "Strategic Intelligence in Law Enforcement: A Review." *Journal of Policing, Intelligence, and Counter Terrorism* 6, no. 1 (2011): 23–39.

Criminal Code of Canada, Part XXIII Sentencing, Purpose and Principles of Sentencing.

Crouch, Ben M. "Is Incarceration Really Worse? Analysis of Offenders' Preferences for Prison over Probation." *Justice Quarterly* 10, no. 1 (1993): 67–88.

Daily Maverick. "SA Crime Statistics May Obscure More than They Reveal," September 12, 2013.

Daly, Yvonne Marie. "Judicial Oversight of Policing: Investigations, Evidence and the Exclusionary Rule." *Crime, Law and Social Change* 55, no. 2–3 (2011): 199–215.

Davis, Brent, and Kym Dossetor. "(Mis)perceptions of Crime in Australia." *Trends & Issues in Crime and Criminal Justice*. Australian Institute of Criminology no. 396 (July 2010).

Deutsch, Morton, and Peter T. Coleman. "Some Guidelines for Developing a Creative Approach to Conflict." In *The Handbook of Conflict Resolution: Theory and Practice*, edited by Morton Deutsch and Peter T. Coleman. San Francisco: Jossey-Bass Publishers, 2000: 355–365.

Dickes, Paul, Marie Valentova, and Monique Borsenberger. "A Multidimensional Assessment of Social Cohesion in 47 European Countries." *CEPS/INSTEAD Working Papers* 2011-07 (2011).

Dowden, Craig, and Donald A. Andrews. "The Importance of Staff Practice in Delivering Effective Correctional Treatment: A Meta-Analytic Review of Core Correctional Practice." *International Journal of Offender Therapy and Comparative Criminology* 48, no. 2 (2004): 203–214.

Economist. "Government Surveillance." July 2012.

Ellis, Darren. "Stop and Search: Disproportionality, Discretion and Generalizations." *Police Journal* 83 no. 3 (2010): 199–216.

Ericson, Richard V. "The Police as Reproducers of Order." *T. Newburn, Policing. Key Readings.* Cullompton: Willan (1982).

Eurostat Statistics Explained. "Crime Statistics, Data from January 2014."

Eurostat. European Commission. "Unemployment Statistics." Table 1: Youth Unemployment Figures 2011–2013.

Famega, Christine N., James Frank, and Lorraine Mazerolle. "Managing Police Patrol Time: The Role of Supervisor Directives." *Justice Quarterly* 22, no. 4 (2005).

Fatah, Tarek. "White Liberal Guilt." *Toronto Sun*, May 23, 2012.

Frahm, Jennifer, and Kerry Brown, "First Steps: Linking Change Communication to Change Receptivity." *Journal of Organizational Change Management* 20, no. 3 (2007): 370–387.

Franco-Santos, Monica, Mike Kennerley, Pietro Micheli, Veronica Martinez, Steve Mason, Bernard Marr, Dina Gray, and Andrew Neely. "Towards a Definition of a Business Performance Measurement System." *International Journal of Operations & Production Management* 27, no. 8 (2007): 784–801.

Fraser, Nancy. "Recognition without Ethics?" *Theory, Culture & Society* 18, no. 2–3 (2001): 21–42.

Fraser, Nancy. "Social Justice in the Age of Identity Politics: Redistribution, Recognition, and Participation." The Tannet Lectures on Human Values, Stanford University, April 30–May 2, 1996, 3. www.tannerlectures.utah.edu/lectures/docum.

Fratello, Jennifer, Andrés F. Rengifo, and Jennifer Trone. "Coming of Age with Stop and Frisk: Experiences, Self-Perceptions, and Public Safety Implications." New York: Vera Institute of Justice, 2013.

Fridell, Lorie A., and Mary Ann Wycoff, eds. "Community Policing: The Past, Present, and Future." Annie E. Casey Foundation and Police Executive Research Forum, 2004.

Furlong, Gary T.. *The Boundary Model, The Conflict Resolution Toolbox*. John Wiley and Sons, 2005.

Gascon, George, and Todd Foglesong. "Making Policing More Affordable: Managing Costs and Measuring Value in Policing," 2010.

Geoghegan, Tom. "US Crime Figures: Why the Drop?" *BBC News*. Washington DC., 2011. http://www.bbc.co.uk/news/world-us-canada-13799616.

Gilmore, Stan. "Why We Trust Police: Police Governance and the Problem of Trust," 2008.

Gilmour, Stan. "Why We Trussed the Police: Police Governance and the Problem of Trust." *International Journal of Police Science and Management* 10, no. 1 (2008): 51–64.

Global Justice Information Sharing Initiative. "Fusion Centre Guidelines—Developing and Sharing Information in a New Era." United States Department of Justice. Washington, DC (2006).

Gottuck, Susanne, and Hans-Uwe Otto. "Editorial: Creating Capabilities for Socially Vulnerable Youth in Europe." *Social Work & Society* 12, no. 2 (2014).

Graham, John, Bruce Amos, and Tim Plumptre. "Principles for Good Governance in the 21st Century." Policy Brief No. 15. Institute on Governance. August 2003.

Hanggi, Heiner. "Conceptualizing Security Sector Reform and Reconstruction."

Harari, Edwin. "Whose Evidence? Lessons from the Philosophy of Science and the Epistemology of Medicine." *Australian and New Zealand Journal of Psychiatry* 35, no. 6 (2001): 724–730.

Harris, Peter, Brian Weagant, David Cole, and Fern Weinper. "'Working in the Trenches' with the YCJA." *Canadian Journal of Criminology and Criminal Justice* 46, no. 3 (2004): 367–390.

Harvard Kennedy School. National Institute of Justice.

Healy, Tom, and Sylvain Côté. "The Well-Being of Nations: The Role of Human and Social Capital." Education and Skills. Organisation for Economic Cooperation and Development. 2 Rue Andre Pascal, F-75775, Paris Cedex 16, France, 2001.

Herbert, Steve. "Police Subculture Reconsidered." *Criminology* 36, no. 2 (1998): 343–370.

Hinds, Lyn. "Public Satisfaction with Police: The Influence of General Attitudes and Police-Citizen Encounters." *International Journal of Police Science & Management* 11, no. 1 (2009).

Hirschfield, Alexander, and Kate J. Bowers. "The Effect of Social Cohesion on Levels of Recorded Crime in Disadvantaged Areas." *Urban Studies* 34, no. 8 (1997): 1275–1295.

Hough, Mike, Jackson J, Bradford B., Myhill A, Quinton P. "Procedural Justice, Trust and Institutional Legitimacy," 2010.

Howell, Gwyneth V.J., and Rohan Miller. "Maple Leaf Foods: Crisis and Containment." *Public Communication Review* (University of Sydney, Australia) 1, no. 1 (2010): 47–56.

Innes, Martin, and Colin Roberts. "Community Intelligence in the Policing of Community Safety." *Community Safety: Innovation and Evaluation* (2007).

Innes, Martin. "Why 'Soft' Policing Is Hard: On the Curious Development of Reassurance Policing, How It Became Neighbourhood Policing and What This Signifies about the Politics of Police Reform." *Journal of Community & Applied Social Psychology* 15, no. 3 (2005): 156–169.

Intelligence-Led Policing: The New Intelligence Architecture. US Department of Justice, Office of Justice Assistance, 2005.

Jackson, Andrew, G. Fawcett, A. Milan, P. Roberts, S. Schetagne, K. Scott, and S. Tsoukalas. "Social Cohesion in Canada: Possible Indicators." *Ottawa: Canadian Council on Social Development* (2000).

Jackson, Jonathan, and Ben Bradford. "Crime, Policing and Social Order: On the Expressive Nature of Public Confidence in Policing." *The British Journal of Sociology* 60, no. 3 (2009): 493–521.

Jackson, Jonathan, Ben Bradford, Mike Hough, Andy Myhill, Paul Quinton, and Tom R. Tyler. "Why Do People Comply with the Law? Legitimacy and the Influence of Legal Institutions." *British Journal of Criminology* (2012).

James, Darlene, and Sawka Ed. "Drug Treatment Courts." Substance Abuse Intervention within the Justice System. Alberta Alcohol and Drug Abuse Commission. Canadian Centre on Substance Abuse National Working Group on Addictions. Policy, November 2000. www.ccsa.ca/pdf/ccsa-008697-2000.pdf.

Jang, Hyunseok, Larry T. Hoover, and Joo Hee-Jong. "An Evaluation of CompStat's Effect on Crime: The Fort Worth Experience." *Police Quarterly* 13, no.4.

Jenson, Jane. "Mapping Social Cohesion: The State of Canadian Research." Canadian Policy Research Networks Inc., 1998.

Journal of Epidemiology and Health 58, no. 6 (2004).

Joustra, Robert J. "The Tenth Man." The Center for Public Justice. November 1, 2013. http://www.capitalcommentary.org/israel/tenth-man.

Kelling, George L. "'Broken Windows' and Police Discretion." National Justice Institute. US Department of Justice (October 1999).

Kleinig, John. "The Ethical Perils of Knowledge Acquisition." *Criminal Justice Ethics* 28, no. 2 (2009): 201–222.

Koonce, Kelly A. "Social Cohesion as the Goal: Can Social Cohesion Be Directly Pursued?" *Peabody Journal of Education* 86 (2011): 144–154.

Kotter, John P. "Leading Change: Why Transformation Efforts Fail." *Harvard Business Review* (2007).

Kruger, J. "The Tapestry of Culture: A Design for the Assessment of Intercultural Disputes." *Dispute Resolution Readings and Case Studies*.

Laegaard, Sune. "Immigration, Social Cohesion, and Naturalization." *Ethnicities* 10, no. 4 (2010): 452–469.

Larsen, James E., and John P. Blair. "The Importance of Police Performance as a Determinant of Satisfaction with Police." *American Journal of Economics and Business Administration* 1, no. 1 (2009): 1–10.

Latimer, Jeff, Craig Dowden, and Danielle Muise. "The Effectiveness of Restorative Justice Practices: A Meta-Analysis." *The Prison Journal* 85, no. 2 (2005).

Law Commission of Canada. "Transforming Relationships through Participatory Justice," (2003). Available at http://www.lcc.gc.ca/about/transform_toc-en.asp.

Layton, Catherine, and Christine Jennett. "Partnerships in Policing and Evidence-Based Practices in Crime Prevention: Are They Incompatible?" Australian Institute of Criminology, 2005.

Lederach, J.P. "Preparing for Peace: Conflict Transformation across Cultures." In Macfarlane, Julie. *Dispute Resolution: Readings and Case Studies.* 2nd Edition. Emond Montgomery Publications Limited, 2003.

Leggett, Ted. "What Do the Police Do?" Institute for Security Studies, 2003. ISSN: 1026-0404.

Lewicki, Roy J., and Carolyn Wiethoff. "Trust, Trust Development, and Trust Repair." In Deutsch, Morton, and Peter T. Coleman, eds. *The Handbook of Conflict Resolution: Theory and Practice.* San Francisco: Jossey-Bas Publishers, 2000.

Loader, Ian. "Policing, Recognition, and Belonging." *The Annals of the American Academy of Political and Social Science* 605, no. 1 (2006): 201–221.

Macfarlane, Julie. *Dispute Resolution: Readings and Case Studies.* 2nd Edition. Emond Montgomery Publications Limited, 2003.

Mackenzie, Simon, and Alistair Henry. *Community Policing: A Review of the Evidence.* Scottish Government, 2009.

Magers, Jeffrey S. "CompStat: A New Paradigm for Policing or a Repudiation of Community Policing?" *Journal of Contemporary Criminal Justice* 20, no. 1 (2004).

Mansur, Salim. *Detectable Lies: A Liberal Repudiation of Multiculturalism.*

Marion, Nancy. "Effectiveness of Community Based Correctional Programs: A Case Study." *The Prison Journal* 82, no. 4 (2002): 478–497.

Markowitz, Fred E., Paul E. Bellair, Allen E. Liska, and Jianhong Liu. "Extending Social Disorganization Theory: Modeling the Relationships between Cohesion, Disorder, and Fear." *Criminology* 39, no. 2 (2001): 293–319.

Martin, Roger. *The Opposable Mind.* Boston: Harvard Business School Press, 2007.

McDonald, Susan, Andrea Wobick, and Janet Graham. Research Report, *Bill C-46: Records Applications Post-Mills, A Case Law Review.* Department of Justice, Canada, 2004, 2006.

Murji, Karim. "Working Together: Governing and Advising the Police." *The Police Journal* 84, no. 3 (2011): 256–271.

Murphy, Gerard, Shannon McFadden, and Molly Griswold. "Police and Immigration: How Chiefs Are Leading Their Communities through the Challenges." Police Executive Research Forum, 2010.

Neely, Andy, and Mohammed Al Najjar. "Management Learning Not Management Control: The True Role of Performance Management." University of California, Berkeley 48, no.3. (2003).

Neely, Andy. "Measuring Business Performance: Why, What, and How." London: The Economist Books, 1998.

Nevin, Rick. "Understanding International Crime Trends: The Legacy of Preschool Lead Exposure." *Environmental Research* 104.

Norton, David, and Robert Kaplan. "Putting the Balanced Scorecard to Work." *Harvard Business Review* 71, no. 5 (1993): 134–140.

Novak, Kenneth J., Leanne Fiftal Alarid, and Wayne L. Lucas. "Exploring Officers' Acceptance of Community Policing: Implications for Policy Implementation." *Journal of Criminal Justice* 31, no. 1 (2003): 57–71.

Office for National Statistics. "Personal Well-Being Across the UK, 2012/13."

Office for National Statistics. "Statistical Bulletin: Crime in England and Wales, Year Ending September 2013."

Ontario Association of Chiefs of Police. "Crime Prevention in Ontario: A Framework for Action."

Ontario Ministry of Children and Youth Services. "Review of the Root of Youth Violence: Literature Review." Volume 5. Chapter 4.

Operation Spring Board. Community Benefits from Cannabis Diversion Program. Part XXIII Sentencing, Purpose and Principles of Sentencing, Criminal Code of Canada.

Pasoline, Eugene A., Stephanie M. Myers, and Robert E. Worden. "Police Culture, Individualism, and Community Policing: Evidence from Two Police Departments." *Justice Quarterly* 17, no. 3 (2000): 576–605.

Petersilia, Joan, and Elizabeth Piper Deschenes. "Perceptions of Punishment: Inmates and Staff Rank the Severity of Prison Versus Intermediate Sanctions." *The Prison Journal* 74, no. 3 (1994): 306–328.

Pfeffer, Jeffrey, and Robert I. Sutton. *The Knowing-Doing Gap: How Smart Companies Turn Knowledge into Action*. Harvard Business Press, 2013.

Phillips, Ann. *Multiculturalism without Culture*. Princeton University Press, 2007.

Pickering, Sharon, Jude McCulloch, and David Wright-Neville. "Counter-terrorism Policing: Towards Social Cohesion." *Crime, Law and Social Change* 50, no. 1–2 (2008): 91–109.

Plant, Joel B., and Michael S. Scott. *Effective Policing and Crime Prevention: A Problem-Oriented Guide for Mayors, City Managers, and County Executives*. US Department of Justice, 2009.

Police Discretion, page 321.

Police Reform, A Police Service for the Twenty-First Century (White Paper). Secretary of State for the Home Department. London, 1993.

R v. Askov [1990] 2 S.C.R. 1199.

R. v. Beaudry, [2007] 1 S.C.R. 190, 2007 SCC 5.

Recasens, Amadeu. "The Control of Police Powers." *European Journal on Criminal Policy and Research* (2000), 8, no. 3.

Reform. "Value for Money in Policing: From Efficiency to Transformation," 2011.

Reiner, Robert. "Let's Admit It: Most Police Work Does Not Involve Catching Criminals." *Guardian*, October 28, 2011. http://www.guardian.co.uk/uk/2011/oct/28/admit-police-work-catching-criminals.

Reisig, Michael D., and Roger B. Parks. "Experience, Quality of Life, and Neighborhood Context: A Hierarchical Analysis of Satisfaction with Police." *Justice Quarterly* 17, no. 3 (2000): 607–630.

Reno, Janet, Raymond C. Fisher, Laurie Robinson, Noel Brennan, and Jeremy Travis. "US Department of Justice." (1999).

Research Report, *Bill C-46: Records Applications Post-Mills, A Case Law Review*. Department of Justice, Canada, 2004.

Resolution: Readings and Case Studies. 2nd Edition. Emond Montgomery Publications Limited, 2003.

Rosenbaum, Dennis P., Amie M. Schuck, Sandra K. Costello, Darnell F. Hawkins, and Marianne K. Ring. "Attitudes towards the Police: The Effects of Direct and Vicarious Experience." *Police Quarterly* 8, no. 3 (2005): 343–365.

Royer, Isabelle. "Why Bad Projects Are So Hard to Kill." *Harvard Business Review* 81, no. 2 (2003): 48–57.

Schafer, Joseph A. "'I'm Not against It in Theory ...': Global and Specific Community Policing Attitudes." *Policing: An International Journal of Police Strategies & Management* 25, no. 4 (2002): 669–686.

Schafer, Joseph A., Beth M. Huebner, and Timothy S. Bynum. "Citizen Perceptions of Police Services: Race, Neighborhood Context, and Community Policing." *Police Quarterly* 6, no. 4 (2003): 440–468.

Shonholtz, Raymond. "Constructive Response to Conflict in Emerging Democracies: Distinguishing between Conflict and Dispute." http://www.partnersglobal.org/resources/article8.html.

Shonholtz, Raymond. "Neighbourhood Justice Systems," 420–427. In Macfarlane, Julie, *Dispute Resolution: Readings and Case Studies*. Emond Montgomery Publication, 2003.

Simons, Robert. "Control in an Age of Empowerment." *Harvard Business Review* 73, no. 2 (March 1995).

Statistics Canada. "Juristat-Family Violence in Canada: A Statistical Profile, 2010." Catalogue no. 85-002-X, 2010.

Statistics Canada. "Projections of the Diversity of the Canadian Population 2006–2031." Catalogue no. 91-551-X, 2010.

Stiglitz, Joseph E., Amartya Sen, and Jean-Paul Fitoussi. "Report by the Commission on the Measurement of Economic Performance and Social Progress." Commission on the Measurement of Economic Performance and Social Progress, Paris, 2009.

Taylor, Gilbert. "The Importance of Developing Correctional Plans for Offenders." In *Forum on Corrections Research* 13, no. 1 (2001): 14–17. Correctional Services of Canada.

Transforming Relationships through Participatory Justice. Law Commission of Canada, 2003.

Travers, Julie. "Global Focus—Sexual Assault Rape." *Globe and Mail*, October 5, 2013.

Travis, Allan. "Significant Proportion of Children Distrust Police, Inquiry Finds. Travis, Jeremy. "'Broken Windows' and Police Discretion." National Justice Institute, US Department of Justice, 1999.

Tseloni, Andromachi, Jen Mailley, Graham Farrell, and Nick Tilley. "Exploring the International Decline in Crime Rates." *European Journal of Criminology* 7, no. 5 (2010): 375–394.

Umbreti, Mark. "Mediation of Victim Offender Conflict." *Journal of Dispute Resolution* (1988): 84, 1t87, 102, and 103–105.

Umbreit, Mark S. "Restorative Justice through Victim-Offender Mediation: A Multi-Site Assessment." *Western Criminology Review* 1, no. 1 (1998): 1–29.

Uniform Crime Reporting Survey (UCR). Statistics Canada.

United Nations. "Public Security in the Americas: Challenges and Opportunities." General Secretariat Organization of American States. 2nd Edition. December 2008.

United Nations. *World Crime Trends and Emerging Issues and Responses in the Field of Crime Prevention and Criminal Justice.* Economic and Social Council. E/CN.15/2011/10. January 24, 2011.

US Department of Justice. Center for Program Evaluation and Performance Measurement. "What Have We Learned from Evaluations of Place-Based Policing Strategies?" 2012.

US Department of Justice. Uniform Crime Reports. "Crime in the United States," 2013.

Verini, James. "The Obama Effect: A Surprising New Theory for the Continuing Crime Decline among Black Americans." Slate.com, October 5, 2010.

Vetten, Lisa. "Rape and Other Forms of Violence in South Africa." Institute for Security Studies. Policy Brief 72 (2014).

Walker, Samuel. *Taming the System: The Control of Discretion in Criminal Justice, 1950–1990.* New York: Oxford University Press, 1992.

Welsh, Brandon, and David Farrington. "Evidence-Based Crime Prevention: Conclusions and Directions for a Safer Society." *Canadian Journal of Criminology and Criminal Justice* 47, no. 2 (2005): 337–354.

Wemmers, Jo-Anne, and Katie Cyr. "Can Mediation Be Therapeutic for Crime Victims? An Evaluation of Victims' Experiences in Mediation with Young Offenders." *Canadian Journal of Criminology and Criminal Justice* 47, no. 3 (2005): 527–544.

Westin, Susan S. *Performance Measurement and Evaluation: Definitions and Relationships*. GAO/GGD-98-26. Washington, DC: US Government Printing Office, 1998.

Willis, James J., and Stephen D. Mastrofski. "CompStat and the New Penology: A Paradigm Shift in Policing?" *British Journal of Criminology* 52, no. 1 (2012): 73–92.

Willis, James J., David Weisburd, and Stephen D. Mastrofski. *CompStat in Practice: An In-Depth Analysis of Three Cities*, 2003.

Wisler, Dominique, and Ihekwoaba D. Onwudiwe. "Community Policing: A Comparative View" 1. *IPES Working Paper* 6, 2007.

Wulf, Herbert. "Security Sector Reform in Developing and Transitional Countries." Berghof Research Centre for Constructive Conflict Management, 2004.

www.operationspringboard.on.ca.

ENDNOTES

1. Kenneth Davis, "Discretionary Justice: A Preliminary Inquiry" (Baton Rouge, LA: Louisiana State University Press, 1969): 166 (as cited in Kelling, George L., "'Broken Windows' and Police Discretion," National Justice Institute, US Department of Justice (October 1999): 2, https://www.ncjrs.gov/pdffiles1/nij/178259.pdf, accessed June 25, 2015.
2. Sarah Botterman, Marc Hooghe, and Tim Reeskens, "'One Size Fits All'? An Empirical Study into the Multidimensionality of Social Cohesion Indicators in Belgian Local Communities," *Urban Studies* 49, no. 1 (2012): 185–202.
3. Roy J. Lewicki and Carolyn Wiethoff, "Trust, Trust Development, and Trust Repair," in Morton Deutsch and Peter T. Coleman, eds., *The Handbook of Conflict Resolution: Theory and Practice* (San Francisco: Jossey-Bas Publishers, 2000)): 86–107.

    The authors define trust as "an individual's belief in, and willingness to act on the basis of, the words, actions, and decisions of another." Lewicki and Wiethoff note that distrust is not merely the absence of trust but is an active negative expectation regarding another. They identify two bases for trust (or distrust). *Calculus-based trust* rests on assessments of costs and rewards for violating or sustaining trust and is more typical of professional relationships. *Identification-based trust* rests on the parties' mutual understanding and affinity and is more typical of personal relationships, such as friendship. Identification-based trust can be fostered if the parties take time to develop their common interests, values, perceptions, motives, and goals. Identification-based trust has a strong emotional component and so is sensitive to a number of nonlogical factors. This makes managing identification-based distrust difficult. One strategy is to increase the parties' calculus-based trust. Another is to openly acknowledge areas of distrust and jointly develop ways to work around those areas.
4. Ibid.
5. Ibid.
6. Ibid.

7   Jonathan Jackson et al., "Why Do People Comply with the Law? Legitimacy and the Influence of Legal Institutions," *British Journal of Criminology* (2012).
8   Tom Healy and Sylvain Côté, "The Well-Being of Nations: The Role of Human and Social Capital. Education and Skills," Organisation for Economic Cooperation and Development, 2 rue Andre Pascal, F-75775 Paris Cedex 16, France (2001).
9   Stan Gilmour, "Why We Trussed the Police: Police Governance and the Problem of Trust," *International Journal of Police Science and Management* 10, no. 1 (2008): 51–64.
10 "Trust in the Police in 16 European Countries: A Multilevel Analysis," *European Journal of Criminology* (2008): 413.
11 John Graham, Bruce Amos, and Tim Plumptre, "Principles for Good Governance in the 21st Century," Policy Brief No. 15—Institute on Governance (August, 2003).
12 Lyn Hinds, "Public Satisfaction with Police: The Influence of General Attitudes and Police-Citizen Encounters," *International Journal of Police Science & Management* 11, no. 1 (2009): 57.
13 Dennis P. Rosenbaum et al., "Attitudes towards the Police: The Effects of Direct and Vicarious Experience," *Police Quarterly* 8, no. 3 (2005): 359.
14 Michael D. Reisig and Roger B. Parks, "Experience, Quality of Life, and Neighbourhood Context: A Hierarchical Analysis of Satisfaction with Police," *Justice Quarterly* 17, no. 3 (2000): 626.
15 Stan Gilmour, "Why We Trussed the Police: Police Governance and the Problem of Trust," *International Journal of Police Science and Management* 10, no. 1 (2008): 51–64.
16 Andromachi Tseloni et al., "Exploring the International Decline in Crime Rates," *European Journal of Criminology* 7, no. 5 (2010): 375–394.
17 John William Coyne and Peter Bell, "Strategic Intelligence in Law Enforcement: A Review," *Journal of Policing, Intelligence, and Counter Terrorism* 6, no. 1 (2011): 23–39.
18 Heiner Hänggi, "Conceptualising Security Sector Reform and Reconstruction," *Reform and Reconstruction of the Security Sector* 6 (2004).
19 Herbert Wulf, "Security Sector Reform in Developing and Transitional Countries," Berghof Research Centre for Constructive Conflict Management (July 2004), available at http://www.berghof-handbook.net/documents/publications/wulf_handbookII.pdf.
20 Heiner Hänggi, "Conceptualising Security Sector Reform and Reconstruction," *Reform and Reconstruction of the Security Sector* 6 (2004).
21 Alexander Hirschfield and Kate J. Bowers, "The Effect of Social Cohesion on Levels of Recorded Crime in Disadvantaged Areas," *Urban Studies* 34, no. 8 (1997): 1275–1295.

22 Fred E. Markowitz et al., "Extending Social Disorganization Theory: Modeling the Relationships between Cohesion, Disorder, and Fear," *Criminology* 39, no. 2 (2001): 293–319.
23 Canadian Council on Social Development, *Social Cohesion in Canada: Possible Indicators*, Canadian Council on Social Development for Social Cohesion Network, Department of Canadian Heritage and Department of Justice, Ottawa (2000): 3, available at http://www.ccsd.ca/pubs/2001/si/sra-543.pdf.
24 Ibid.
25 Kelly A. Koonce, "Social Cohesion as the Goal: Can Social Cohesion Be Directly Pursued?" *Peabody Journal of Education* 86 (2011): 144–154.
26 Jonathan Jackson and Ben Bradford, "Crime, Policing and Social Order: On the Expressive Nature of Public Confidence in Policing," *The British Journal of Sociology* 60, no. 3 (2009): 496.
27 Steve Herbert, "Police Subculture Reconsidered," *Criminology* 36, no. 2 (1998): 360.
28 George L. Kelling, "'Broken Windows' and Police Discretion," National Justice Institute, US Department of Justice (October 1999): 2, available at https://www.ncjrs.gov/pdffiles1/nij/178259.pdf, accessed June 25, 2015.
29 George L. Kelling, "'Broken Windows' and Police Discretion," National Justice Institute, US Department of Justice (October 1999): 7, available at https://www.ncjrs.gov/pdffiles1/nij/178259.pdf, accessed June 25, 2015.
30 *Community* here refers to a neighborhood from which the affected parties come. While "community" may be defined in different ways, depending on the context, it is the assertion of this work that *community* should be used in broader terms than simply referring to the service community represented by the formalized institutions in a given jurisdiction.
31 A landmark decision on the legalization of abortion by the Supreme Court in the United States (Stephen Levitt).
32 Tom Geoghegan, "US Crime Figures: Why the Drop?" *BBC News*, Washington DC (2011), available at www.bbc.co.ok/news/world-us-canada-13799616, accessed October 14, 2012.

   The Obama Effect: a theory for the continuing crime decline among black Americans. In general terms, the Obama effect refers to increased aspirations and achievement among black youth attributed to the role model of President Obama.
33 Nevin Rick, "Understanding International Crime Trends: The Legacy of Preschool Lead Exposure," *Environmental Research* 104, no. 3 (2007): 315–336.
34 US Department of Justice, Uniform Crime Reports, Crime in the United States 2013, https://www.fbi.gov/about-us/cjis/ucr/crime-in-the-u.s/2013/

crime-in-the-u.s.-2013/violent-crime/violent-crime-topic-page/violentcrimemain_final, accessed June 26, 2015.

35. United Nations, *World Crime Trends and Emerging Issues and Responses in the Field of Crime Prevention and Criminal Justice*, Economic and Social Council, E/CN.15/2011/10 (January 24, 2011), available at https://www.unodc.org/pdf/criminal_justice/Secretariat Note World crime trends and emerging issues and responses in CP and CJ.pdfhttp://www.unodc.org/documents/data-and-analysis/Crime-statistics/V1180272.pdf

36. Office for National Statistics, "Statistical Bulletin: Crime in England and Wales (Year Ending September 2013)," http://www.ons.gov.uk/ons/rel/crime-stats/crime-statistics/period-ending-september-2013/stb-crime-in-england-and-wales--year-ending-sept-2013.html#tab-Summary, accessed June 26, 2015.

37. Eurostat Statistics Explained, Crime Statistics, Data from January 2014, http://ec.europa.eu/eurostat/statistics-explained/index.php/Crime_statistics#Violent_crime, accessed June 15, 2015.

38. Ibid.

39. Shannon Brennan and Mia Dauvergne, *Police-Reported Crime Statistics in Canada, 2010*, Statistics Canada, catalogue no. 85-002-X, ISSN 1209-6393 (July 21, 2010), available at http://www.statcan.gc.ca/pub/85-002-x/2011001/article/11523-eng.pdf, 12.

40. Jillian Boyce, Adam Cotter, and Samuel Perreault, Canadian Centre for Justice Statistics, "Police-Reported Crime Statistics in Canada" 34, no.1 (2014), http://www.statcan.gc.ca/access_acces/alternative_alternatif.action?l=eng&loc=/pub/85-002-x/2014001/article/14040-eng.pdf, accessed June 27, 2015.

41. Rupert Chaplin, John Flatley, and Kevin Smith, *Crime in England and Wales 2010/11, Findings from the British Crime Survey and Police Recorded Crime* (2nd Edition), Home Office Statistics Bulletin, UK, HOSB:10/11 (July 2010): 23.

42. Shannon Brennan and Mia Dauvergne, *Police-Reported Crime Statistics in Canada, 2010*, Statistics Canada, Catalogue no. 85-002-X, ISSN 1209-6393 (July 21, 2010), available at http://www.statcan.gc.ca/pub/85-002-x/2011001/article/11523-eng.pdf, 5.

43. Brent Davis and Kym Dossetor, "(Mis)perceptions of Crime in Australia," *Trends & Issues in Crime and Criminal Justice*, Australian Institute of Criminology, no. 396 (July 2010), available at http://www.aic.gov.au/media_library/publications/tandi_pdf/tandi396.pdf, 2.

44. Australian Institute of Criminology, "Australian Crime: Facts & Figures: 2013," http://www.aic.gov.au/publications/current%20series/facts/1-20/2013.html?, accessed June 26, 2015.

45 Ontario Association of Chiefs of Police, *Crime Prevention in Ontario: A Framework for Action*, available at http://www.mcscs.jus.gov.on.ca/stellent/groups/public/@mcscs/@www/@com/documents/webasset/ec157730.pdf, 40.
46 Ontario Ministry of Children and Youth Services, *Review of the Root of Youth Violence: Literature Review,* Volume 5, Chapter 4.
47 James Verini, "The Obama Effect: A Surprising New Theory for the Continuing Crime Decline among Black Americans," Slate.com, available at www.slate.com/articles/news-and-politics/crime/2011/10/the_obama_effect_a _surprising_new_theory_for_the_continuing_crime.html, accessed November 1, 2012.
48 George Gascon and Todd Foglesong, "Making Policing More Affordable: Managing Costs and Measuring Value in Policing," *New Perspectives on Policing*, Harvard Kennedy School, National Institute of Justice (2010), available at https://ncjrs.gov/pdffiles1/nij/231096.pdf, accessed June 23, 2015.
49 Ian Loader, "Policing, Recognition, and Belonging," *The Annals of the American Academy of Political and Social Science* 605, no. 1 (2006): 201–221.
50 Tom Carter et al., *"Different Groups" Perception of Panhandling in Winnipeg*, The Institute of Urban Studies, The University of Winnipeg, available at http://www.homelesshub.ca/Library/Research-Highlights-Different-Groups-Perception-of-Panhandling-in-Winnipeg-34887.aspx, accessed November 2, 2012.
51 Rupert Chaplin, John Flatley, and Kevin Smith, *Crime in England and Wales 2010/11, Findings from the British Crime Survey and Police Recorded Crime* (2nd Edition), Home Office Statistics Bulletin, UK (July 2010), HOSB:10/11, 21.
52 Statistics Canada, "Juristat-Family Violence in Canada: A Statistical Profile, 2010," Catalogue no. 85-002-X (2010), available at http://www.statcan.gc.ca/pub/85-002-x/2012001/article/11643-eng.pdf, 70.
53 Research Report, *Bill C-46: Records Applications Post-Mills, A Case Law Review,* Department of Justice, Canada, 2004, 14.
54 Susan McDonald, Andrea Wobick, and Janet Graham, Research Report, *Bill C-46: Records Applications Post-Mills, A Case Law Review*, Department of Justice, Canada, 2004 (2006), 14.
55 Julie Travers, "Global Focus-Sexual Assault Rape," *Globe and Mail*, October 5, 2013.
56 Comment on domestic abuse in certain ethnic/immigrant communities.
57 Julie Travers, "Global Focus-Sexual Assault Rape," *Globe and Mail*, October 5, 2013.
58 Allan Travis, ed., "Significant Proportion of Children Distrust Police, Inquiry Finds, All-Party Parliamentary Report Says that Many under-18s Have Negative Experience of Police," *Guardian*, October 28, 2014, http://www.theguardian.com/uk-news/2014/oct/28/significant-proportion-children-distrust-police-inquiry-all-party-parliamentary-report.

59 Jennifer Fratello, Andrés F. Rengifo, and Jennifer Trone, "Coming of Age with Stop and Frisk: Experiences, Self-Perceptions, and Public Safety Implications" (New York, NY: Vera Institute of Justice, 2013).
60 James E. Larsen and John P. Blair, "The Importance of Police Performance as a Determinant of Satisfaction with Police," *American Journal of Economics and Business Administration* 1, no. 1 (2009): 1–10.
61 Uniform Crime Reporting Survey (UCR), Statistics Canada, http://www.23.statcan.gc.ca/imdb/p2SV.pl?Function=getSurvey&SSDS=3302&itemId=1044&lang=en#a2, accessed February 28, 2013.
62 Daily Maverick, "SA Crime Statistics May Obscure More than They Reveal," September 12, 2013, http://www.dailymaverick.co.za/article/2013-09-12-sa-crime-statistics-may-obscure-more-than-they-reveal/#.VY8l9GA5N5h, accessed June 27, 2015.
63 Lisa Vetten, "Rape and Other Forms of Violence in South Africa," Institute for Security Studies, Policy Brief 72 (2014), http://www.issafrica.org/uploads/PolBrief72.pdf, accessed June 27, 2015.
64 Lorie A. Fridell and Mary Ann Wycoff, eds., "Community Policing: The Past, Present, and Future," Annie E. Casey Foundation and Police Executive Research Forum (2004), 122.
65 Lorie A. Fridell and Mary Ann Wycoff, eds., "Community Policing: The Past, Present, and Future," Annie E. Casey Foundation and Police Executive Research Forum, 2004.
66 United Nations. "Public Security in the Americas: Challenges and Opportunities," General Secretariat Organization of American States, 2nd Edition (December 2008), 73.
67 John Kleining, "The Ethical Perils of Knowledge Acquisition," *Criminal Justice Ethics* 28, no. 2 (2009): 201–222.
68 Egon Bittner, "Florence Nightingale in Pursuit of Willie Sutton: A Theory of the Police," *The Potential for Reform of Criminal Justice* 3 (1974): 233–68.
69 Police Reform, *A Police Service for the Twenty-First Century* (White Paper), Secretary of State for the Home Department, London (1993), 4.
70 Jonathan Jackson and Ben Bradford, "Crime, Policing and Social Order: On the Expressive Nature of Public Confidence in Policing," *The British Journal of Sociology* 60, no. 3 (2009): 493–521, 497.
71 Robert Reiner, "Let's Admit It: Most Police Work Does Not Involve Catching Criminals," *Guardian*, October 28, 2011, available at hhtp://www.guardian.co.uk/uk/2011/oct/28/admit-police-work-catching-criminals, accessed November 2, 2012.
72 Andy Neely, *Measuring Business Performance: Why, What, and How* (London: The Economist Books, 1998); Monica Franco-Santos, Mike Kennerley, Pietro Micheli, Veronica Martinez, Steve Mason, Bernard Marr, Dina Gray, and Andrew Neely, "Towards a Definition of a Business

Performance Measurement System," *International Journal of Operations & Production Management* 27, no. 8 (2007): 784–801.

73 Susan S. Westin, *Performance Measurement and Evaluation: Definitions and Relationships*, GAO/GGD-98-26 (Washington DC: US Government Printing Office, 1998), available at http://www.gao.gov/special.pubs/gg98026.pdf, accessed August 23, 2015.

74 Annette Binnendijk, "Results Based Management in the Development Cooperation Agencies: A Review of Experience," *Background Report* (2000), available at http://www.oecd.org/development/evaluation/1886527.pdf, accessed August 23, 2015.

75 David Norton and Robert Kaplan, "Putting the Balanced Scorecard to Work," *Harvard Business Review* 71, no. 5 (1993): 134–140.

76 Robert Simons, "Control in an Age of Empowerment," *Harvard Business Review* 73, no. 2 (March 1995), 80–88.

77 Jeffrey S. Magers, "CompStat: A New Paradigm for Policing or a Repudiation of Community Policing?," *Journal of Contemporary Criminal Justice* 20, no. 1 (2004): 70–79.

78 Al Baker and William K. Rashbaum, "New York City to Examine Reliability of Its Crime Reports," *New York Times*, January 5, 2011 (2012), available at www.nytimes.com/2011/01/06/nyregion/06crime.html?pagewanted=all, accessed November 1, 2012.

79 James J. Willis, David Weisburd and Stephen D. Mastrofski, *CompStat in Practice: An In-Depth Analysis of Three Cities* (2003), available at http://www.policefoundation.org/sites/g/files/g798246/f/Willis%20et%20al.%20%282004%29%20-%20CompStat%20in%20Practice.pdf.

80 James J. Willis and Stephen D. Mastrofski, "CompStat and the New Penology: A Paradigm Shift in Policing?," *British Journal of Criminology* 52, no. 1 (2012): 73–92.

81 Hyunseok Jang, Larry T. Hoover, and Joo Hee-Jong, "An Evaluation of CompStat's Effect on Crime: The Fort Worth Experience," *Police Quarterly* 13, no.4, 387–412.

The study notes: "Despite CompStat's popularity, little empirical research has scientifically evaluated the effectiveness of the CompStat strategy. A number of the reviews of CompStat in New York City have been in the form of 'advocacy' books which assume effectiveness. A majority of the existing research has been anecdotal and qualitative, thus lacking generalizability. In addition, a few studies that measured the effectiveness of CompStat in New York City found conflicting results concerning the causal relationship between the CompStat strategy and the decline in crime rates. It is also important to recognize the potential role of other social structural variables in the reduction of crime rates in New York. Fagan, Zimring, and Kim (1998) reported that no firearm homicides began to decline in New York City prior to the implementation of the CompStat strategy."

82   Andy Neely and Mohammed Al Najjar, *Management Learning Not Management Control: The True Role of Performance Management*, University of California, Berkeley 48, no.3. (2003).

83   Moments of truth include service contact and experience opportunities: ticket purchase, check-in service, departure, aircraft condition, in-flight service, meal rating, baggage claim, and executive club membership.

84   Ontario Association of Chiefs of Police, *Crime Prevention in Ontario: A Framework for Action*, available at: http://www.mcscs.jus.gov.on.ca/stellent/groups/public/@mcscs/@www/@com/documents/webasset/ec157730.pdf, 9.

85   Richard V. Ericson, "The Police as Reproducers of Order," *T. Newburn, Policing. Key Readings. Cullompton: Willan* (1982), 215.

86   *Police Reform, A Police Service for the Twenty-First Century* (White Paper), Secretary of State for the Home Department, London (1993), 4.

87   Richard V. Ericson, "The Police as Reproducers of Order," *T. Newburn, Policing. Key Readings. Cullompton: Willan* (1982), 215.

88   James J. Willis, David Weisburd, and Stephen D. Mastrofski, *CompStat in Practice: An In-Depth Analysis of Three Cities* (2003), available at http://www.policefoundation.org/sites/g/files/g798246/f/Willis%20et%20al.%20%282004%29%20-%20CompStat%20in%20Practice.pdf, 18.

89   Richard V. Ericson, "The Police as Reproducers of Order," *T. Newburn, Policing. Key Readings. Cullompton: Willan* (1982), 235.

90   Robert Simons, "Control in an Age of Empowerment," *Harvard Business Review* 73, no. 2 (March 1995), 80–88.

91   Roy J. Lewicki and Carolyn Wiethoff, "Trust, Trust Development, and Trust Repair," in Morton Deutsch and Peter T. Coleman, eds., *The Handbook of Conflict Resolution: Theory and Practice* (San Francisco: Jossey-Bas Publishers, 2000): 86–107.

The authors define trust as "an individual's belief in, and willingness to act on the basis of, the words, actions, and decisions of another." Roy Lewicki and Carolyn Wiethoff note that distrust is not merely the absence of trust but is an active negative expectation regarding another. They identify two bases for trust (or distrust). Calculus-based trust rests on assessments of costs and rewards for violating or sustaining trust and is more typical of professional relationships. Identification-based trust rests on the parties' mutual understanding and affinity and is more typical of personal relationships, such as friendship. Identification-based trust can be fostered if the parties take time to develop their common interests, values, perceptions, motives, and goals. Identification-based trust has a strong emotional component and so is sensitive to a number of nonlogical factors. This makes managing identification-based distrust difficult. One strategy is to increase the parties' calculus-based trust. Another is to openly acknowledge areas of distrust and jointly develop ways to work around those areas.

92 Amadeu Recasens, "The Control of Police Powers," *European Journal on Criminal Policy and Research* 8, no. 3 (2000): 247–269 (page 253).

93 *Police Reform, A Police Service for the Twenty-First Century* (White Paper), Secretary of State for the Home Department, London (1993) 1–2, available at http://www.official-documents.gov.uk/document/cm22/2281/2281.pdf.

94 Yvonne Marie Daly, "Judicial Oversight of Policing: Investigations, Evidence, and the Exclusionary Rule," *Crime, Law and Social Change* 55, no. 2–3 (2011): 199–215 (page 199).

95 Richard V. Ericson, "The Police as Reproducers of Order," *T. Newburn, Policing. Key Readings. Cullompton: Willan* (1982), 231–233.

96 Ibid., 232, 235.

97 Rupert F. Chisholm, "Quality of Working Life: Critical Issue for the 80s," *Public Productivity Review* (1983): 10–25 (page 23).

98 Sune Laegaard, "Immigration, Social Cohesion, and Naturalization," *Ethnicities* 10, no. 4 (2010): 452–469.

99 Edwin Harari, "Whose Evidence? Lessons from the Philosophy of Science and the Epistemology of Medicine," *Australian and New Zealand Journal of Psychiatry* 35, no. 6 (2001): 724–730 (page 35).

100 Robert Simons, "Control in an Age of Empowerment," *Harvard Business Review* 73, no. 2 (March 1995), 80–88.

101 Peter T. Coleman and Morton Deutsch, "Some Guidelines for Developing a Creative Approach to Conflict," *The Handbook of Conflict Resolution* (San Francisco: Jossey-Bass Publishers, 2000): 355–365.

102 Robert Simons, "Control in an Age of Empowerment," *Harvard Business Review* 73, no. 2 (March 1995): 80–88.

103 Ibid.

104 George L. Kelling, "'Broken Windows' and Police Discretion," National Justice Institute, US Department of Justice (October 1999), 2, available at https://www.ncjrs.gov/pdffiles1/nij/178259.pdf, accessed June 25, 2015.

105 David Cox, "Educating Police for Uncertain Times: The Australian Experience and Case for 'Normative' Approach," *Journal of Police Intelligence and Counter Terrorism* 6, no. 1 (April 2011): 3–22.

106 Richard V. Ericson, "The Police as Reproducers of Order," *T. Newburn, Policing. Key Readings. Cullompton: Willan* (1982).

107 Egon Bittner, "Florence Nightingale in Pursuit of Willie Sutton: A Theory of the Police," *The Potential for Reform of Criminal Justice* 3 (1974): 233–68.

108 Famega, Christine N., James Frank, and Lorraine Mazerolle. "Managing Police Patrol Time: The Role of Supervisor Directives." *Justice Quarterly* 22, no. 4 (2005).

109 Egon Bittner, "Florence Nightingale in Pursuit of Willie Sutton: A Theory of the Police," *The Potential for Reform of Criminal Justice* 3 (1974): 233–68.
110 Robert Simons, "Control in an Age of Empowerment," *Harvard Business Review* 73, no. 2 (March 1995): 80–88.
111 Ibid.
112 Ibid.
113 John P. Kotter, "Leading Change: Why Transformation Efforts Fail," *Harvard Business Review* (2007): 92–107.
114 Jeffrey Pfeffer and Robert I. Sutton, *The Knowing-Doing Gap: How Smart Companies Turn Knowledge into Action*, Harvard Business Press, 2013.
115 Ibid.
116 Robert Simons, "Control in an Age of Empowerment," *Harvard Business Review* 73, no. 2 (March 1995): 80–88.
117 Ibid.
118 Gwyneth V.J. Howell and Rohan Mille, "Maple Leaf Foods: Crisis and Containment Case Study," *Public Communication Review* 1, no. 1 (2010): 47–56.
119 "Boston Police Accept 'Full Responsibility' in Death of Red Sox Fan," cnn.com, October 22, 2004, www.cnn.com/2004/us/10/22/fan.death/.
120 Jennifer Frahm and Kerry Brown, "First Steps: Linking Change Communication to Change Receptivity," *Journal of Organizational Change Management* 20, no. 3 (2007): 370–387.
121 CBC News, "Police Chief Bill Blair on the Rob Ford Video," October 31, 2013, available at http://www.cbc.ca/news/canada/toronto/police-chief-bill-blair-on-the-rob-ford-video-1.2303505, accessed November 28, 2013.
122 Conrad Black, "Conrad Black: The Salvation of Rob Ford," *National Post*, November 13, 2013, available at http://fullcomment.nationalpost.com/2013/11/23/conrad-black-salvation-of-rob-ford/, accessed November 28, 2013.
123 Robert Simons, "Control in an Age of Empowerment," *Harvard Business Review* 73, no. 2 (March 1995): 80–88.
124 Ibid.
125 Roger Martin, *The Opposable Mind* (Boston: Harvard Business School Press, 2007): 20–29.
126 Ibid.
127 J. Kruger, "The Tapestry of Culture: A Design for the Assessment of Intercultural Disputes," *Dispute Resolution Readings and Case Studies*, 738.
   Identifying who the stakeholders are and what role they should play in the resolution of conflict is often a difficult task. It is sometimes suggested that a good benchmark for determining stakeholders is to pose the question: "Does this (individual, group) need to be part of creating a solution because they can otherwise thwart its intent or derail it?" Deciding who should have

a seat at the table and in what authentic representative capacity is a complex challenge for anyone committed to client-centered design.

128 James J. Willis, David Weisburd, and Stephen D. Mastrofski, *CompStat in Practice: An In-Depth Analysis of Three Cities* (2003), available at http://www.policefoundation.org/sites/g/files/g798246/f/Willis%20et%20al.%20%282004%29%20-%20CompStat%20in%20Practice.pdf, 19.

129 United Nations, "World Crime Trends and Emerging Issues and Responses in the Field of Crime Prevention and Criminal Justice," *Economic and Social Council* (January 24, 2011), 14.

130 Rupert F. Chisholm, "Quality of Working Life: Critical Issue for the 80s," *Public Productivity Review* (1983): 10–25 (page 23).

    For clarity, it should be noted that this report, on page 23 (Conclusion A Paragraph 45), also concludes: "As demonstrated by victimization surveys, addressing crime and violence in all its manifestations in Africa requires the development of just, accountable and effective law enforcement and criminal justice institutions. Although persons may express confidence in police services, in practice, both violent and property crime is reported to the police in only about one third of cases in countries surveyed in Africa. Building public trust in the criminal justice system through strengthened capacity and integrity is crucial to effective crime prevention and sustainable security and development."

131 Isabelle Royer, "Why Bad Projects Are So Hard to Kill," *Harvard Business Review* 81, no. 2 (2003): 48–57.

132 Roger Martin, *The Opposable Mind* (Boston: Harvard Business School Press, 2007): 20–29.

133 Robert J. Joustra, "The Tenth Man," The Center for Public Justice (November 1, 2013), http://www.capitalcommentary.org/israel/tenth-man.

134 James J. Willis and Stephen D. Mastrofski, "CompStat and the New Penology: A Paradigm Shift in Policing?," *British Journal of Criminology* 52, no. 1 (2012): 73–92.

135 Ibid.

136 Maureen Brosnahan, "Canada's Prison Population at All-Time High," CBC News online, posted November 25, 2013, 9:20 p.m., available at http://www.cbc.ca/news/canada-s-prison-population-at-all-time-high-1.2440039, accessed November 26, 2013.

137 Mark S. Umbreit, "Restorative Justice through Victim-Offender Mediation: A Multi-Site Assessment," *Western Criminology Review* 1, no.1 (1998): 1–29.

138 Eugene A. Pasoline, Stephanie M. Myers, and Robert E. Worden, "Police Culture, Individualism, and Community Policing: Evidence from Two Police Departments," *Justice Quarterly* 17, no. 3 (2000): 575–605. In a more recent article, Martin Innes, in "Why 'Soft' Policing Is Hard: On the Curious Development of Reassurance Policing, How It Became Neighbourhood

Policing and What This Signifies about the Politics of Police Reform" (*Journal of Community & Applied Social Psychology* 15 (2005): 156–169) also notes: "And yet, despite the manifest benefits that flow from effective soft policing, research shows that trying to introduce a style of policing that promotes soft policing and in the process challenges the cultural sustained orthodoxy of what constitutes 'real' police work in the eyes of 'street cops' tends to result in significant tension and oftentimes implementation failure (Irving et al., 1989)."

139 Joseph A. Schafer, "'I'm Not Against It in Theory …': Global and Specific Community Policing Attitudes," *Policing: An International Journal of Police Strategies & Management* 25, no. 4 (2002): 669–686. Notes: "The police were primarily oriented towards controlling crime; they viewed themselves as experts on crime and sought to limit the information they shared with the public. Police organizations were quasi-military bureaucracies which sought to restrict the freedom and discretion of front line employees. Supervisors and subordinates had 'command and obey' relationships; the relationship between front line employees and department leaders was characterized by a high degree of tension."

140 Bonnie Bacqueroux, "Community Criminal Justice: What Community Policing Teaches," http://www.policing.com/articles/ccj.html, accessed June 24, 2015.

141 Albert Cardarelli, Jack McDevitt, and Katrina Baum, "The Rhetoric and Reality of Community Policing in Small and Medium-Sized Cities and Towns," *Policing: An International Journal of Police Strategies & Management* 21, no. 3(1998): 397–415.

As a case in point, a survey of 170 police departments in the United States, conducted by Albert Cardarelli (1998), found that there were a variety of interpretations for community policing. This diversity has, however, been suggestive of a healthy application of subjective criteria in the interpretation and design of community programs, and despite the variety of characterizations, it is possible to identify some common elements in providing a more comprehensive picture of what community policing entails.

142 Raymond Shonholtz, "Neighbourhood Justice Systems," 420–427, in Julie Macfarlane, *Dispute Resolution: Readings and Case Studies* (Emond Montgomery Publication, 2003).

143 Ibid.

144 Lorie A. Fridell and Mary Ann Wycoff, eds., "Community Policing: The Past, Present, and Future," Annie E. Casey Foundation and Police Executive Research Forum (2004).

145 John William Coyne and Peter Bell, "Strategic Intelligence in Law Enforcement: A Review," *Journal of Policing, Intelligence, and Counter Terrorism* 6, no. 1 (2011): 23–39.

146 Ibid., 25.
147 *Intelligence-Led Policing: The New Intelligence Architecture*, US Department of Justice, Office of Justice Assistance (2005), 9.
148 Global Justice Information Sharing Initiative, "Fusion Centre Guidelines—Developing and Sharing Information in a New Era," United States Department of Justice, Washington DC (2006).
149 John William Coyne and Peter Bell, "Strategic Intelligence in Law Enforcement: A Review," *Journal of Policing, Intelligence, and Counter Terrorism* 6, no. 1 (April 2011): 23–39 (page 27).
150 Ibid., 31.
151 Marilyn Peterson, *Intelligence-Led Policing: The New Intelligence Architecture*, US Department of Justice, Office of Justice Programs (2005), 19.
152 Ibid., 12.
153 Ibid.
154 John William Coyne and Peter Bell, "Strategic Intelligence in Law Enforcement: A Review," *Journal of Policing, Intelligence, and Counter Terrorism* 6, no. 1 (April 2011): 23–39 (page 25).
155 Marilyn Peterson, *Intelligence-Led Policing: The New Intelligence Architecture*, US Department of Justice, Office of Justice Programs (2005), 12.
156 Jeffrey S. Magers, "CompStat: A New Paradigm for Policing or a Repudiation of Community Policing?," *Journal of Contemporary Criminal Justice* 20, no. 1 (2004): 70–79 (page 77).
157 Jonathan Jackson and Ben Bradford, "Crime, Policing and Social Order: On the Expressive Nature of Public Confidence in Policing," *The British Journal of Sociology* 60, no. 3 (2009): 493–521 (page 496).
158 Steve Herbert, "Police Subculture Reconsidered," *Criminology* 36, no. 2 (1998): 343–370 (page 360).
159 Roger Bohn, "Stop Fighting Fires," *Harvard Business Review*, 179.
160 John William Coyne and Peter Bell, "Strategic Intelligence in Law Enforcement: A Review," *Journal of Policing, Intelligence, and Counter Terrorism* 6, no. 1 (2011): 23–39 (page 24).
161 *Intelligence-Led Policing: The New Intelligence Architecture*, US Department of Justice, Office of Justice Assistance (2005), xvi.
162 Sharon Pickering, Jude McCulloch, and David Wright-Neville, "Counter-terrorism Policing: Towards Social Cohesion," *Crime, Law and Social Change* 50, no. 1–2 (2008): 91–109.
163 John Kleining, "The Ethical Perils of Knowledge Acquisition," *Criminal Justice Ethics* 28, no. 2 (2009): 201–222.
164 *Economist*, "Government Surveillance," July, 2012, http://www.economist.com/blogs/democracyinamerica/2012/07/government-surveillance, accessed August 7, 2015.

165 Kenneth J. Novak, Leanne Fiftal Alarid, and Wayne L. Lucas, "Exploring Officers' Acceptance of Community Policing: Implications for Policy Implementation," *Journal of Criminal Justice* 31, no. 1 (2003): 57–71 (page 57).

166 Simon Mackenzie and Alistair Henry, *Community Policing: A Review of the Evidence*, Scottish Government (2009), 6.

167 Joseph A. Schafer, Beth M. Huebner, and Timothy S. Bynum, "Citizen Perceptions of Police Services: Race, Neighborhood Context, and Community Policing," *Police Quarterly* 6, no. 4 (2003): 440–468 (page 461).

168 Albert Cardarelli, Jack McDevitt, and Katrina Baum, "The Rhetoric and Reality of Community Policing in Small and Medium-Sized Cities and Towns," *Policing: An International Journal of Police Strategies & Management* 21, no. 3 (1998), 397–415.

As a case in point, a survey of 170 police departments in the United States, conducted by Albert Cardarelli (1998), found that there were a variety of interpretations for community policing. This diversity has, however, been suggestive of a healthy application of subjective criteria in the interpretation and design of community programs, and despite the variety of characterizations, it is possible to identify some common elements in providing a more comprehensive picture of what community policing entails.

169 Martin Innes and Colin Roberts, "Community Intelligence in the Policing of Community Safety," *Community Safety: Innovation and Evaluation* (2007): 183 (page 3).

170 Law Commission of Canada, "Transforming Relationships through Participatory Justice" (2003), xiii, available at http://www.lcc.gc.ca/about/transform_toc-en.asp.

171 Jeff Latimer, Craig Dowden, and Danielle Muise, "The Effectiveness of Restorative Justice Practices: A Meta-Analysis," *The Prison Journal* 85, no. 2 (2005): 127–144 (page 127).

172 Ibid., page 127–139.

173 Brandon Welsh and David Farrington, "Evidence-Based Crime Prevention: Conclusions and Directions for a Safer Society," *Canadian Journal of Criminology and Criminal Justice* 47, no. 2 (2005): 337–354.

174 John Braithwaite, "Restorative Justice and Social Justice," *Saskatchewan Law Review* 63 (2000): 185.

175 Criminal Code of Canada, Part XXIII Sentencing, Purpose and Principles of Sentencing.

176 Law Commission of Canada, "Transforming Relationships through Participatory Justice" (2003), xii, available at http://www.lcc.gc.ca/about/transform_toc-en.asp.

177 Mark Umberti, "Mediation of Victim Offender Conflict," *Journal of Dispute Resolution* 84 (1987, 1988), 102, and 103–105, in Julie Macfarlane, *Dispute*

Resolution: Readings and Case Studies (Emond Montgomery Publication, 2003): 427–433.

178 Brandon Welsh and David Farrington, "Evidence-Based Crime Prevention: Conclusions and Directions for a Safer Society," *Canadian Journal of Criminology and Criminal Justice* 47, no. 2 (2005): 337–354.

179 Mark S. Umbreit, "Restorative Justice through Victim-Offender Mediation: A Multi-Site Assessment," *Western Criminology Review* 1, no. 1 (1998): 1–29.

180 Ibid., 2.

181 Joan Petersilia, Elizabeth Piper, and Deschenes Rand, "Perceptions of Punishment: Inmates and Staff Rank the Severity of Prison Versus Intermediate Sanctions," *The Prison Journal* 74, no. 3 (1994): 306–328.

182 Ben M. Crouch, "Is Incarceration Really Worse? Analysis of Offenders' Preferences for Prison over Probation," *Justice Quarterly* 10, no. 1 (1993): 67–88 (page 68).

183 Ibid., 79.

184 Joan Petersilia, Elizabeth Piper, and Deschenes Rand, "Perceptions of Punishment: Inmates and Staff Rank the Severity of Prison Versus Intermediate Sanctions," *The Prison Journal* 74, no. 3 (1994): 309.

185 Ibid., 310.

186 Craig Dowden and D. A. Andrews, "The Importance of Staff Practice in Delivering Effective Correctional Treatment: A Meta-Analytic Review of Core Correctional Practice," *International Journal of Offender Therapy and Comparative Criminology* 48, no. 2 (2004): 203–214 (pages 204–207).

187 Gilbert Taylor, "The Importance of Developing Correctional Plans for Offenders," in Forum on Corrections Research 13, no. 1 (2001): 14–17, Correctional Services of Canada (2001), http://www.csc-scc.gc.ca/research/forum/e131/131e_e.pdf, accessed July 18, 2015.

188 Craig Dowden and D.A. Andrews, "The Importance of Staff Practice in Delivering Effective Correctional Treatment: A Meta-Analytic Review of Core Correctional Practice," *International Journal of Offender Therapy and Comparative Criminology* 48, no. 2 (2004): 203–214 (pages 204–207).

189 Ibid.

190 Ibid.

191 Jo-Anne Wemmers and Katie Cyr, "Can Mediation Be Therapeutic for Crime Victims? An Evaluation of Victims' Experiences in Mediation with Young Offenders," *Canadian Journal of Criminology and Criminal Justice* 47, no. 3 (2005): 527–544 (page 529).

192 Supreme Court of Canada. R v. Askov [1990] 2 S.C.R. 1199.

193 Operation Spring Board, Community Benefits from Cannabis Diversion Program, www.operationspringboard.on.ca.

194 Peter Harris et al., "'Working in the Trenches' with the YCJA," *Canadian Journal of Criminology and Criminal Justice* 46, no. 3 (2004): 367–390 (page 370).
195 Nancy Marion, "Effectiveness of Community Based Correctional Programs: A Case Study," *The Prison Journal* 82, no. 4 (2002): 478–497 (page 493).
196 Joan Petersilia, Elizabeth Piper, and Deschenes Rand, "Perceptions of Punishment: Inmates and Staff Rank the Severity of Prison Versus Intermediate Sanctions," *The Prison Journal* 74, no. 3 (1994): 309–310.
197 Mark S. Umbreit, "Restorative Justice through Victim-Offender Mediation: A Multi-Site Assessment," *Western Criminology Review* 1, no. 1 (1998): 1–29.
198 Jo-Anne Wemmers and Katie Cyr, "Can Mediation Be Therapeutic for Crime Victims? An Evaluation of Victims' Experiences in Mediation with Young Offenders," *Canadian Journal of Criminology and Criminal Justice* 47, no. 3 (2005): 527–544 (page 528).
199 Raymond Shonholtz, "Neighbourhood Justice Systems," *Dispute Resolution: Readings and Case Studies*, 420–427.
200 Darlene James and Sawka Ed, "Drug Treatment Courts," *Substance Abuse Intervention within the Justice System*, Alberta Alcohol and Drug Abuse Commission, Canadian Centre on Substance Abuse National Working Group on Addictions Policy (November 2000), www.ccsa.ca/pdf/ccsa-008697-2000.pdf.

Although these types of programs may be considered community justice programs, viewed from the perspective of police involvement (personnel), police policies, and resource expenditure, they are inclusive of a larger community policing function. This category of programs is exemplified by the types of initiatives represented by the Toronto Drug Treatment Court (TDTC) and the postcharge diversion-sentencing program in Toronto. TDTC, for instance, operates as a collaborative venture between the Center for Addiction and Mental Health, the criminal justice system, the Toronto Police Service, and the City of Toronto Public Health Department.

A noted goal of the TDTC includes demonstrating the cost-effectiveness of judicially supervised treatment as an alternative to incarceration.
201 Richard V. Ericson, "The Police as Reproducers of Order," *T. Newburn, Policing. Key Readings. Cullompton: Willan* (1982), 215.
202 According to Census Canada, 73 percent of the population in 1951 claimed their origins as British, whereas in 2001, only 12 percent reported their origins as British. By 2001, diversity within Canada had enlarged to include those with Southern European origins to 19 percent, East and Southeast Asian origins to 18 percent, South Asian origins to 13 percent, and Eastern European origins to 6 percent. Similarly, in 1951, only 85 FNP were recorded as residing in Toronto. By 1961, that number had grown to 1,196 and then to over 20,000 by 1971. Today, there are over 100,000 FNP in the Metropolitan Toronto area, including status and nonstatus Indian, Metis, and Inuit. Furthermore,

2001 data indicates that 44 percent of Toronto's population was born outside Canada and that one in five people living in Toronto have been in the country for less than ten years. Significantly, the proportion of newcomers to Toronto unable to speak either English or French increased from 38.0 percent in 1997 to 46.8 percent in 2001.

This diversity is not unique to Toronto, and these numbers emphasize the evolution of large metropolitan centers like Toronto as being richly multicultural. This increasing diversity is reflective of globalization and repeated in major metropolitan centers across North America and Europe. Oakland, California, for instance, according to a census conducted in 2000, indicated that its population was 34.7 percent Caucasian, 37.6 percent African American, 17.4 percent Asia Pacific Islander, and 14.1 percent American Indian and Alaskan Native. This survey also indicated that 43.1 percent of the youth between the ages of 5 and 17 consisted of African American, 27.5 percent Hispanic, 26.3 percent Caucasian, 15.3 percent Asian, 1.2 percent Pacific Islander, 1.9 percent Native American, and 18 percent other (Lai 2005). Similarly, according to a 2001 census, 26 percent of persons born in Australia had at least one immigrant parent.

203 Paul Dicks, Marie Vallentova, and Monique Borsenberger, "A Multidimensional Assessment of Social Cohesion in 47 European Countries," *CEPS/INSTEAD Working Papers* 2011-07 (2011); also Jane Jenson, "Mapping Social Cohesion: The State of Canadian Research," Canadian Policy Research Networks Inc. (1998).

204 Kelly A. Koonce, "Social Cohesion as the Goal: Can Social Cohesion Be Directly Pursued?," *Peabody Journal of Education* 86 (2011): 144–154.

205 Jane Jenson, "Mapping Social Cohesion: The State of Canadian Research," Canadian Policy Research Networks Inc. (1998), v.

206 Office for National Statistics, "Personal Well-Being across the UK, 2012/13," http://www.ons.gov.uk/ons/dcp171778_328486.pdf.

207 Joseph E. Stiglitz, Amartya Sen, and Jean-Paul Fitoussi, "The Measurement of Economic Performance and Social Progress Revisited," *Reflections and Overview: Commission on the Measurement of Economic Performance and Social Progress, Paris* (2009): 41.

208 Gerard Murphy, Shannon McFadden, and Molly Griswold, "Police and Immigration: How Chiefs Are Leading Their Communities through the Challenges," Police Executive Research Forum (2010), 6.

209 Ian Loader, "Policing, Recognition, and Belonging," *The Annals of the American Academy of Political and Social Science* 605, no. 1 (2006): 201–221.

210 Kelly A. Koonce, "Social Cohesion as the Goal: Can Social Cohesion Be Directly Pursued?," *Peabody Journal of Education* 86, no. 2 (2011): 144–154.

211 Gerard Murphy, Shannon McFadden, and Molly Griswold, "Police and Immigration: How Chiefs Are Leading Their Communities through the Challenges," Police Executive Research Forum (2010), iii.
212 Ibid., 4.
213 Alexander Hirschfield and Kate J. Bowers, "The Effect of Social Cohesion on Levels of Recorded Crime in Disadvantaged Areas," *Urban Studies* 34, no. 8 (1997): 1275–1295.
214 Paul Dicks, Marie Vallentova, and Monique Borsenberger, "A Multidimensional Assessment of Social Cohesion in 47 European Countries," *CEPS/INSTEAD Working Papers* 2011-07 (2011).
215 Paul Dicks, Marie Vallentova, and Monique Borsenberger, "A Multidimensional Assessment of Social Cohesion in 47 European Countries," *CEPS/INSTEAD Working Papers* 2011-07 (2011).
216 Paul Dicks, Marie Vallentova, and Monique Borsenberger, "A Multidimensional Assessment of Social Cohesion in 47 European Countries," *CEPS/INSTEAD Working Papers* 2011-07 (2011); also Jane Jenson, "Mapping Social Cohesion: The State of Canadian Research," Canadian Policy Research Networks Inc. (1998).
217 Jane Jenson, "Mapping Social Cohesion: The State of Canadian Research," Canadian Policy Research Networks Inc. (1998).
218 Andrew G., Jackson, G. Fawcett, A. Milan, P. Roberts, S. Schetagne, K. Scott, and S. Tsoukalas, "Social Cohesion in Canada: Possible Indicators," Ottawa: Canadian Council on Social Development (2000), 3.
219 "Extending Social Disorganization Theory: Modeling the Relationships between Cohesion, Disorder, and Fear," *Criminology* 39, no. 2 (2001), 293.
220 Steve Herbert, "Police Subculture Reconsidered," *Criminology* 36, no. 2 (1998): 343–370 (page 360).
221 Mathieu Charron, "Neighbourhood Characteristics and the Distribution of Crime in Toronto: Additional Analysis on Youth Crime," Canadian Centre for Justice Statistics, Catalogue no. 85-561-M, no. 22, December 2011, http://www.statcan.gc.ca/pub/85-561-m/2011022/part-partie1-eng.htm#h2_1.
222 Kelly A. Koonce, "Social Cohesion as the Goal: Can Social Cohesion Be Directly Pursued?," *Peabody Journal of Education* 86, no. 2 (2011): 144–154.
223 Ibid.
224 Sarah Botterman, Marc Hooghe, and Tim Reeskens, "'One Size Fits All'? An Empirical Study into the Multidimensionality of Social Cohesion Indicators in Belgian Local Communities," *Urban Studies* 49, no. 1 (2012): 185–202.
225 Gerard Murphy, Shannon McFadden, and Molly Griswold, "Police and Immigration: How Chiefs Are Leading Their Communities through the Challenges," Police Executive Research Forum (2010).

226 Raymond Shonholtz, "Constructive Response to Conflict in Emerging Democracies: Distinguishing between Conflict and Dispute," http://www.partnersglobal.org/resources/article8.html.

Shonholtz writes: "In the pre-democratic period, issues became conflicts when they were managed through forms of repression, violence, avoidance, or ideology. Issues become disputes when they are managed through transparent rule of law systems. The difference is that the latter system is designed to resolve differences peacefully, while the former system is designed to manipulate or suppress them at all costs."

227 John Bollard and Deborah McCallum, "Neighboring and Community Mobilization in High-Poverty Inner-City Neighborhoods," *Urban Affairs Review* 38, no. 1 (September 2002): 42–69.

228 Dominique Wisler and Ihekwoaba D. Onwudiwe, "Community Policing: A Comparative View" 1, *IPES Working Paper* 6 (2007), www.IPES.info.

229 Dominique Wisler and Ihekwoaba D. Onwudiwe, "Community Policing: A Comparative View" 1, *IPES Working Paper* 6 (2007), www.IPES.info.

230 John Braithwaite, *Crime, Shame and Reintegration* (Cambridge University Press, 1989).

231 Joel B. Plant and Michael S. Scott, *Effective Policing and Crime Prevention: A Problem-Oriented Guide for Mayors, City Managers, and County Executives*, US Department of Justice, Office of Community Oriented Policing Services (2009), 13.

232 Jane Jenson, "Mapping Social Cohesion: The State of Canadian Research," Canadian Policy Research Networks Inc. (1998).

233 Bonnie Bacqueroux, "Community Criminal Justice: What Community Policing Teaches," *On Restorative Justice* online, http://www.restorativejustice.org/articlesdb/articles/257, accessed June 25, 2015.

The health of a community to engage in collaborative practices is dependent on opportunity and capability and according to Public Safety Canada can be summarized to include the following:

human capital—the skills, knowledge, attitudes, and understanding of people who are part of the community, which may include those who are resident and nonresident

social capital—the breadth and depth of social relationships and the extent to which these are integrated within the community and can be used to promote collective identity, common values, trust, and participation

spiritual/cultural capital—includes values, symbols, rituals, traditions, art, and language that are used to promote identity and common visions

234 John Braithwaite, *Crime, Shame and Reintegration* (Cambridge University Press, 1989).

235 Jane Jenson, "Mapping Social Cohesion: The State of Canadian Research," Canadian Policy Research Networks Inc. (1998), 36.

236 Kelly A. Koonce, "Social Cohesion as the Goal: Can Social Cohesion Be Directly Pursued?," *Peabody Journal of Education* 86, no. 2 (2011): 144–154.

237 Bonnie Bacqueroux, "Community Criminal Justice: What Community Policing Teaches," *On Restorative Justice* online, http://www.restorativejustice.org/articlesdb/articles/257, accessed June 25, 2015.

The health of a community to engage in collaborative practices is dependent on opportunity and capability and according to Public Safety Canada can be summarized to include the following:

human capital—the skills, knowledge, attitudes, and understanding of people who are part of the community, which may include those who are resident and nonresident

social capital—the breadth and depth of social relationships and the extent to which these are integrated within the community and can be used to promote collective identity, common values, trust, and participation

spiritual/cultural capital—includes values, symbols, rituals, traditions, art, and language that are used to promote identity and common visions

238 Andrew G. Jackson, G. Fawcett, A. Milan, P. Roberts, S. Schetagne, K. Scott, and S. Tsoukalas, "Social Cohesion in Canada: Possible Indicators," Ottawa: Canadian Council on Social Development (2000), 3.

239 Canadian Council on Social Development, *Social Cohesion in Canada: Possible Indicators*, Canadian Council on Social Development for Social Cohesion Network, Department of Canadian Heritage and Department of Justice, Ottawa (2000), 3, available at http://www.ccsd.ca/pubs/2001/si/sra-543.pdf (page 3).

240 Fred E. Markowitz et al., "Extending Social Disorganization Theory: Modeling the Relationships between Cohesion, Disorder, and Fear," *Criminology* 39, no. 2 (2001): 293–319 (page 294).

241 Eurostat, European Commission, Unemployment Statistics, Table 1: Youth Unemployment Figures 2011–2013Q, http://ec.europa.eu/eurostat/statistics-explained/index.php/Unemployment_statistics, accessed January 24, 2015.

242 Susanne Gottuck and Hans-Uwe Otto, "Editorial: Creating Capabilities for Socially Vulnerable Youth in Europe," *Social Work & Society* 12, no. 2 (2014), http://www.socwork.net/sws/issue/current, accessed June 25, 2015.

243 Susanne Gottuck and Hans-Uwe Otto, "Editorial: Creating Capabilities for Socially Vulnerable Youth in Europe," *Social Work & Society* 12, no. 2 (2014), http://www.socwork.net/sws/issue/current, accessed June 25, 2015.

244 Joel B. Plant and Michael S. Scott, *Effective Policing and Crime Prevention: A Problem-Oriented Guide for Mayors, City Managers, and County Executives*, US Department of Justice, Office of Community Oriented Policing Services (2009), 16.

245 Janet Reno, Raymond C. Fisher, Laurie Robinson, Noel Brennan, and Jeremy Travis, "US Department of Justice" (1999), available at http://www.popcenter.org/problems/panhandling/PDFs/Kelling_1999.pdf, accessed August 8, 2015.
246 Samuel Walker, "Taming the System: The Control of Discretion in Criminal Justice, 1950–1990" (New York: Oxford University Press, 1992: 7–8), in Janet Reno, Raymond C. Fisher, Laurie Robinson, Noel Brennan, and Jeremy Travis, "US Department of Justice," (1999), available at http://www.popcenter.org/problems/panhandling/PDFs/Kelling_1999.pdf, accessed August 8, 2015.
247 Simon Bronitt and Philip Stenning, "Understanding Discretion in Modern Policing," *Criminal Law Journal* 35, no. 6 (2011): 319–332.
248 Canadian Supreme Court of Canada, Regina vs. Beare [1988] 2SCR 387, available at: https://scc-csc.lexum.com/scc-csc/scc-csc/en/item/374/index.do, accessed August 23, 2015.
249 Darren Ellis, "Stop and Search: Disproportionality, Discretion and Generalizations," *Police Journal* 83 no. 3 (2010): 199–216 (page 202).
250 Joel B. Plant and Michael S. Scott, *Effective Policing and Crime Prevention: A Problem-Oriented Guide for Mayors, City Managers, and County Executives*, US Department of Justice, Office of Community Oriented Policing Services (2009), 13.
251 Canadian Supreme Court of Canada. R. v. Beaudry, [2007] 1 S.C.R. 190, 2007 SCC 5, available at http://scc-csc.lexum.com/scc-csc/scc-csc/en/item/2340/index.do, accessed August 23, 2015.
252 Canadian Supreme Court of Canada. R. v. Beaudry, [2007] 1 S.C.R. 190, 2007 SCC 5, available at http://scc-csc.lexum.com/scc-csc/scc-csc/en/item/2340/index.do, accessed August 23, 2015.
253 Ibid.
254 George L. Kelling, "'Broken Windows' and Police Discretion," National Justice Institute, US Department of Justice (October 1999), 2, https://www.ncjrs.gov/pdffiles1/nij/178259.pdf, accessed June 25, 2015.
255 *Police Reform, A Police Service for the Twenty-First Century* (White Paper), Secretary of State for the Home Department, London (1993) 4.
256 Darren Ellis, "Stop and Search: Disproportionality, Discretion and Generalizations," *Police Journal* 83, no. 3 (2010): 199–216 (page 202).
257 Ibid.
258 George L. Kelling, "'Broken Windows' and Police Discretion," National Justice Institute, US Department of Justice (October 1999), 2, https://www.ncjrs.gov/pdffiles1/nij/178259.pdf, accessed June 25, 2015.
259 Ibid., 13.
260 Darren Ellis, "Stop and Search: Disproportionately, Discretion and Generalizations," *The Police Journal* 83 (2010): 199–216.
261 Ibid.

262 George L. Kelling, "'Broken Windows' and Police Discretion," National Justice Institute, US Department of Justice (October 1999), 2, https://www.ncjrs.gov/pdffiles1/nij/178259.pdf, accessed June 25, 2015.

263 James J. Willis, David Weisburd, and Stephen D. Mastrofski, *CompStat in Practice: An In-Depth Analysis of Three Cities* (2003), available at http://www.policefoundation.org/sites/g/files/g798246/f/Willis%20et%20al.%20%282004%29%20-%20CompStat%20in%20Practice.pdf, accessed August 5, 2015.

264 Karim Murji, "Working Together: Governing and Advising the Police," *The Police Journal* 84, no. 3 (2011): 256–271.

265 Sherri R. Arnstein, "A Ladder of Citizen Participation," *Journal of the American Institute of Planners* 35, no. 4 (1969): 216–224.

266 Catherine Layton and Christine Jennett, "Partnerships in Policing and Evidence-Based Practices in Crime Prevention: Are They Incompatible?" Australian Institute of Criminology (2005), 6–7, http://www.aic.gov.au/media_library/conferences/2005-cp/jennett.pdf, accessed June 25, 2015.

267 David Cox, "Educating Police for Uncertain Times: The Australian Experience and Case for 'Normative' Approach," *Journal of Police Intelligence and Counter Terrorism* 6, no. 1 (April 2011): 3–22.

268 Ted Leggett, "What Do the Police Do? Performance Measurement and the SAPS," *Institute for Security Studies Papers* 66 (2003): 15–p., (page 3), available at http://www.issafrica.org/uploads/PAPER66.pdf.

269 Reform, "Value for Money in Policing: From Efficiency to Transformation" (2011), 31, http://www.reform.uk/wp-content/uploads/2014/10/VfMinPolicing.pdf, accessed June 15, 2015.

270 *Police Reform, A Police Service for the Twenty-First Century* (White Paper), Secretary of State for the Home Department, London (1993), 4.

271 Andreas Cebulla and Mike Stephens, "Public Perceptions of the Police: Effects of Police Investigations and Police Resources," *Internet Journal of Criminology* (2010), available at www.internetjournalofcriminology.com/Stephens_Cebulla_Public_Perceptions_of_the_Police_October_2010.pdf, accessed June 25, 2015.

272 US Department of Justice, Center for Program Evaluation and Performance Measurement, "What Have We Learned from Evaluations of Place-Based Policing Strategies?" (2012), available at https://www.bja.gov/evaluation/program-law-enforcement/place-based2.htm, accessed June 25, 2015.

273 Anthony Braga, Andrew Papachristos, and David Hureau, "Hot Spots Policing Effects on Crime," *Campbell Systematic Reviews* 8, no. 8 (2012): 1–96.

274 City of Toronto, "Wellbeing Toronto," City of Toronto (2012), available at www.map.toronto.ca/wellbeing/, accessed December 7, 2012.

275 Ibid.

276 Jonathan Jackson and Ben Bradford, "Crime, Policing and Social Order: On the Expressive Nature of Public Confidence in Policing," *The British Journal of Sociology* 60, no. 3 (2009): 493–521 (page 497).
277 Ibid.
278 Jonathan Jackson et al., "Why Do People Comply with the Law? Legitimacy and the Influence of Legal Institutions," *British Journal of Criminology* (2012).
279 Nancy Fraser, "Recognition without Ethics?," *Theory, Culture & Society* 18, no. 2–3 (2001): 21–42.
280 Raj Bhopal, "Glossary of Terms Relating to Ethnicity and Race: For Reflection and Debate," *Journal of Epidemiology and Community Health* 58, no. 6 (2004): 441–445.